JUMP
AT HOME
GRADE
5

NEW EDITION

D0730787

JUMP AT HOME GRADE 5

NEW EDITION

Worksheets for the JUMP Math Program

JOHN MIGHTON

ANANSI

First published in 2004 by House of Anansi Press Inc.

Revised edition published in 2010 by
House of Anansi Press Inc.
110 Spadina Avenue, Suite 801
Toronto, ON, M5V 2K4
Tel. 416-363-4343
Fax 416-363-1017
www.anansi.ca

Distributed in Canada by
HarperCollins Canada Ltd.
1995 Markham Road
Scarborough, ON, M1B 5M8
Toll free tel. 1-800-387-0117

Distributed in the United States by
Publishers Group West
1700 Fourth Street
Berkeley, CA 94710
Toll free tel. 1-800-788-3123

House of Anansi Press is committed to protecting our natural environment. As part of our efforts, this book is printed on Ancient Forest Friendly paper that contains 100% recycled fibres (40% post-consumer waste and 60% pre-consumer waste) and is processed chlorine-free.

Some of the material in this book has previously been published by JUMP Math.

Every reasonable effort has been made to contact the holders of copyright for materials reproduced in this work. The publishers will gladly receive information that will enable them to rectify any inadvertent errors or omissions in subsequent editions.

14 13 12 11 10   1 2 3 4 5

Library and Archives Canada Cataloguing in Publication

Cataloguing data available from Library and Archives Canada

Library of Congress Control Number: 2010924084

Acknowledgements
Authors – Dr. John Mighton (Ph.D. Mathematics, Ashoka Fellow, Fellow of the Fields Institute for Research in Mathematical Sciences), Dr. Sindi Sabourin (Ph.d. Mathematics, B.Ed.), and Dr. Anna Klebanov (Ph.D. Mathematics)
Consultant – Jennifer Wyatt (M.A. Candidate, B.Ed.)
Contributors – Betony Main, Lisa Hines, and Sheila Mooney
Layout – Katie Baldwin, Rita Camacho, Tony Chen, Lyubava Fartushenko, and Pam Lostracco

This book, like the JUMP program itself, is made possible by the efforts of the volunteers and staff of JUMP Math.

 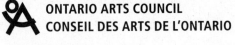

We acknowledge for their financial support of our publishing program the Canada Council for the Arts, the Ontario Arts Council, and the Government of Canada through the Canada Book Fund.

Printed and bound in Canada

Contents

Unit 2: Number Sense 1

Unit 3: Logic and Systematic Search 1

Unit 4: Patterns & Algebra 2

Unit 5: Number Sense 2

Introduction: **About JUMP Math**

There is a prevalent myth in our society that people are born with mathematical talent, and others simply do not have the ability to succeed. Recent discoveries in cognitive science are challenging this myth of ability. The brain is not hard-wired, but continues to change and develop throughout life. Steady, incremental learning can result in the emergence of new abilities.

The carefully designed mathematics in the JUMP Math program provide the necessary skills and knowledge to give your child the joy of success in mathematics. Through step-by-step learning, students celebrate success with every question, thereby increasing achievement and reducing math anxiety.

John Mighton: Founder of JUMP Math

"Nine years ago I was looking for a way to give something back to my local community. It occurred to me that I should try to help kids who needed help with math. Mathematicians don't always make the best teachers because mathematics has become obvious to them; they can have trouble seeing why their students are having trouble. But because I had struggled with math myself, I wasn't inclined to blame my students if they couldn't move forward."

— John Mighton, *The End of Ignorance*

JUMP Math, a national charity dedicated to improving mathematical literacy, was founded by John Mighton, a mathematician, bestselling author, and award-winning playwright. The organization grew out of John's work with a core group of volunteers in a "tutoring club"; their goal was to meet the needs of the most challenged students from local schools. Over the next three years John developed the early material — simple handouts for the tutors to use during their one-on-one teaching sessions with individual students. This period was one of experimentation in developing the JUMP Math method. Eventually, John began to work in local inner-city schools, by placing tutors in the classrooms. This led to the next period of innovation: using the JUMP Math method on small groups of students.

Teachers responded enthusiastically to the success they saw in their students and wanted to adapt the method for classroom use. In response, the needs of the teachers for curriculum-based resources were met by the development of workbooks. These started out as a series of three remedial books with limited accompanying teacher materials, released in fall 2003. The effectiveness of these workbooks led quickly to the development of grade-specific, curriculum-based workbooks. The grade-specific books were first released in 2004. Around that time, the power of teacher networks in creating learning communities was beginning to take shape.

Inspired by the work he has done with thousands of students over the past twenty years, John has systematically developed an approach to teaching mathematics that is based on fostering brain plasticity and emergent intelligence, and on the idea that children have more potential in mathematics than is generally believed. Linking new research in cognitive science to his extensive observations of students, John calls for a re-examination of the assumptions that underlie current methods of teaching mathematics.

JUMP Math, as a program and as an organization, developed in response to the needs of the students, teachers, schools, and communities where John and the volunteers were working. Recognizing the potential of all students to succeed in mathematics, and to succeed in school, was the motivation that John needed to dedicate more than ten years of his life developing a mathematics program that achieved his vision.

JUMP Math: An Innovative Approach

In only ten years, JUMP Math has gone from John's kitchen table to a thriving organization reaching more than 50,000 students with high-quality learning resources and training for 2,000 teachers. It continues to work with community organizations to reach struggling students through homework clubs and after-school programs. Through the generous support of our sponsors, JUMP Math donates resources to classrooms and homework clubs across Canada. The organization has also inspired thousands of community volunteers and teachers to donate their time as tutors, mentors, and trainers.

JUMP Math is unique; it builds on the belief that every child can be successful at mathematics by
- Promoting positive learning environments and building confidence through praise and encouragement;
- Maintaining a balanced approach to mathematics by concurrently addressing conceptual and procedural learning;
- Achieving understanding and mastery by breaking mathematics down into small sequential steps;
- Keeping all students engaged and attentive by "raising the bar" incrementally; and,
- Guiding students strategically to explore and discover the beauty of mathematics.

JUMP Math recognizes the importance of reducing math anxiety. Research in psychology has shown that our brains are extremely fallible: our working memories are poor, we are easily overwhelmed by too much new information, and we require a good deal of practice to consolidate skills and concepts. These mental challenges are compounded when we are anxious. The JUMP approach has been shown to reduce math anxiety significantly.

JUMP Math scaffolds mathematical concepts rigorously and completely. The materials were designed by a team of mathematicians and educators who have a deep understanding of and a love for mathematics. Concepts are introduced in rigorous steps, and prerequisite skills are included in the lesson. Breaking down concepts and skills into steps is often necessary even with the more able students. Math is a subject in which a gifted student can become a struggling student almost overnight, because mathematical knowledge is cumulative.

Consistent with emerging brain research, JUMP Math provides materials and methods that minimize differences between students, allowing teachers, tutors, and parents to more effectively improve student performance in mathematics. Today, parents have access to this unique innovation in mathematics learning with the revised JUMP at Home books.

JUMP Math at Home

JUMP at Home has been developed by mathematicians and educators to complement the mathematics curriculum that your child learns at school. Each grade covers core skills and knowledge to help your child succeed in mathematics. The program focuses on building number sense, pattern recognition, and foundations for algebra.

JUMP at Home is designed to boost every student's confidence, skills, and knowledge. Struggling students will benefit from practice in small steps, while good students will be provided with new ways to understand concepts that will help them enjoy mathematics even more and to exceed their own expectations.

JUMP Math in Schools

JUMP Math also publishes full curriculum-based resources — including student workbooks, teacher guides with daily lesson plans, and blackline masters — that cover all of the Ontario and the Western Canada mathematics curriculum. For more information, please visit the JUMP Math website, www.jumpmath.org, to find out how to order.

Evidence that JUMP Math Works

JUMP Math is a leader in promoting third-party research about its work. A recent study by researchers at the Ontario Institute for Studies in Education (OISE), the University of Toronto, and Simon Fraser University found that in JUMP Math classrooms conceptual understanding improved significantly for weaker students. In Lambeth, England, researchers reported that after using JUMP Math for one year, 69 percent of students who were two years behind were assessed at grade level.

Cognitive scientists from The Hospital for Sick Children in Toronto recently conducted a randomized-controlled study of the effectiveness of the JUMP math program. Studies of such scientific rigour remain relatively rare in mathematics education research in North America. The results showed that students who received JUMP instruction outperformed students who received the methods of instruction their teachers would normally use, on well-established measures of math achievement.

Using JUMP at Home

Helping your child discover the joy of mathematics can be fun and productive. You are not the teacher but the tutor. When having fun with mathematics, remember the JUMP Math T.U.T.O.R. principles:

Take responsibility for learning:

If your child doesn't understand a concept, it can always be clarified further or explained differently. As the adult, you are responsible for helping your child understand. If they don't get it, don't get frustrated — get creative!

Use positive reinforcement:

Children like to be rewarded when they succeed. Praise and encouragement build excitement and foster an appetite for learning. The more confidence a student has, the more likely they are to be engaged.

Take small steps:

In mathematics, it is always possible to make something easier. Always use the JUMP Math worksheets to break down the question to a series of small steps. Practice, practice, practice!

Only indicate correct answers:

Your child's confidence can be shaken by a lack of success. Place checkmarks for correct answers, then revisit questions that your child is having difficulty with. Never use Xs!

Raise the bar:

When your child has mastered a particular concept, challenge them by posing a question that is slightly more difficult. As your child meets these small challenges, you will see their focus and excitement increase.

And remember: if your child is falling behind, teach the number facts! It is a serious mistake to think that students who don't know their number facts can always get by in mathematics using a calculator or other aids. Students can certainly perform operations on a calculator, but they cannot begin to solve problems if they lack a sense of numbers. Students need to be able to see patterns in numbers, and to make estimates and predictions about numbers, in order to have any success in mathematics.

Introductory Unit on Fractions

"In the twenty years that I have been teaching mathematics to children, I have never met an educator who would say that students who lack confidence in their intellectual or academic abilities are likely to do well in school. Our introductory unit has been carefully designed and tested with thousands of students to boost confidence. It has proven to be an extremely effective tool for convincing even the most challenged student that they can do well in mathematics."

— John Mighton

Cognitive scientists have discovered that in order for the brain to be "ready to learn" it cannot be distracted by anxiety. If your child struggles with mathematics or has "math anxiety," be sure to start JUMP Math with the introductory unit on Fractions found on page xxxii.

In recent years, research has shown that students are more apt to do well in subjects when they believe they are capable of doing well. It seems obvious, then, that any math program that aims to harness the potential of every student must start with an exercise that builds the *confidence* of every student. The introductory unit on Fractions was designed for this purpose. It has proven to be an extremely effective tool for convincing even the most challenged students that they can do well in mathematics.

The method used in the introductory unit can be described as *guided discovery*. The individual steps that you will follow in teaching the unit are extremely small, so even the weakest student needn't be left behind. Throughout the unit, students are expected to

- Discover or extend patterns or rules on their own;
- See what changes and what stays the same in sequences of mathematical expressions; and
- Apply what they have learned to new situations.

Students become very excited at making these discoveries and meeting these challenges as they learn the material. For many, it is the first time they have ever been motivated to pay attention to mathematical rules and patterns or to try to extend their knowledge in new cases.

How Does the Introductory Unit Build Confidence?

The introductory unit on Fractions has been specifically designed to build confidence by

- **Requiring that students possess only a few very simple skills.** To achieve a perfect score on the final test in the unit, students need only possess three skills. These skills can be taught to the most challenged students in a very short amount of time. Students must be able to do these three things:
  1) Skip count on their fingers;
  2) Add one-digit numbers; and
  3) Subtract one-digit numbers.
- **Eliminating heavy use of language.** Mathematics functions as its own symbolic language. Since the vast majority of children are able to perform the most basic operations (counting and grouping objects into sets) long before they become expert readers, mathematics is the lone subject in which the vast majority of kids are naturally equipped to excel at an early age. By removing language as a barrier, students can realize their full potential in mathematics.
- **Allowing you to continually provide feedback.** Moving on too quickly is both a hindrance to a student's confidence and an impediment to their eventual success. In the introductory unit, the mathematics are broken down into small steps so that you can quickly identify difficulties and help as soon as they arise.
- **Keeping the student engaged through the excitement of small victories.** Children respond more quickly to praise and success than to criticism and threats. If students are encouraged, they feel an incentive to learn. Students enjoy exercising their minds and showing off to a caring adult.

Since the introductory unit is about building confidence, work with your child to ensure that they are successful. Celebrate every correct answer. Take your time. Encourage your child. And, most importantly, have fun!

Work on Mental Math

Included in *JUMP at Home Grade 5* is a Mental Math unit, which will provide you with strategies and techniques for sharpening your child's math brain. Mental math is the foundation for all further study in mathematics. Students who cannot see number patterns often become frustrated and disillusioned with their work. Consistent practice in mental math allows students to become familiar with the way numbers interact, enabling them to make simple calculations quickly and effectively without always having to recall their number facts.

Mental math confronts people at every turn, making the ability to quickly calculate numbers an invaluable asset. Calculating how much change you are owed at a grocery store or deciding how much of a tip to leave at a restaurant are both real-world examples of mental math in action. For this reason, it may be the single most relevant strand of mathematics to everyday life.

How Can a Parent Best Use Math Time?

To keep your child engaged and attentive, consider breaking up your half-hour math time together into thirds:

- **First 10 Minutes:** Use this time to focus on Mental Math. This will sharpen your child's mental number skills, and they will find the remainder of the session much more enjoyable if they are not constantly struggling to remember their number facts.

- **Second 10 Minutes:** Use this time to work on grade-specific material. These worksheets have been designed by mathematicians and educators to fill gaps in learning, strengthen basic skills, and reinforce fundamental concepts.

- **Final 10 Minutes:** Save this portion of the session for math games, cards, or board games.

It is important to remember that mathematics can be fun! Liven up things by playing games and being as active as possible. If the opportunity to visually demonstrate a concept arises, JUMP at it! Have your child sort out change, look around them for geometric objects, or pace out a perimeter.

"Children will never fulfill their extraordinary potential until we remember how it felt to have so much potential ourselves. There was nothing we weren't inspired to look at or hold, or that we weren't determined to find out how to do. Open the door to the world of mathematics so your child can pass through."

— John Mighton

Mental Math Skills: **Addition and Subtraction**

PARENT:
If your child doesn't know their addition and subtraction facts, teach them to add and subtract using their fingers by the methods taught below. You should also reinforce basic facts using drills, games, and flash cards. There are mental math strategies that make addition and subtraction easier. Some effective strategies are taught in the next section. (Until your child knows all their facts, allow them to add and subtract on their fingers when necessary.)

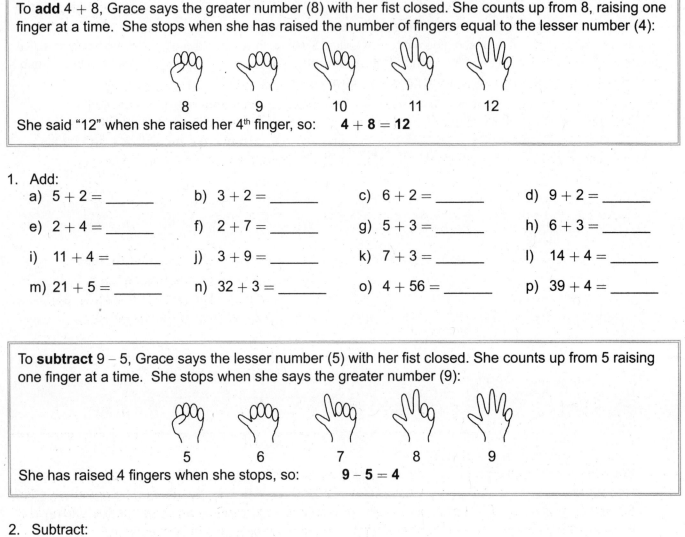

To **add** $4 + 8$, Grace says the greater number (8) with her fist closed. She counts up from 8, raising one finger at a time. She stops when she has raised the number of fingers equal to the lesser number (4):

| 8 | 9 | 10 | 11 | 12 |

She said "12" when she raised her 4th finger, so: $4 + 8 = 12$

1. Add:
   a) $5 + 2 =$ _____   b) $3 + 2 =$ _____   c) $6 + 2 =$ _____   d) $9 + 2 =$ _____

   e) $2 + 4 =$ _____   f) $2 + 7 =$ _____   g) $5 + 3 =$ _____   h) $6 + 3 =$ _____

   i) $11 + 4 =$ _____   j) $3 + 9 =$ _____   k) $7 + 3 =$ _____   l) $14 + 4 =$ _____

   m) $21 + 5 =$ _____   n) $32 + 3 =$ _____   o) $4 + 56 =$ _____   p) $39 + 4 =$ _____

To **subtract** $9 - 5$, Grace says the lesser number (5) with her fist closed. She counts up from 5 raising one finger at a time. She stops when she says the greater number (9):

| 5 | 6 | 7 | 8 | 9 |

She has raised 4 fingers when she stops, so: $9 - 5 = 4$

2. Subtract:
   a) $7 - 5 =$ _____   b) $8 - 6 =$ _____   c) $5 - 3 =$ _____   d) $5 - 2 =$ _____

   e) $9 - 6 =$ _____   f) $10 - 5 =$ _____   g) $11 - 7 =$ _____   h) $17 - 14 =$ _____

   i) $33 - 31 =$ _____   j) $27 - 24 =$ _____   k) $43 - 39 =$ _____   l) $62 - 58 =$ _____

PARENT:
To prepare for the next section (Mental Math), teach your child to add 1 to any number mentally (by counting forward by 1 in their head) and to subtract 1 from any number (by counting backward by 1).

Mental Math Skills: **Addition and Subtraction** *(continued)*

PARENT: Children who don't know how to add, subtract, or estimate readily are at a great disadvantage in mathematics. Children who have trouble memorizing addition and subtraction facts can still learn to mentally add and subtract numbers in a short time if they are given daily practice in a few basic skills.

SKILL 1 – Adding 2 to an Even Number

This skill has been broken down into a number of sub-skills. After teaching each sub-skill, you should give your child a short diagnostic quiz to verify that they have learned the skill. I have included sample quizzes for Skills 1 to 4.

i)   *Naming the next one-digit even number:*

Numbers that have ones digit 0, 2, 4, 6, or 8 are called *even numbers*. Using drills or games, teach your child to say the sequence of one-digit even numbers without hesitation. Ask them to imagine the sequence going on in a circle so that the next number after 8 is 0 (0, 2, 4, 6, 8, 0, 2, 4, 6, 8, . . .). Then play the following game: name a number in the sequence and ask your child to give the next number in the sequence. Don't move on until they have mastered the game.

ii)   *Naming the next greatest two-digit even number:*

Case 1 – Numbers that end in 0, 2, 4, or 6
Write an even two-digit number that ends in 0, 2, 4, or 6 on a piece of paper. Ask your child to name the next greatest even number. They should recognize that if a number ends in 0, then the next even number ends in 2; if it ends in 2, then the next even number ends in 4, etc. For instance, the number 54 has ones digit 4, so the next greatest even number will have ones digit 6.

> **QUIZ** Name the next greatest even number:
>
> a) 52 : _____   b) 64 : _____   c) 36 : _____   d) 22 : _____   e) 80 : _____

Case 2 – Numbers that end in 8
Write the number 58 on a piece of paper. Ask your child to name the next greatest even number. Remind them that even numbers must end in 0, 2, 4, 6, or 8. But 50, 52, 54, and 56 are all less than 58, so the next greatest even number is 60. Your child should see that an even number ending in 8 is always followed by an even number ending in 0 (with a tens digit that is one higher).

> **QUIZ** Name the next greatest even number:
>
> a) 58 : _____   b) 68 : _____   c) 38 : _____   d) 48 : _____   e) 78 : _____

iii)   *Adding 2 to an even number:*

Point out to your child that adding 2 to any even number is equivalent to finding the next even number: e.g., $46 + 2 = 48$, $48 + 2 = 50$, etc. Knowing this, your child can easily add 2 to any even number.

QUIZ

Add:

a) $26 + 2 =$ ___   b) $82 + 2 =$ ___   c) $40 + 2 =$ ___   d) $58 + 2 =$ ___   e) $34 + 2 =$ ___

SKILL 2 – Subtracting 2 from an Even Number

i) *Finding the preceding one-digit even number:*

Name a one-digit even number and ask your child to give the preceding number in the sequence. For instance, the number that comes before 4 is 2, and the number that comes before 0 is 8. (Remember: the sequence is circular.)

ii) *Finding the preceding two-digit even number:*

Case 1 – Numbers that end in 2, 4, 6, or 8
Write a two-digit number that ends in 2, 4, 6, or 8 on a piece of paper. Ask your child to name the preceding even number. They should recognize that if a number ends in 2, then the preceding even number ends in 0; if it ends in 4, then the preceding even number ends in 2, etc. For instance, the number 78 has ones digit 8, so the preceding even number has ones digit 6.

QUIZ

Name the preceding even number:

a) 48 : _____   b) 26 : _____   c) 34 : _____   d) 62 : _____   e) 78 : _____

Case 2 – Numbers that end in 0
Write the number 80 on a piece of paper and ask your child to name the preceding even number. They should recognize that if an even number ends in 0, then the preceding even number ends in 8 (but the ones digit is one less). So the even number that comes before 80 is 78.

QUIZ

Name the preceding even number:

a) 40 : _____   b) 60 : _____   c) 80 : _____   d) 50 : _____   e) 30 : _____

iii) *Subtracting 2 from an even number:*

Point out to your child that subtracting 2 from any even number is equivalent to finding the preceding even number: e.g., $48 - 2 = 46$, $46 - 2 = 44$, etc.

QUIZ

Subtract:

a) $58 - 2 =$ ___   b) $24 - 2 =$ ___   c) $36 - 2 =$ ___   d) $42 - 2 =$ ___   e) $60 - 2 =$ ___

Mental Math Skills: **Addition and Subtraction** *(continued)*

SKILL 3 – Adding 2 to an Odd Number

i) *Naming the next one-digit odd number:*

Numbers that have ones digit 1, 3, 5, 7, 9 are called *odd numbers*. Using drills or games, teach your child to say the sequence of one-digit odd numbers without hesitation. Ask them to imagine the sequence going on in a circle so that the next number after 9 is 1 (1, 3, 5, 7, 9, 1, 3, 5, 7, 9, . . .). Then play the following game: name a number in the sequence and ask your child to give the next number in the sequence. Don't move on until they have mastered the game.

ii) *Naming the next greatest two-digit odd number:*

Case 1 – Numbers that end in 1, 3, 5, or 7
Write an odd two-digit number that ends in 1, 3, 5, or 7 on a piece of paper. Ask your child to name the next greatest odd number. They should recognize that if a number ends in 1, then the next odd number ends in 3; if it ends in 3, then the next odd number ends in 5, etc. For instance, the number 35 has ones digit 5, so the next greatest odd number will have ones digit 7.

> **QUIZ**
>
> Name the next greatest odd number:
>
> a) 51 : _____   b) 65 : _____   c) 37 : _____   d) 23 : _____   e) 87 : _____

Case 2 – Numbers that end in 9
Write the number 59 on a piece of paper. Ask your child to name the next greatest odd number. Remind them that odd numbers must end in 1, 3, 5, 7, or 9. But 51, 53, 55, and 57 are all less than 59. The next greatest odd number is 61. Your child should see that an odd number ending in 9 is always followed by an odd number ending in 1 (with a tens digit that is one higher).

> **QUIZ**
>
> Name the next greatest odd number:
>
> a) 59 : _____   b) 69 : _____   c) 39 : _____   d) 49 : _____   e) 79 : _____

iii) *Adding 2 to an odd number:*
Point out to your child that adding 2 to any odd number is equivalent to finding the next odd number: e.g., $47 + 2 = 49$, $49 + 2 = 51$, etc. Knowing this, your child can easily add 2 to any odd number.

> **QUIZ**
>
> Add:
>
> a) $27 + 2 = $ ___   b) $83 + 2 = $ ___   c) $41 + 2 = $ ___   d) $59 + 2 = $ ___   e) $35 + 2 = $ ___

SKILL 4 – Subtracting 2 from an Odd Number

i) *Finding the preceding one-digit odd number:*

Name a one-digit odd number and ask your child to give the preceding number in the sequence. For instance, the number that comes before 3 is 1, and the number that comes before 1 is 9. (Remember: the sequence is circular.)

ii) *Finding the preceding two-digit odd number:*

Case 1 – Numbers that end in 3, 5, 7, or 9
Write a two-digit number that ends in 3, 5, 7, or 9 on a piece of paper. Ask your child to name the preceding odd number. They should recognize that if a number ends in 3, then the preceding odd number ends in 1; if it ends in 5, then the preceding odd number ends in 3, etc. For instance, the number 79 has ones digit 9, so the preceding odd number has ones digit 7.

QUIZ

Name the preceding odd number:

a) 49 : _____   b) 27 : _____   c) 35 : _____   d) 63 : _____   e) 79 : _____

Case 2 – Numbers that end in 1
Write the number 81 on a piece of paper and ask your child to name the preceding odd number. They should recognize that if an odd number ends in 1, then the preceding odd number ends in 9 (but the ones digit is one less). So the odd number that comes before 81 is 79.

QUIZ

Name the preceding odd number:

a) 41 : _____   b) 61 : _____   c) 81 : _____   d) 51 : _____   e) 31 : _____

iii) *Subtracting 2 from an odd number:*

Point out to your child that subtracting 2 from any odd number is equivalent to finding the preceding odd number: e.g., $49 - 2 = 47$, $47 - 2 = 45$, etc.

QUIZ

Subtract:

a) $59 - 2 =$ ___   b) $25 - 2 =$ ___   c) $37 - 2 =$ ___   d) $43 - 2 =$ ___   e) $61 - 2 =$ ___

SKILLS 5 and 6

Once your child can add and subtract the numbers 1 and 2, then they can easily add and subtract the number 3: Add 3 to a number by first adding 2, then adding 1 (e.g., $35 + 3 = 35 + 2 + 1$). Subtract 3 from a number by subtracting 2, then subtracting 1 (e.g., $35 - 3 = 35 - 2 - 1$).

Mental Math Skills: Addition and Subtraction *(continued)*

PARENT: All of the addition and subtraction tricks you teach your child should be reinforced with drills, flashcards and tests. Eventually they should memorize their addition and subtraction facts and shouldn't have to rely on the mental math tricks. One of the greatest gifts you can give your child is to teach them their number facts.

SKILLS 7 and 8

Add 4 to a number by adding 2 twice (e.g., $51 + 4 = 51 + 2 + 2$). Subtract 4 from a number by subtracting 2 twice (e.g., $51 - 4 = 51 - 2 - 2$).

SKILLS 9 and 10

Add 5 to a number by adding 4 then 1. Subtract 5 by subtracting 4 then 1.

SKILL 11

Your child can add pairs of identical numbers by doubling (e.g., $6 + 6 = 2 \times 6$). They should either memorize the 2 times table or they should double numbers by counting on their fingers by 2s.

Add a pair of numbers that differ by 1 by rewriting the larger number as 1 plus the smaller number, then use doubling to find the sum: e.g., $6 + 7 = 6 + 6 + 1 = 12 + 1 = 13$; $7 + 8 = 7 + 7 + 1 = 14 + 1 = 15$.

SKILLS 12, 13, and 14

Add a one-digit number to 10 by simply replacing the zero in 10 with the one-digit number: e.g., $10 + 7 = 17$.

Add 10 to any two-digit number by simply increasing the tens digit of the two-digit number by 1: e.g., $53 + 10 = 63$.

Add a pair of two-digit numbers (with no carrying) by adding the ones digits of the numbers and then adding the tens digits: e.g., $23 + 64 = 87$.

SKILLS 15 and 16

To add 9 to a one-digit number, subtract 1 from the number and then add 10: e.g., $9 + 6 = 10 + 5 = 15$; $9 + 7 = 10 + 6 = 16$. (Essentially, your child simply has to subtract 1 from the number and then stick a 1 in front of the result.)

To add 8 to a one-digit number, subtract 2 from the number and add 10: e.g., $8 + 6 = 10 + 4 = 14$; $8 + 7 = 10 + 5 = 15$.

SKILLS 17 and 18

To subtract a pair of multiples of ten, simply subtract the tens digits and add a zero for the ones digit: e.g., $70 - 50 = 20$.

To subtract a pair of two-digit numbers (without carrying or regrouping), subtract the ones digit from the ones digit and the tens digit from the tens digit: e.g., $57 - 34 = 23$.

Mental Math — Further Strategies

Further Mental Math Strategies

1. Your child should be able to explain how to use the strategy of "rounding the subtrahend (i.e., the number you are subtracting) up to the nearest multiple of ten."
   Examples:

   Subtrahend   Subtrahend rounded to the nearest tens

   a) $37 - 19 = 37 - 20 + 1$ ◄——— You must add 1 because 20 is 1 greater than 19.
   b) $64 - 28 = 64 - 30 + 2$ ◄——— You must add 2 because 30 is 2 greater than 28.
   c) $65 - 46 = 65 - 50 + 4$

   Practice Questions:
   a) $27 - 17 = 27 -$ ____ $+$ ____   d) $84 - 57 = 84 -$ ____ $+$ ____
   b) $52 - 36 = 52 -$ ____ $+$ ____   e) $61 - 29 = 61 -$ ____ $+$ ____
   c) $76 - 49 = 76 -$ ____ $+$ ____   f) $42 - 18 = 42 -$ ____ $+$ ____

   PARENT: This strategy works well with numbers that end in 6, 7, 8, or 9.

2. Your child should be able to explain how to subtract by thinking of adding.
   Examples:

   Count by ones from 45 to the nearest tens (50).   Count from 50 until you reach the first number (62).

   a) $62 - 45 = 5 + 12 = 17$ ◄——— The sum of counting up to the nearest ten and the original number is the difference.
   b) $46 - 23 = 3 + 20 = 23$ ⎫
   c) $73 - 17 = 6 + 50 = 56$ ⎭ ——— What method did we use here?

   Practice Questions:
   a) $88 - 36 =$ ____ $+$ ____ $=$ ____   d) $74 - 28 =$ ____ $+$ ____ $=$ ____
   b) $58 - 21 =$ ____ $+$ ____ $=$ ____   e) $93 - 64 =$ ____ $+$ ____ $=$ ____
   c) $43 - 17 =$ ____ $+$ ____ $=$ ____   f) $82 - 71 =$ ____ $+$ ____ $=$ ____

3. Your child should be able to explain how to "use doubles."
   Examples:

   Minuend   If you add the subtrahend to itself, and the sum is equal to the minuend, then the subtrahend is the same as the difference.

   a) $12 - 6 = 6$ $6 + 6 = 12$ ◄——— Same value as minuend
   b) $8 - 4 = 4$

   Subtrahend plus itself

   Practice Questions:
   a) $6 - 3 =$ ____   d) $18 - 9 =$ ____
   b) $10 - 5 =$ ____   e) $16 - 8 =$ ____
   c) $14 - 7 =$ ____   f) $20 - 10 =$ ____

Mentel Math Exercises

PARENT: Teaching the material on these Mental Math worksheets may take several lessons. Your child will need more practice than is provided on these pages. These pages are intended as a test to be given when you are certain your child has learned the materials fully.

- -

PARENT: Teach skills 1, 2, 3, and 4 as outlined on pages xv–xviii before you allow your child to answer Questions 1 through 12:

1. Name the <u>even</u> number that comes <u>after</u> the number. Answer in the blank provided:

    a) 32 _____   b) 46 _____   c) 14 _____   d) 92 _____   e) 56 _____

    f) 30 _____   g) 84 _____   h) 60 _____   i) 72 _____   j) 24 _____

2. Name the <u>even</u> number that comes <u>after</u> the number:

    a) 28 _____   b) 18 _____   c) 78 _____   d) 38 _____   e) 68 _____

3. Add:
    REMEMBER: Adding 2 to an even number is the same as finding the next even number.

    a) $42 + 2 =$ _____   b) $76 + 2 =$ _____   c) $28 + 2 =$ _____   d) $16 + 2 =$ _____

    e) $68 + 2 =$ _____   f) $12 + 2 =$ _____   g) $36 + 2 =$ _____   h) $90 + 2 =$ _____

    i) $70 + 2 =$ _____   j) $24 + 2 =$ _____   k) $66 + 2 =$ _____   l) $52 + 2 =$ _____

4. Name the <u>even</u> number that comes <u>before</u> the number:

    a) **38** _____   b) **42** _____   c) **56** _____   d) **72** _____   e) **98** _____

    f) **48** _____   g) **16** _____   h) **22** _____   i) **66** _____   j) **14** _____

5. Name the <u>even</u> number that comes <u>before</u> the number:

    a) **30** _____   b) **70** _____   c) **60** _____   d) **10** _____   e) **80** _____

6. Subtract:
    REMEMBER: Subtracting 2 from an even number is the same as finding the preceding even number.

    a) $46 - 2 =$ _____   b) $86 - 2 =$ _____   c) $90 - 2 =$ _____   d) $14 - 2 =$ _____

    e) $54 - 2 =$ _____   f) $72 - 2 =$ _____   g) $12 - 2 =$ _____   h) $56 - 2 =$ _____

    i) $32 - 2 =$ _____   j) $40 - 2 =$ _____   k) $60 - 2 =$ _____   l) $26 - 2 =$ _____

7. Name the <u>odd</u> number that comes <u>after</u> the number:

    a) 37 _____   b) 51 _____   c) 63 _____   d) 75 _____   e) 17 _____

    f) 61 _____   g) 43 _____   h) 81 _____   i) 23 _____   j) 95 _____

8. Name the <u>odd</u> number that comes <u>after</u> the number:

    a) 69 _____   b) 29 _____   c) 9 _____   d) 79 _____   e) 59 _____

Mental Math Exercises *(continued)*

9. Add:

   REMEMBER: Adding 2 to an odd number is the same as finding the next odd number.

   a) $25 + 2 =$ _____   b) $31 + 2 =$ _____   c) $47 + 2 =$ _____   d) $33 + 2 =$ _____

   e) $39 + 2 =$ _____   f) $91 + 2 =$ _____   g) $5 + 2 =$ _____   h) $89 + 2 =$ _____

   i) $11 + 2 =$ _____   j) $65 + 2 =$ _____   k) $29 + 2 =$ _____   l) $17 + 2 =$ _____

10. Name the odd number that comes before the number:

    a) **39** _____   b) **43** _____   c) **57** _____   d) **17** _____   e) **99** _____

    f) **13** _____   g) **85** _____   h) **79** _____   i) **65** _____   j) **77** _____

11. Name the odd number that comes before the number:

    a) **21** _____   b) **41** _____   c) **11** _____   d) **91** _____   e) **51** _____

12. Subtract:

    REMEMBER: Subtracting 2 from an odd number is the same as finding the preceding odd number.

    a) $47 - 2 =$ _____   b) $85 - 2 =$ _____   c) $91 - 2 =$ _____   d) $15 - 2 =$ _____

    e) $51 - 2 =$ _____   f) $73 - 2 =$ _____   g) $11 - 2 =$ _____   h) $59 - 2 =$ _____

    i) $31 - 2 =$ _____   j) $43 - 2 =$ _____   k) $7 - 2 =$ _____   l) $25 - 2 =$ _____

PARENT: Teach skills 5 and 6 as outlined on page xviii before you allow your child to answer Questions 13 and 14.

13. Add 3 to the number by adding 2, then adding 1 (e.g., $35 + 3 = 35 + 2 + 1$):

    a) $23 + 3 =$ _____   b) $36 + 3 =$ _____   c) $29 + 3 =$ _____   d) $16 + 3 =$ _____

    e) $67 + 3 =$ _____   f) $12 + 3 =$ _____   g) $35 + 3 =$ _____   h) $90 + 3 =$ _____

    i) $78 + 3 =$ _____   j) $24 + 3 =$ _____   k) $6 + 3 =$ _____   l) $59 + 3 =$ _____

14. Subtract 3 from the number by subtracting 2, then subtracting 1 (e.g., $35 - 3 = 35 - 2 - 1$):

    a) $46 - 3 =$ _____   b) $87 - 3 =$ _____   c) $99 - 3 =$ _____   d) $14 - 3 =$ _____

    e) $8 - 3 =$ _____   f) $72 - 3 =$ _____   g) $12 - 3 =$ _____   h) $57 - 3 =$ _____

    i) $32 - 3 =$ _____   j) $40 - 3 =$ _____   k) $60 - 3 =$ _____   l) $28 - 3 =$ _____

15. Fred has 49 stamps. He gives 2 stamps away. How many stamps does he have left?

16. There are 25 minnows in a tank. Alice adds 3 more to the tank. How many minnows are now in the tank?

Mental Math Exercises *(continued)*

PARENT: Teach skills 7 and 8 as outlined on page xix.

17. Add 4 to the number by adding 2 twice (e.g., $51 + 4 = 51 + 2 + 2$):

a) $42 + 4 =$ _____   b) $76 + 4 =$ _____   c) $27 + 4 =$ _____   d) $17 + 4 =$ _____

e) $68 + 4 =$ _____   f) $11 + 4 =$ _____   g) $35 + 4 =$ _____   h) $8 + 4 =$ _____

i) $72 + 4 =$ _____   j) $23 + 4 =$ _____   k) $60 + 4 =$ _____   l) $59 + 4 =$ _____

18. Subtract 4 from the number by subtracting 2 twice (e.g., $26 - 4 = 26 - 2 - 2$):

a) $46 - 4 =$ _____   b) $86 - 4 =$ _____   c) $91 - 4 =$ _____   d) $15 - 4 =$ _____

e) $53 - 4 =$ _____   f) $9 - 4 =$ _____   g) $13 - 4 =$ _____   h) $57 - 4 =$ _____

i) $40 - 4 =$ _____   j) $88 - 4 =$ _____   k) $69 - 4 =$ _____   l) $31 - 4 =$ _____

PARENT: Teach skills 9 and 10 as outlined on page xix.

19. Add 5 to the number by adding 4, then adding 1 (or add 2 twice, then add 1):

a) $84 + 5 =$ _____   b) $27 + 5 =$ _____   c) $31 + 5 =$ _____   d) $44 + 5 =$ _____

e) $63 + 5 =$ _____   f) $92 + 5 =$ _____   g) $14 + 5 =$ _____   h) $16 + 5 =$ _____

i) $9 + 5 =$ _____   j) $81 + 5 =$ _____   k) $51 + 5 =$ _____   l) $28 + 5 =$ _____

20. Subtract 5 from the number by subtracting 4, then subtracting 1 (or subtract 2 twice, then subtract 1):

a) $48 - 5 =$ _____   b) $86 - 5 =$ _____   c) $55 - 5 =$ _____   d) $69 - 5 =$ _____

e) $30 - 5 =$ _____   f) $13 - 5 =$ _____   g) $92 - 5 =$ _____   h) $77 - 5 =$ _____

i) $45 - 5 =$ _____   j) $24 - 5 =$ _____   k) $91 - 5 =$ _____   l) $8 - 5 =$ _____

PARENT: Teach skill 11 as outlined on page xix.

21. Add:

a) $6 + 6 =$ _____   b) $7 + 7 =$ _____   c) $8 + 8 =$ _____

d) $5 + 5 =$ _____   e) $4 + 4 =$ _____   f) $9 + 9 =$ _____

22. Add by thinking of the larger number as a sum of two smaller numbers. The first one is done for you:

a) $6 + 7 = 6 + 6 + 1$ b) $7 + 8 =$ _____   c) $6 + 8 =$ _____

d) $4 + 5 =$ _____   e) $5 + 7 =$ _____   f) $8 + 9 =$ _____

Mental Math Exercises *(continued)*

PARENT: Teach skills 12, 13, and 14 as outlined on page xix.

23. a) $10 + 3 =$ _____ b) $10 + 7 =$ _____ c) $5 + 10 =$ _____ d) $10 + 1 =$ _____

    e) $9 + 10 =$ _____ f) $10 + 4 =$ _____ g) $10 + 8 =$ _____ h) $10 + 2 =$ _____

24. a) $10 + 20 =$ _____ b) $40 + 10 =$ _____ c) $10 + 80 =$ _____ d) $10 + 50 =$ _____

    e) $30 + 10 =$ _____ f) $10 + 60 =$ _____ g) $10 + 10 =$ _____ h) $70 + 10 =$ _____

25. a) $10 + 25 =$ _____ b) $10 + 67 =$ _____ c) $10 + 31 =$ _____ d) $10 + 82 =$ _____

    e) $10 + 43 =$ _____ f) $10 + 51 =$ _____ g) $10 + 68 =$ _____ h) $10 + 21 =$ _____

    i) $10 + 11 =$ _____ j) $10 + 19 =$ _____ k) $10 + 44 =$ _____ l) $10 + 88 =$ _____

26. a) $20 + 30 =$ _____ b) $40 + 20 =$ _____ c) $30 + 30 =$ _____ d) $50 + 30 =$ _____

    e) $20 + 50 =$ _____ f) $40 + 40 =$ _____ g) $50 + 40 =$ _____ h) $40 + 30 =$ _____

    i) $60 + 30 =$ _____ j) $20 + 60 =$ _____ k) $20 + 70 =$ _____ l) $60 + 40 =$ _____

27. a) $20 + 23 =$ _____ b) $32 + 24 =$ _____ c) $51 + 12 =$ _____ d) $12 + 67 =$ _____

    e) $83 + 14 =$ _____ f) $65 + 24 =$ _____ g) $41 + 43 =$ _____ h) $70 + 27 =$ _____

    i) $31 + 61 =$ _____ j) $54 + 33 =$ _____ k) $28 + 31 =$ _____ l) $42 + 55 =$ _____

PARENT: Teach skills 15 and 16 as outlined on page xix.

28. a) $9 + 3 =$ _____ b) $9 + 7 =$ _____ c) $6 + 9 =$ _____ d) $4 + 9 =$ _____

    e) $9 + 9 =$ _____ f) $5 + 9 =$ _____ g) $9 + 2 =$ _____ h) $9 + 8 =$ _____

29. a) $8 + 2 =$ _____ b) $8 + 6 =$ _____ c) $8 + 7 =$ _____ d) $4 + 8 =$ _____

    e) $5 + 8 =$ _____ f) $8 + 3 =$ _____ g) $9 + 8 =$ _____ h) $8 + 8 =$ _____

PARENT: Teach skills 17 and 18 as outlined on page xix.

30. a) $40 - 10 =$ _____ b) $50 - 10 =$ _____ c) $70 - 10 =$ _____ d) $20 - 10 =$ _____

    e) $40 - 20 =$ _____ f) $60 - 30 =$ _____ g) $40 - 30 =$ _____ h) $60 - 50 =$ _____

31. a) $57 - 34 =$ _____ b) $43 - 12 =$ _____ c) $62 - 21 =$ _____ d) $59 - 36 =$ _____

    e) $87 - 63 =$ _____ f) $95 - 62 =$ _____ g) $35 - 10 =$ _____ h) $17 - 8 =$ _____

Mental Math (Advanced)

Multiples of Ten

NOTE: In the exercises below, you will learn several ways to use multiples of ten in mental addition or subtraction.

I $542 + 214 = 542 + 200 + 10 + 4 = 742 + 10 + 4 = 752 + 4 = 756$

       $827 - 314 = 827 - 300 - 10 - 4 = 527 - 10 - 4 = 517 - 4 = 513$

       Sometimes you will need to carry:

       $545 + 172 = 545 + 100 + 70 + 2 = 645 + 70 + 2 = 715 + 2 = 717$

1. Warm up:

    a) $536 + 100 = $ _____   b) $816 + 10 = $ _____   c) $124 + 5 = $ _____   d) $540 + 200 = $ _____

    e) $234 + 30 = $ _____   f) $345 + 300 = $ _____   g) $236 - 30 = $ _____   h) $442 - 20 = $ _____

    i) $970 - 70 = $ _____   j) $542 - 400 = $ _____   k) $160 + 50 = $ _____   l) $756 + 40 = $ _____

2. Write the second number in expanded form and add or subtract one digit at a time. The first one is done for you:

    a) $564 + 215 = $ _____ $564 + 200 + 10 + 5$ _____ $= $ _____ 779 _____

    b) $445 + 343 = $ _____ $= $ _____

    c) $234 + 214 = $ _____ $= $ _____

3. Add or subtract mentally (one digit at a time):

    a) $547 + 312 = $ _____   b) $578 - 314 = $ _____   c) $845 - 454 = $ _____

II   If one of the numbers you are adding or subtracting is close to a number that is a multiple of ten, add the multiple of ten and then add or subtract an adjustment factor:

         $645 + 99 = 645 + 100 - 1 = 745 - 1 = 744$

         $856 + 42 = 856 + 40 + 2 = 896 + 2 = 898$

III   Sometimes in subtraction it helps to think of a multiple of ten as a sum of 1 and a number consisting entirely of 9s (e.g., $100 = 1 + 99$; $1000 = 1 + 999$). You never have to borrow or exchange when you are subtracting from a number consisting entirely of 9s.

         $100 - 43 = 1 + 99 - 43 = 1 + 56 = 57$ ⟵   *Do the subtraction, using 99 instead of 100, and then add 1 to your answer.*

         $1000 - 543 = 1 + 999 - 543 = 1 + 456 = 457$

4. Use the tricks you've just learned:

    a) $845 + 91 = $ _____   b) $456 + 298 = $ _____   c) $100 - 84 = $ _____   d) $1000 - 846 = $ _____

Mental Math Game: Modified Go Fish

PURPOSE:

If children know the pairs of one-digit numbers that add up to particular **target numbers**, they will be able to mentally break sums into easier sums.

EXAMPLE:

As it is easy to add any one-digit number to 10, you can add a sum more readily if you can decompose numbers in the sum into pairs that add to ten. For example:

$$7 + 5 = 7 + 3 + 2 = 10 + 2 = 12$$

These numbers add to 10.

To help children remember pairs of numbers that add up to a given target number, I developed a variation of "Go Fish" that I have found very effective.

THE GAME:

Pick any target number and remove all the cards with value greater than or equal to the target number out of the deck. In what follows, I will assume that the target number is 10, so you would take all the tens and face cards out of the deck (aces count as one).

The dealer gives each player six cards. If a player has any pairs of cards that add to 10, they are allowed to place these pairs on the table before play begins.

Player 1 selects one of the cards in their hand and asks Player 2 for a card that adds to 10 with the chosen card. For instance, if Player 1's chosen card is a 3, they may ask Player 2 for a 7.

If Player 2 has the requested card, Player 1 takes it and lays it down along with the card from their hand. Player 1 may then ask for another card. If Player 2 does not have the requested card, they say, "Go fish," and Player 1 must pick up a card from the top of the deck. (If this card adds to 10 with a card in Player 1's hand, they may lay down the pair right away.) It is then Player 2's turn to ask for a card.

Play ends when one player lays down all of their cards. Players receive 4 points for laying down all of their cards first and 1 point for each pair they have laid down.

PARENT: If your child is having difficulty, I would recommend that you start with pairs of numbers that add to 5. Take all cards with value greater than 4 out of the deck. Each player should be dealt only four cards to start with.

I have worked with several children who have had a great deal of trouble sorting their cards and finding pairs that add to a target number. I have found that the following exercise helps:

Give your child only three cards, two of which add to the target number. Ask them to find the pair that adds to the target number. After your child has mastered this step with three cards, repeat the exercise with four cards, then five cards, and so on.

PARENT: You can also give your child a list of the pairs that add to the target number. As your child gets used to the game, gradually remove pairs from the list so that they learn the pairs by memory.

Hundreds Charts

1	2	3	4	5	6	7	8	9	10
11	12	13	14	15	16	17	18	19	20
21	22	23	24	25	26	27	28	29	30
31	32	33	34	35	36	37	38	39	40
41	42	43	44	45	46	47	48	49	50
51	52	53	54	55	56	57	58	59	60
61	62	63	64	65	66	67	68	69	70
71	72	73	74	75	76	77	78	79	80
81	82	83	84	85	86	87	88	89	90
91	92	93	94	95	96	97	98	99	100

1	2	3	4	5	6	7	8	9	10
11	12	13	14	15	16	17	18	19	20
21	22	23	24	25	26	27	28	29	30
31	32	33	34	35	36	37	38	39	40
41	42	43	44	45	46	47	48	49	50
51	52	53	54	55	56	57	58	59	60
61	62	63	64	65	66	67	68	69	70
71	72	73	74	75	76	77	78	79	80
81	82	83	84	85	86	87	88	89	90
91	92	93	94	95	96	97	98	99	100

1	2	3	4	5	6	7	8	9	10
11	12	13	14	15	16	17	18	19	20
21	22	23	24	25	26	27	28	29	30
31	32	33	34	35	36	37	38	39	40
41	42	43	44	45	46	47	48	49	50
51	52	53	54	55	56	57	58	59	60
61	62	63	64	65	66	67	68	69	70
71	72	73	74	75	76	77	78	79	80
81	82	83	84	85	86	87	88	89	90
91	92	93	94	95	96	97	98	99	100

1	2	3	4	5	6	7	8	9	10
11	12	13	14	15	16	17	18	19	20
21	22	23	24	25	26	27	28	29	30
31	32	33	34	35	36	37	38	39	40
41	42	43	44	45	46	47	48	49	50
51	52	53	54	55	56	57	58	59	60
61	62	63	64	65	66	67	68	69	70
71	72	73	74	75	76	77	78	79	80
81	82	83	84	85	86	87	88	89	90
91	92	93	94	95	96	97	98	99	100

How to Learn Your Times Tables in 5 Days

PARENT:

Trying to do math without knowing your times tables is like trying to play the piano without knowing the location of the notes on the keyboard. Your child will have difficulty seeing patterns in sequences and charts, solving proportions, finding equivalent fractions, decimals and percents, solving problems, etc., if they don't know their tables.

Using the method below, you can teach your child their tables in a week or so. (If you set aside five or ten minutes a day to work with them, the pay-off will be enormous.) There is really no reason for your child not to know their tables!

DAY 1: Counting by 2s, 3s, 4s, and 5s

If you have completed the JUMP Fractions unit you should already know how to count and multiply by 2s, 3s, 4s, and 5s. If you do not know how to count by these numbers, you should memorize the hands:

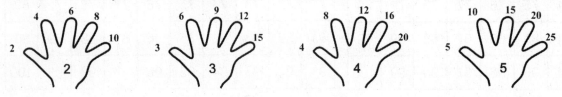

If you know how to count by 2s, 3s, 4s, and 5s, then you can multiply by any combination of these numbers. For instance, to find the product of 3×2, count by 2s until you have raised 3 fingers:

$$3 \times 2 = 6$$

DAY 2: The 9 Times Table

The numbers you say when you count by 9s are called the **multiples** of 9 (0 is also a multiple of 9). The first ten multiples of 9 (after 0) are 9, 18, 27, 36, 45, 54, 63, 72, 81, and 90. What happens when you add the digits of any of these multiples of 9 (such as $1 + 8$ or $6 + 3$)? The sum is always 9!

Here is another useful fact about the 9 times table: Multiply 9 by any number between 1 and 10 and look at the tens digit of the product. The tens digit is always one less than the number you multiplied by:

$9 \times 4 = 36$

3 is one less than 4.

$9 \times 8 = 72$

7 is one less than 8.

$9 \times 2 = 18$

1 is one less than 2.

You can find the product of 9 and any number by using the two facts given above. For example, to find 9×7, follow these steps:

Step 1: $9 \times 7 = $ __ __

Subtract 1 from the number
you are multiplying by 9: $\mathbf{7 - 1 = 6}$

$9 \times 7 = $ __ __

Now you know the tens digit
of the product.

How to Learn Your Times Tables in 5 Days *(continued)*

Step 2: $9 \times 7 = \underline{6}\ \underline{}$ $9 \times 7 = \underline{6}\ \underline{3}$

These two digits add to 9.   So the missing digit is $9 - 6 = 3$.
(You can do the subtraction on your fingers if necesary.)

Practise these two steps for all of the products of 9: 9×2, 9×3, 9×4, and so on.

DAY 3: The 8 Times Table

There are two patterns in the digits of the 8 times table. Knowing these patterns will help you remember how to count by 8s.

Step 1: You can find the ones digit of the first five multiples of 8 by starting at 8 and counting backwards by 2s.

8
6
4
2
0

Step 2: You can find the tens digit of the first five multiples of 8 by starting at 0 and counting up by 1s.

08
16
24
32
40

Step 3: You can find the ones digit of the next five multiples of 8 by repeating step 1.

8
6
4
2
0

Step 4: You can find the remaining tens digits by starting at 4 and counting by 1s.

48
56
64
72
80

(Of course, you do not need to write the 0 in front of the 8 for the product 1×8.)

Practise writing the multiples of 8 (up to 80) until you have memorized the complete list. Knowing the patterns in the digits of the multiples of 8 will help you memorize the list very quickly. Then you will know how to multiply by 8.

$8 \times 6 = 48$

Count by 8 until you have 6 fingers up: 8, 16, 24, 32, 40, 48.

How to Learn Your Times Tables in 5 Days *(continued)*

DAY 4: The 6 Times Table

If you have learned the 8 and 9 times tables, then you already know 6×9 and 6×8.

And if you know how to multiply by 5 up to 5×5, then you also know how to multiply by 6 up to 6×5! That is because you can always calculate 6 times a number by calculating 5 times the number and then adding the number itself to the result. The pictures below show how this works for 6×4:

$$6 \times 4 \left\{ \begin{array}{cccc} \bullet & \bullet & \bullet & \bullet \\ \bullet & \bullet & \bullet & \bullet \\ \bullet & \bullet & \bullet & \bullet \\ \bullet & \bullet & \bullet & \bullet \\ \bullet & \bullet & \bullet & \bullet \\ \bullet & \bullet & \bullet & \bullet \end{array} \right. $$

5×4

$\leftarrow$ plus one more 4

5 fours

$6 \times 4 = 4 + 4 + 4 + 4 + 4 + 4$

plus one more 4

$6 \times 4 = 5 \times 4 + 4 = 20 + 4 = 24$

Similarly: $\quad 6 \times 2 = 5 \times 2 + 2; \qquad 6 \times 3 = 5 \times 3 + 3; \qquad 6 \times 5 = 5 \times 5 + 5.$

Knowing this, you only need to memorize 2 facts:

$$6 \times 6 = 36 \qquad 6 \times 7 = 42$$

Or, if you know 6×5, you can find 6×6 by calculating $6 \times 5 + 5$.

DAY 5: The 7 Times Table

If you have learned the 6, 8, and 9 times tables, then you already know 6×7, 8×7, and 9×7.

And since you also already know $1 \times 7 = 7$, you only need to memorize 5 facts:

$$2 \times 7 = 14 \qquad 3 \times 7 = 21 \qquad 4 \times 7 = 28 \qquad 5 \times 7 = 35 \qquad 7 \times 7 = 49$$

If you are able to memorize your own phone number, then you can easily memorize these 5 facts!

NOTE: You can use doubling to help you learn the facts above: 4 is double 2, so 4×7 (28) is double 2×7 (14); 6 is double 3, so 6×7 (42) is double 3×7 (21).

Try this test every day until you have learned your times tables.

1. $3 \times 5 =$ _____	2. $8 \times 4 =$ _____	3. $9 \times 3 =$ _____	4. $4 \times 5 =$ _____
5. $2 \times 3 =$ _____	6. $4 \times 2 =$ _____	7. $8 \times 1 =$ _____	8. $6 \times 6 =$ _____
9. $9 \times 7 =$ _____	10. $7 \times 7 =$ _____	11. $5 \times 8 =$ _____	12. $2 \times 6 =$ _____
13. $6 \times 4 =$ _____	14. $7 \times 3 =$ _____	15. $4 \times 9 =$ _____	16. $2 \times 9 =$ _____
17. $9 \times 9 =$ _____	18. $3 \times 4 =$ _____	19. $6 \times 8 =$ _____	20. $7 \times 5 =$ _____
21. $9 \times 5 =$ _____	22. $5 \times 6 =$ _____	23. $6 \times 3 =$ _____	24. $7 \times 1 =$ _____
25. $8 \times 3 =$ _____	26. $9 \times 6 =$ _____	27. $4 \times 7 =$ _____	28. $3 \times 3 =$ _____
29. $8 \times 7 =$ _____	30. $1 \times 5 =$ _____	31. $7 \times 6 =$ _____	32. $2 \times 8 =$ _____

Base Ten Blocks

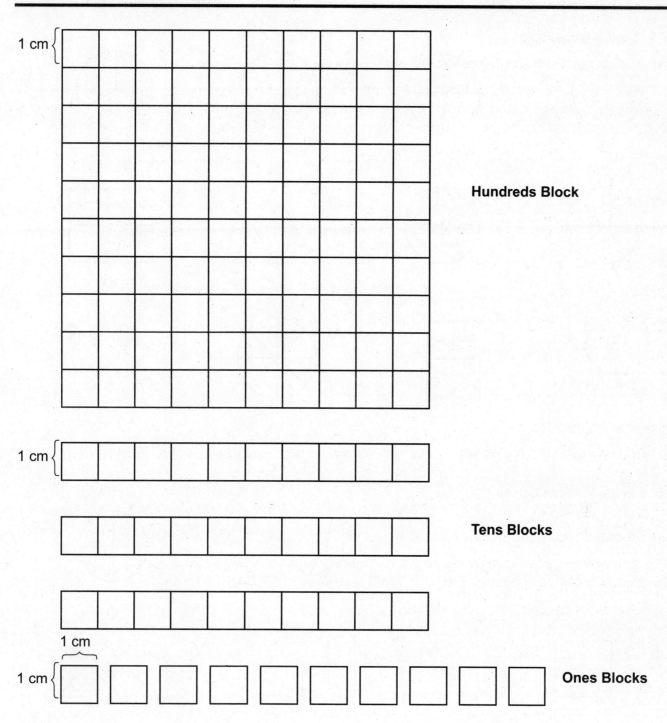

1 cm

Hundreds Block

1 cm

Tens Blocks

1 cm

1 cm

Ones Blocks

Fractions

1. Name the following fractions.

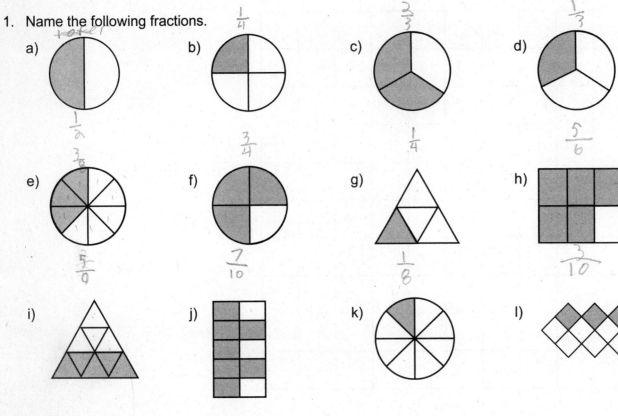

a) $\frac{1}{2}$

b) $\frac{1}{4}$ $\frac{3}{4}$

c) $\frac{2}{3}$ $\frac{1}{4}$

d) $\frac{1}{3}$ $\frac{5}{6}$

e) $\frac{3}{8}$ $\frac{5}{8}$

f) $\frac{7}{10}$

g) $\frac{1}{8}$

h) $\frac{3}{10}$

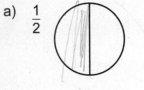 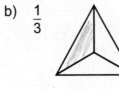

i)

j)

k)

l)

2. Shade the fractions named.

a) $\frac{1}{2}$ 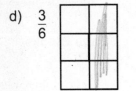

b) $\frac{1}{3}$

c) $\frac{3}{4}$

d) $\frac{3}{6}$

e) $\frac{2}{5}$

f) $\frac{5}{9}$ 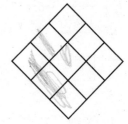

Fractions *(continued)*

3. Add.

   a) $\dfrac{1}{3} + \dfrac{1}{3}$

   b) $\dfrac{2}{7} + \dfrac{3}{7}$

   c) $\dfrac{2}{11} + \dfrac{1}{11}$

   d) $\dfrac{2}{5} + \dfrac{2}{5}$

   e) $\dfrac{2}{11} + \dfrac{3}{11}$

   f) $\dfrac{3}{8} + \dfrac{4}{8}$

   g) $\dfrac{3}{17} + \dfrac{2}{17}$

   h) $\dfrac{1}{21} + \dfrac{4}{21}$

   i) $\dfrac{4}{9} + \dfrac{3}{9}$

4. Subtract.

   a) $\dfrac{3}{5} - \dfrac{1}{5}$

   b) $\dfrac{2}{7} - \dfrac{1}{7}$

   c) $\dfrac{4}{11} - \dfrac{2}{11}$

   d) $\dfrac{5}{8} - \dfrac{2}{8}$

   e) $\dfrac{6}{17} - \dfrac{2}{17}$

   f) $\dfrac{5}{9} - \dfrac{1}{9}$

5. **Advanced:** Add or Subtract.

   a) $\dfrac{1}{7} + \dfrac{1}{7} + \dfrac{1}{7}$

   b) $\dfrac{1}{7} + \dfrac{2}{7} + \dfrac{3}{7}$

   c) $\dfrac{1}{15} + \dfrac{2}{15} + \dfrac{5}{15}$

   BONUS:

   d) $\dfrac{16}{21} - \dfrac{5}{21} - \dfrac{3}{21}$

   e) $\dfrac{7}{9} - \dfrac{4}{9} + \dfrac{2}{9}$

   f) $\dfrac{2}{11} + \dfrac{5}{11} - \dfrac{3}{11}$

Fractions *(continued)*

6. Write times signs beside the fractions.

   Example: $\dfrac{1}{5} + \dfrac{1}{3} \longrightarrow {}^\times_\times \dfrac{1}{5} + \dfrac{1}{3} {}^\times_\times$

$\dfrac{1}{2} + \dfrac{1}{3}$	$\dfrac{1}{2} + \dfrac{1}{5}$	$\dfrac{1}{3} + \dfrac{1}{5}$

7. Switch the bottom numbers.

   Example: $\dfrac{1}{5} + \dfrac{1}{3} \longrightarrow \dfrac{3 \times 1}{3 \times 5} + \dfrac{1 \times 5}{3 \times 5}$

${}^\times_\times \dfrac{1}{2} + \dfrac{1}{3} {}^\times_\times$	${}^\times_\times \dfrac{1}{2} + \dfrac{1}{5} {}^\times_\times$	${}^\times_\times \dfrac{1}{3} + \dfrac{1}{5} {}^\times_\times$

8. Write times signs and switch the numbers.

   Example: $\dfrac{1}{5} + \dfrac{1}{3} \longrightarrow \dfrac{3 \times 1}{3 \times 5} + \dfrac{1 \times 5}{3 \times 5}$

$\dfrac{1}{2} + \dfrac{1}{3}$	$\dfrac{1}{2} + \dfrac{1}{5}$	$\dfrac{1}{3} + \dfrac{1}{5}$
$\dfrac{2}{3} + \dfrac{1}{2}$	$\dfrac{2}{3} + \dfrac{1}{5}$	$\dfrac{2}{5} + \dfrac{1}{3}$

9. Perform the multiplications.

   Example: $\dfrac{1}{5} + \dfrac{1}{3} \longrightarrow \dfrac{3 \times 1}{3 \times 5} + \dfrac{1 \times 5}{3 \times 5}$

   $$= \dfrac{3}{15} + \dfrac{5}{15}$$

$\dfrac{3 \times 1}{3 \times 2} + \dfrac{1 \times 2}{3 \times 2}$ $= \underline{} + \underline{}$	$\dfrac{5 \times 1}{5 \times 2} + \dfrac{1 \times 2}{5 \times 2}$ $= \underline{} + \underline{}$	$\dfrac{5 \times 1}{5 \times 3} + \dfrac{1 \times 3}{5 \times 3}$ $= \underline{} + \underline{}$

Fractions *(continued)*

$$\frac{2}{2} \times \frac{2}{3} + \frac{1}{2} \times \frac{3}{3}$$

$$= \frac{}{} + \frac{}{}$$

$$\frac{5}{5} \times \frac{2}{3} + \frac{1}{5} \times \frac{3}{3}$$

$$= \frac{}{} + \frac{}{}$$

$$\frac{3}{3} \times \frac{2}{5} + \frac{1}{3} \times \frac{5}{5}$$

$$= \frac{}{} + \frac{}{}$$

10. Perform the additions.

Example: $\dfrac{1}{5} + \dfrac{1}{3} \longrightarrow \dfrac{3}{3} \times \dfrac{1}{5} + \dfrac{1}{3} \times \dfrac{5}{5}$

$$= \frac{3}{15} + \frac{5}{15} = \frac{8}{15}$$

$$\frac{3}{3} \times \frac{1}{2} + \frac{1}{3} \times \frac{2}{2}$$

$$= \frac{3}{6} + \frac{2}{6} = \underline{\quad}$$

$$\frac{5}{5} \times \frac{1}{2} + \frac{1}{5} \times \frac{2}{2}$$

$$= \frac{5}{10} + \frac{2}{10} = \underline{\quad}$$

$$\frac{5}{5} \times \frac{1}{3} + \frac{1}{5} \times \frac{3}{3}$$

$$= \frac{5}{15} + \frac{3}{15} = \underline{\quad}$$

$$\frac{2}{2} \times \frac{2}{3} + \frac{1}{2} \times \frac{3}{3}$$

$$= \frac{4}{6} + \frac{3}{6} = \underline{\quad}$$

$$\frac{5}{5} \times \frac{2}{3} + \frac{1}{5} \times \frac{3}{3}$$

$$= \frac{10}{15} + \frac{3}{15} = \underline{\quad}$$

$$\frac{3}{3} \times \frac{2}{5} + \frac{1}{3} \times \frac{5}{5}$$

$$= \frac{6}{15} + \frac{5}{15} = \underline{\quad}$$

11. Perform the multiplications and the additions.

Example: $\dfrac{1}{5} + \dfrac{1}{3} \longrightarrow \dfrac{3}{3} \times \dfrac{1}{5} + \dfrac{1}{3} \times \dfrac{5}{5}$

$$= \frac{3}{15} + \frac{5}{15} = \frac{8}{15}$$

$$\frac{3}{3} \times \frac{1}{2} + \frac{1}{3} \times \frac{2}{2}$$

$$= \frac{}{} + \frac{}{} = \frac{}{}$$

$$\frac{5}{5} \times \frac{1}{2} + \frac{1}{5} \times \frac{2}{2}$$

$$= \frac{}{} + \frac{}{} = \frac{}{}$$

$$\frac{5}{5} \times \frac{1}{3} + \frac{1}{5} \times \frac{3}{3}$$

$$= \frac{}{} + \frac{}{} = \frac{}{}$$

$$\frac{2}{2} \times \frac{2}{3} + \frac{1}{2} \times \frac{3}{3}$$

$$= \frac{}{} + \frac{}{} = \frac{}{}$$

$$\frac{5}{5} \times \frac{2}{3} + \frac{1}{5} \times \frac{3}{3}$$

$$= \frac{}{} + \frac{}{} = \frac{}{}$$

$$\frac{3}{3} \times \frac{2}{5} + \frac{1}{3} \times \frac{5}{5}$$

$$= \frac{}{} + \frac{}{} = \frac{}{}$$

Introduction

Fractions *(continued)*

12. Add.

a) $\frac{1}{2} + \frac{1}{3}$

b) $\frac{1}{3} + \frac{1}{5}$

c) $\frac{1}{2} + \frac{1}{5}$

13. **Advanced:** Add or Subtract.

a) $\frac{2}{5} + \frac{1}{3}$

b) $\frac{3}{5} + \frac{1}{2}$

c) $\frac{2}{3} + \frac{1}{2}$

d) $\frac{1}{5} + \frac{2}{3}$

d) $\frac{4}{5} + \frac{1}{2}$

f) $\frac{2}{3} + \frac{2}{5}$

BONUS:

a) $\frac{1}{2} - \frac{1}{3}$

b) $\frac{2}{3} - \frac{1}{2}$

c) $\frac{3}{5} - \frac{1}{2}$

Fractions *(continued)*

14. Write how many times the lesser denominator goes into the greater denominator.

Example: $\dfrac{1}{2} + \dfrac{1}{10} \longrightarrow \begin{array}{c}\mathbf{5} \\ \mathbf{5}\end{array} \times \dfrac{1}{2} + \dfrac{1}{10}$

$\dfrac{1}{2} + \dfrac{1}{10}$	$\dfrac{1}{5} + \dfrac{1}{10}$	$\dfrac{1}{2} + \dfrac{1}{8}$
$\dfrac{1}{3} + \dfrac{1}{6}$	$\dfrac{1}{5} + \dfrac{1}{20}$	$\dfrac{1}{2} + \dfrac{1}{6}$
$\dfrac{2}{5} + \dfrac{1}{25}$	$\dfrac{3}{5} + \dfrac{1}{15}$	$\dfrac{1}{2} + \dfrac{7}{8}$

15. Change the fraction with the lesser denominator and keep the other fraction the same.

Example: $\dfrac{1}{2} + \dfrac{1}{10} \longrightarrow \begin{array}{c}\mathbf{5} \\ \mathbf{5}\end{array} \times \dfrac{1}{2} + \dfrac{1}{10}$

$$= \dfrac{5}{10} + \dfrac{1}{10}$$

$\dfrac{1}{2} + \dfrac{1}{10}$	$\dfrac{1}{5} + \dfrac{1}{10}$	$\dfrac{1}{2} + \dfrac{1}{8}$
$\dfrac{1}{3} + \dfrac{1}{6}$	$\dfrac{1}{5} + \dfrac{1}{20}$	$\dfrac{1}{2} + \dfrac{1}{6}$
$\dfrac{2}{5} + \dfrac{1}{25}$	$\dfrac{3}{5} + \dfrac{1}{15}$	$\dfrac{1}{2} + \dfrac{7}{8}$

Fractions *(continued)*

16. Add. (Remember to change only one denominator.)

a) $\dfrac{1}{2} + \dfrac{1}{10}$

b) $\dfrac{1}{5} + \dfrac{1}{10}$

c) $\dfrac{1}{2} + \dfrac{1}{8}$

d) $\dfrac{1}{3} + \dfrac{1}{6}$

e) $\dfrac{1}{5} + \dfrac{1}{20}$

f) $\dfrac{1}{2} + \dfrac{1}{6}$

17. **Advanced:** Add or Subtract.

a) $\dfrac{2}{3} + \dfrac{1}{15}$

b) $\dfrac{2}{5} + \dfrac{1}{10}$

c) $\dfrac{3}{5} + \dfrac{2}{15}$

d) $\dfrac{2}{3} + \dfrac{1}{12}$

e) $\dfrac{1}{4} + \dfrac{3}{8}$

f) $\dfrac{1}{4} + \dfrac{3}{12}$

g) $\dfrac{3}{4} + \dfrac{1}{2}$

h) $\dfrac{4}{25} + \dfrac{1}{5}$

i) $\dfrac{3}{15} + \dfrac{4}{5}$

BONUS:

j) $\dfrac{7}{20} - \dfrac{1}{5}$

k) $\dfrac{3}{8} - \dfrac{1}{4}$

l) $\dfrac{1}{2} - \dfrac{3}{10}$

Fractions *(continued)*

18. Write **yes** beside the number in bold if you say the number when counting by 2s.
    If you don't, write **no**.

    a) **6** _____   b) **3** _____   c) **9** _____   d) **8** _____

    e) **10** _____   f) **4** _____   g) **5** _____   h) **7** _____

19. Write **yes** beside the given number if you say the number when counting by 3s.
    If you don't, write **no**.

    a) **9** _____   b) **4** _____   c) **12** _____   d) **13** _____

    e) **6** _____   f) **5** _____   g) **8** _____   h) **14** _____

20. Write **yes** beside the given number if you say the number when counting by 5s.
    If you don't, write **no**.

    a) **10** _____   b) **12** _____   c) **15** _____   d) **8** _____

    e) **20** _____   f) **9** _____   g) **14** _____   h) **11** _____

21. Circle the smaller denominator. The first one has been done for you.

    a) $\frac{1}{②} + \frac{1}{3}$ b) $\frac{1}{3} + \frac{1}{5}$ c) $\frac{2}{6} + \frac{1}{2}$

    d) $\frac{1}{4} + \frac{1}{8}$ e) $\frac{3}{5} + \frac{1}{2}$ f) $\frac{1}{2} + \frac{1}{8}$

22. Count by the lesser denominator, and write **yes** if you say the greater denominator.
    Write **no** if you don't. The first one has been done for you.

    a) ___*no*___   b) _____   c) _____

    $\frac{1}{②} + \frac{1}{3}$ $\frac{1}{③} + \frac{1}{5}$ $\frac{2}{6} + \frac{1}{②}$

    d) _____   e) _____   f) _____

    $\frac{1}{4} + \frac{1}{8}$ $\frac{3}{5} + \frac{1}{2}$ $\frac{1}{2} + \frac{1}{8}$

    g) _____   h) _____   i) _____

    $\frac{1}{2} + \frac{1}{8}$ $\frac{3}{15} + \frac{1}{3}$ $\frac{1}{5} + \frac{1}{9}$

Fractions *(continued)*

23. Count by the lesser denominator until you reach the greater denominator. Write the number of fingers you have raised beside the times signs.

a) ___yes___

$$\begin{array}{l}\times\ 1\\ \times\ 2\end{array} + \dfrac{1}{6}$$

b) ___yes___

$$\begin{array}{l}\times\ 1\\ \times\ 5\end{array} + \dfrac{1}{10}$$

c) ___yes___

$$\begin{array}{l}\times\ 1\\ \times\ 3\end{array} + \dfrac{1}{9}$$

24. Complete the first step of addition by multiplying each fraction by the opposite denominator.

a) ___no___

$$\begin{array}{l}\times\ 1\\ \times\ 2\end{array} + \begin{array}{l}1\ \times\\ 6\ \times\end{array}$$

b) ___no___

$$\begin{array}{l}\times\ 1\\ \times\ 5\end{array} + \begin{array}{l}1\ \times\\ 10\ \times\end{array}$$

c) ___no___

$$\begin{array}{l}\times\ 1\\ \times\ 3\end{array} + \begin{array}{l}1\ \times\\ 9\ \times\end{array}$$

25. Write **yes** or **no** above the following fractions. If you wrote **yes**, then complete the first step of addition as in Question 23 above. If you wrote **no**, complete the first step as in Question 24.

a) _____

$$\dfrac{1}{3} + \dfrac{1}{5}$$

b) _____

$$\dfrac{3}{5} + \dfrac{1}{10}$$

c) _____

$$\dfrac{1}{2} + \dfrac{1}{4}$$

d) _____

$$\dfrac{1}{3} + \dfrac{1}{4}$$

BONUS:

e) _____

$$\dfrac{3}{15} + \dfrac{1}{5}$$

f) _____

$$\dfrac{1}{10} + \dfrac{1}{5}$$

26. Add or Subtract. Change *one* denominator or change *both*. (For each question you have to decide what to do. Start by writing **yes** or **no** above the fraction.)

a) _____

$$\dfrac{1}{4} + \dfrac{1}{5}$$

b) _____

$$\dfrac{2}{3} + \dfrac{1}{5}$$

c) _____

$$\dfrac{2}{5} + \dfrac{1}{20}$$

BONUS:

d) _____

$$\dfrac{3}{20} + \dfrac{4}{5}$$

e) _____

$$\dfrac{2}{15} + \dfrac{3}{5}$$

f) _____

$$\dfrac{1}{16} + \dfrac{1}{4}$$

Introduction

Fractions *(continued)*

27. **Advanced:** Add or Subtract. (Change *one* denominator or change *both*.)

   a) $\dfrac{1}{3} + \dfrac{1}{9}$

   b) $\dfrac{2}{3} + \dfrac{1}{5}$

   c) $\dfrac{1}{5} + \dfrac{1}{20}$

   d) $\dfrac{1}{2} + \dfrac{1}{3}$

   e) $\dfrac{1}{4} + \dfrac{1}{5}$

   f) $\dfrac{1}{4} + \dfrac{5}{16}$

   g) $\dfrac{1}{2} - \dfrac{1}{10}$

   h) $\dfrac{3}{4} - \dfrac{1}{3}$

   i) $\dfrac{7}{20} - \dfrac{1}{4}$

28. If the denominators are the same, write **same**. Otherwise change *one* denominator or change *both*. Then complete all the questions.

   a) $\dfrac{1}{3} + \dfrac{1}{12}$

   b) $\dfrac{1}{4} + \dfrac{3}{5}$

   c) $\dfrac{1}{7} + \dfrac{1}{7}$

   d) $\dfrac{2}{3} + \dfrac{1}{2}$

   e) $\dfrac{10}{11} - \dfrac{6}{11}$

   f) $\dfrac{4}{5} - \dfrac{3}{20}$

       Introduction

Fractions *(continued)*

Example: $\frac{1}{2} + \frac{1}{3} + \frac{1}{6} \longrightarrow \frac{\mathbf{3} \times 1}{\mathbf{3} \times 2} + \frac{\mathbf{2} \times 1}{\mathbf{2} \times 3} + \frac{1}{6}$

$\frac{1}{2} + \frac{1}{3} + \frac{1}{6}$	$\frac{1}{3} + \frac{1}{5} + \frac{1}{15}$
$\frac{1}{2} + \frac{1}{4} + \frac{3}{8}$	$\frac{1}{4} + \frac{1}{5} + \frac{1}{20}$
$\frac{2}{3} + \frac{1}{4} + \frac{1}{12}$	$\frac{1}{5} + \frac{3}{10} + \frac{2}{20}$

30. Write times signs and numbers, and carry out multiplication as needed.

Example: $\frac{1}{2} + \frac{1}{3} + \frac{1}{6} \longrightarrow \frac{\mathbf{3} \times 1}{\mathbf{3} \times 2} + \frac{\mathbf{2} \times 1}{\mathbf{2} \times 3} + \frac{1}{6}$

$$= \frac{\mathbf{3}}{\mathbf{6}} + \frac{\mathbf{2}}{\mathbf{6}} + \frac{\mathbf{1}}{\mathbf{6}}$$

$\frac{1}{2} + \frac{1}{3} + \frac{1}{6}$	$\frac{1}{3} + \frac{1}{5} + \frac{1}{15}$
$\frac{1}{2} + \frac{1}{4} + \frac{3}{8}$	$\frac{1}{4} + \frac{1}{5} + \frac{1}{20}$
$\frac{2}{3} + \frac{1}{4} + \frac{1}{12}$	$\frac{1}{5} + \frac{3}{10} + \frac{2}{20}$

Fractions *(continued)*

31. Solve completely.

a) $\dfrac{1}{2} + \dfrac{1}{3} + \dfrac{3}{6}$

b) $\dfrac{1}{3} + \dfrac{1}{5} + \dfrac{1}{15}$

c) $\dfrac{1}{2} + \dfrac{1}{4} + \dfrac{3}{8}$

d) $\dfrac{1}{4} + \dfrac{1}{5} + \dfrac{5}{20}$

e) $\dfrac{2}{3} + \dfrac{1}{4} + \dfrac{1}{12}$

f) $\dfrac{1}{5} + \dfrac{3}{10} + \dfrac{2}{20}$

BONUS:

g) $\dfrac{17}{20} - \dfrac{1}{4} - \dfrac{1}{5}$

h) $\dfrac{3}{4} - \dfrac{1}{8} - \dfrac{1}{2}$

i) $\dfrac{1}{2} - \dfrac{1}{6} + \dfrac{1}{3}$

j) $\dfrac{2}{3} + \dfrac{1}{4} - \dfrac{5}{12}$

 Introduction

Define a Number

A The number is even.	**B** The number is odd.	**C** You can count to the number by 2s.
D You can count to the number by 3s.	**E** You can count to the number by 5s.	**F** You can count to the number by 10s.
G The number is greater than 15.	**H** The number is less than 25.	**I** The number has 1 digit.
J The number has 2 digits.	**K** The number has two digits that are the same.	**L** The number has a zero in it.
M The number is 7.	**N** The number is less than 7.	**O** You can see the number on the face of a clock.
P The ones digit is smaller than 6.	**Q** The sum of its digits is less than 9.	**R** The number is divisible by 2.

1. Write a number that statement **A** applies to. _____

2. Statements **B**, **D**, **H**, and **J** all apply to the number 15.
   Which other statements apply to the number 15 as well? _____

3. Choose a number between 1 and 25 (besides 15).
   Find all the statements that apply to that number.

   Your number: _____ Statements that apply to that number: _____

4. a) Which statements apply to both 3 and 18? _____

   b) Which statements apply to both 7 and 11? _____

5. a) Can you find a number that statements **A**, **E**, **J**, **L**, and **R** apply to?
      (**NOTE:** There may be more than one answer.)

      _____

   b) Can you find a number that statements **B**, **D**, **H**, and **Q** apply to?

      _____

   c) Can you find a number that statements **C**, **K**, **H**, and **P** apply to?

      _____

Define a Number (continued)

PARENT: You should only assign a few questions on this page at a time.

6. a) Is it possible for statements **A** and **B** to both apply to a number? Explain.

   _____

   _____

   b) Is it possible for statements **D** and **E** to both apply to a number? _____

   c) Is it possible for statements **C** and **R** to both apply to a number? _____

7. a) Can you think of a number where statements **E** and **F** apply, but not **H**? _____

   b) Can you think of a number where statements **H** and **K** apply, but not **G**? _____

8. a) If statement **N** applies to a number, does statement **O** always have to apply? _____

   b) If statement **O** applies to a number, does statement **N** always have to apply? _____

9. Fill out the chart below by writing in a number for each statement. Don't use the same number more than once.

A	B	C
D	E	F
G	H	I
J	K	L
M	N	O
P	Q	R

JUMP at Home Grade 5   No unauthorized copying

Introduction

Models of Fractions

1. Give your child a ruler and ask them to solve the following puzzles:

   a. Draw a line 1 cm long. If the line, represents $\frac{1}{4}$, show what a whole line what look like.

   b. Line: 1 cm long. The line represents $\frac{1}{6}$. Show the whole.

   c. Line: 2 cm long. The line represents $\frac{1}{3}$. Show the whole.

   d. Line: 3 cm long. The line represents $\frac{1}{4}$. Show the whole.

   e. Line: $1\frac{1}{2}$ cm long. The line represents $\frac{1}{2}$. Show the whole.

   f. Line: $1\frac{1}{2}$ cm long. The line represents $\frac{1}{4}$. Show the whole.

   g. Line: 3 cm long. The line represents $\frac{1}{4}$. Show $\frac{1}{2}$.

   h. Line: 2 cm long. The line represents $\frac{1}{8}$. Show $\frac{1}{4}$.

2. Give your child counters to make a model of the following problem:
   Postcards come in packs of 4. How many packs would you need to buy to send 15 postcards?
   Write a mixed and improper fraction for the number of packs you would use.

   Your child could use a counter of a particular colour to represent the postcards they have used and a counter of a different colour to represent the postcards left over. After they have made their model, they could fill in the following chart:

Number of postcards	15
Number of packs of 4 postcards (improper fraction)	$\frac{15}{4}$
Number of packs of 4 postcards (mixed fraction)	$3\frac{3}{4}$

   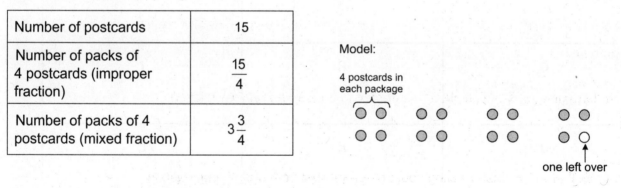

   Model:

   4 postcards in each package

   one left over

   Here is another sample problem your child could try:

   Juice cans come in boxes of 6. How many boxes would you bring if you needed 20 cans?
   What fraction of the boxes would you use?

3. Give your child blocks of 2 colours and have them make models of fractions of whole numbers using the method described at the top of the worksheet. Here are some fractions they might try:

   a) $\frac{3}{4}$ of 15   b) $\frac{3}{4}$ of 16   c) $\frac{3}{5}$ of 20   d) $\frac{2}{7}$ of 21

Models of Fractions (continued)

4. Ask your child to draw 4 boxes of equal length on grid paper and shade 1 box:

Point out to them that $\frac{1}{4}$ of the area of the boxes is shaded. Now ask them to draw the same set of boxes, but in each box to draw a line dividing the box into 2 parts:

Now $\frac{2}{8}$ of the area is shaded. Repeat the exercise, dividing the boxes into 3 equal parts, (roughly: the sketch doesn't have to be perfectly accurate), then 4 parts, then five parts:

$\frac{3}{12}$ of the area is shaded.

$\frac{4}{16}$ of the area is shaded.

$\frac{5}{20}$ of the area is shaded.

Point out to your child that while the appearance of the fraction changes, the same amount of area is represented:

$\frac{1}{4}, \frac{2}{8}, \frac{3}{12}, \frac{4}{16}$, and $\frac{5}{20}$ all represent the same amount; they are equivalent fractions.

Ask your child how each of the denominators in the fractions above can be generated from the initial fraction of $\frac{1}{4}$:

Answer:

Each denominator is a multiple of the denominator 4 in the original fraction:

$$8 = 2 \times 4 \qquad 12 = 3 \times 4 \qquad 16 = 4 \times 4 \qquad 20 = 5 \times 4$$

Then ask them how each fraction could be generated from the original fraction.

Answer:

Multiplying the numerator and denominator of the original fraction by the same number:

$$\frac{1}{4}\begin{smallmatrix}\times 2\\ \times 2\end{smallmatrix} = \frac{2}{8} \qquad \frac{1}{4}\begin{smallmatrix}\times 3\\ \times 3\end{smallmatrix} = \frac{3}{12} \qquad \frac{1}{4}\begin{smallmatrix}\times 4\\ \times 4\end{smallmatrix} = \frac{4}{16} \qquad \frac{1}{4}\begin{smallmatrix}\times 5\\ \times 5\end{smallmatrix} = \frac{5}{20}$$

Models of Fractions *(continued)*

Point out that multiplying the top and bottom of the original fraction by any given number, say 5, corresponds to cutting each box into that number of pieces:

$$\frac{1 \times 5}{4 \times 5}$$ ← There are 5 pieces in each box.
← There are 4 × 5 pieces altogether.

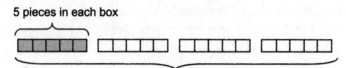

5 pieces in each box

4 × 5 = pieces altogether.

The fractions $\frac{1}{4}, \frac{2}{8}, \frac{3}{12}, \frac{4}{16} \ldots$ form a **family of equivalent fractions**. Notice that no whole number greater than 1 will divide into both the numerator and denominator of $\frac{1}{4} : \frac{1}{4}$ is said to be reduced to lowest terms. By multiplying the top and bottom of a reduced fraction by various whole numbers, you can generate an entire fraction family. For instance, $\frac{2}{5}$ generates this family:

$$\frac{2}{5} \begin{matrix} \times 2 \\ \times 2 \end{matrix} = \frac{4}{10} \qquad \frac{2}{5} \begin{matrix} \times 3 \\ \times 3 \end{matrix} = \frac{6}{15} \qquad \frac{2}{5} \begin{matrix} \times 4 \\ \times 4 \end{matrix} = \frac{8}{20}$$

Elimination Game

Find the special number in each square by reading the clues and eliminating.
REMEMBER: Zero is an even number.

1. Cross out numbers that are…

a)

4	3	9
7	9	8
1	6	5

• Odd
• Less than 4
• Greater than 5
What number is left?

b)

4	2	3
5	1	7
0	9	8

• Even
• Less than 4
• Greater than 6
What number is left?

c)

4	20	9
11	6	16
5	3	18

• Even
• Multiples of 3
• Greater than 10
What number is left?

d)

4	20	9
15	6	16
5	3	18

• Multiples of 2
• Multiples of 3
• Multiples of 4
What number is left?

2. **BONUS:** Cross out numbers **with**…

a)

42	31	92
27	99	88
21	66	52

• Ones digit 2
• Tens digit 2
• Both digits are the same
What number is left?

b)

24	3	9
7	89	83
1	6	52

• One digit
• Tens digit 8
• Ones digit 2
What number is left?

Battleship and Secret Squares

Once your child understands the game, they can play in pairs.

Battleship

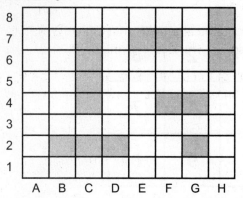

Player 1 and Player 2 each draw a grid as shown. Each player shades:

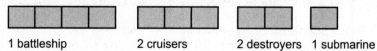

1 battleship   2 cruisers   2 destroyers   1 submarine

(See grid for an example: no square of a ship may be adjacent to a square of another ship, including diagonally.)

Players try to sink all their partner's battleships by guessing their coordinates. If a player's ship is in a square that is called out, the player must say "hit." Otherwise they say "miss."

Each player should keep track of the squares they have guessed on a blank grid by marking hits with ✗'s and misses with ✓'s. The game ends when all of one player's ships are sunk. A ship is sunk when <u>all</u> its squares are hit.

Secret Squares

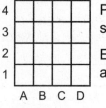

Player 1 draws a 4 × 4 grid as shown and picks a square. Player 2 tries to guess the square by giving its coordinates.

Each time Player 2 guesses, Player 1 writes the distance between the guessed square and the hidden square.

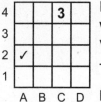

For instance, if Player 1 has chosen square A2 (✓) and Player 2 guesses C4, Player 1 writes 3 in the guessed square. (Distances on the grid are counted horizontally and vertically, <u>never</u> diagonally.)

The game ends when Player 2 guesses the correct square.

PARENT: As a warm-up for the Secret Squares game above, have your child try to guess the locations of each hidden square from the information given in the grids below. In 2 grids, not enough information is given (have your child mark all possible locations for the hidden square) and in one grid too much information is given (have your child identify one piece of redundant information):

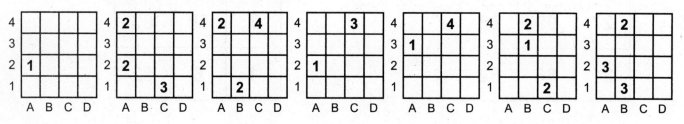

Models of Decimals

Children often make mistakes in comparing decimals where one of the decimals is expressed in tenths and the other in hundredths. (For instance, they will say that .17 is greater than .2.) The following activity will help your child understand the relation between tenths and hundredths.

Give your child a set of play-money dimes and pennies. Explain that a dime is a tenth of a dollar (which is why it is written as $0.10) and a penny is a hundredth of a dollar (which is why it is written as $0.01).

Ask your child to make models of the amounts in the left-hand column of the chart below and to write as many names for the amounts as they can think of in the right-hand columns (sample answers are provided in italics):

Amount	Amount in Pennies	Decimal Names (in words)	Decimal Names (in numbers)
2 dimes	*20 pennies*	*2 tenths (of a dollar)* *20 hundredths*	*.2* *.20*
3 pennies	*3 pennies*	*3 hundredths*	*.03*
4 dimes and 3 pennies	*43 pennies*	*4 tenths and 3 hundredths* *43 hundredths*	*.43* *.43*

You should also write various amounts of money on a sheet of paper and have your child make models of the amounts (e.g., make models of .3 dollars, .27 dollars, .07 dollars, etc.). Also challenge them to make models of amounts that have 2 different decimal representations (e.g., 2 dimes can be written as .2 dollars or .20 dollars).

When you feel your child is able to translate between money and decimal notation, ask them to say whether they would rather have .2 dollars or .17 dollars. In their answer, they should say exactly how many pennies each amount represents (e.g., they must articulate that .2 represents 20 pennies and so it is actually the larger amount).

Amount (in dollars)	Amount (in pennies)
.2	
.15	

For extra practice, ask your child to fill in the right-hand column of the chart and then circle the greater amount. (Create several charts of this sort for them.)

No unauthorized copying **Games, Activities, and Puzzles**

Magic Squares and Number Pyramids

1. In a magic square, the numbers in each row, column, and diagonal all add up to the same number (the "magic number" for the square):

   What is the magic number for this square? _____

2	9	4
7	5	3
6	1	8

2. Complete the magic squares:

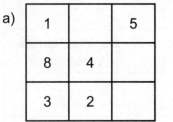

a)

1		5
8	4	
3	2	

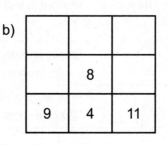

b)

	8	
9	4	11

c)

		9
	11	
13		17

3. Here are some number pyramids:

  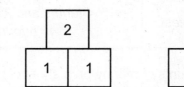

Can you find the rule by which the patterns in the pyramids were made? Describe it here:

4. Using the rule you described in Question 3, find the missing numbers:

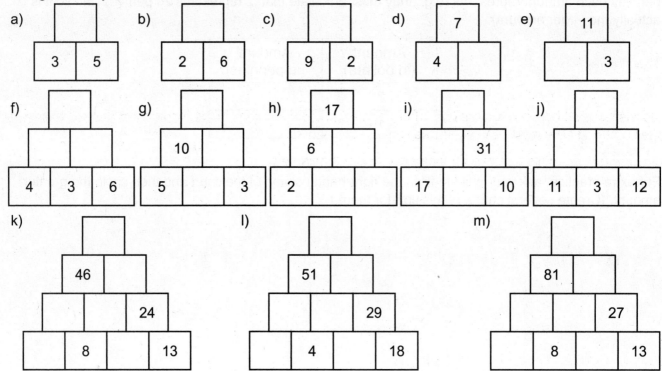

No unauthorized copying   **Games, Activities, and Puzzles**

Magic Trick (Algebra)

In the magic trick below, the magician can always predict the result of a sequence of operations performed on any chosen number. Try the trick with your child, then encourage them to figure out how it works using a block to stand in for the mystery number (give lots of hints).

The Trick		The Algebra
Pick any number.	□	Use a square block to represent the mystery number.
Add 4.	□ ○○○○	Use 4 circles to represent the 4 ones that were added.
Multiply by 2.	□ ○○○○ □ ○○○○	Create 2 sets of blocks to show the doubling.
Subtract 2.	□ ○○○ □ ○○○	Take away 2 circles to show the subtraction.
Divide by 2.	□ ○○○	Remove one set of blocks to show the division.
Subtract the mystery number.	○○○	Remove the square.

The answer is 3!

No matter what number you choose, after performing the operations in the magic trick, you will always get the number 3. The model above shows why the trick works.

Encourage your child to make up their own trick of the same type.

PA5-1: Counting

Jamie finds the **difference** between 15 and 12 by counting on her fingers.
She says "12" with her fist closed, then counts to 15, raising one finger at a time:

When she says "15," she has raised 3 fingers. So the difference or "gap" between 12 and 15 is 3.

----

1. Count the gap between the numbers. Write your answer in the circle:
   HINT: If you know your subtraction facts, you may be able to find the answer without counting.

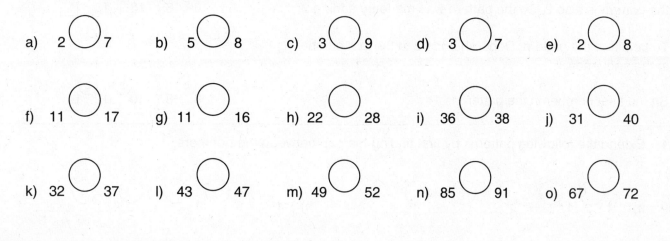

2. Add the number in the circle to the number beside it. Write your answer in the blank:

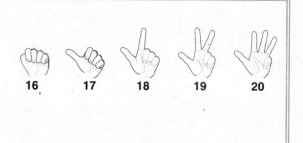

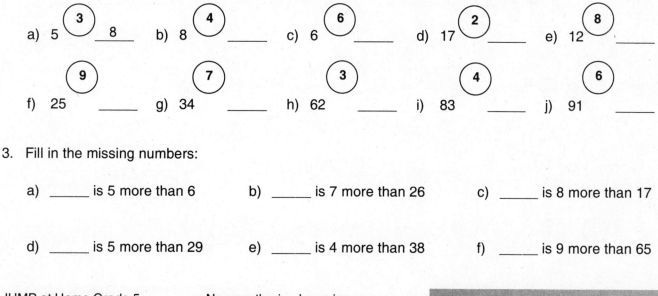

3. Fill in the missing numbers:

   a) _____ is 5 more than 6   b) _____ is 7 more than 26   c) _____ is 8 more than 17

   d) _____ is 5 more than 29   e) _____ is 4 more than 38   f) _____ is 9 more than 65

Patterns & Algebra 1

In an **increasing sequence**, each number is greater than the one before it.

Deborah wants to continue the number pattern:

6 , 8 , 10 , 12 , _?_

She finds the **difference**
between the first two numbers:

6 , 8 , 10 , 12 , _?_

She finds that the difference between the other numbers in
the pattern is also 2. So the pattern was made by adding 2:

6 , 8 , 10 , 12 , _?_

To continue the pattern, Deborah adds 2 to the last number
in the sequence.

So the final number in the pattern is 14:

6 , 8 , 10 , 12 , 14

---

1. Extend the following patterns by first finding the gap between the numbers.

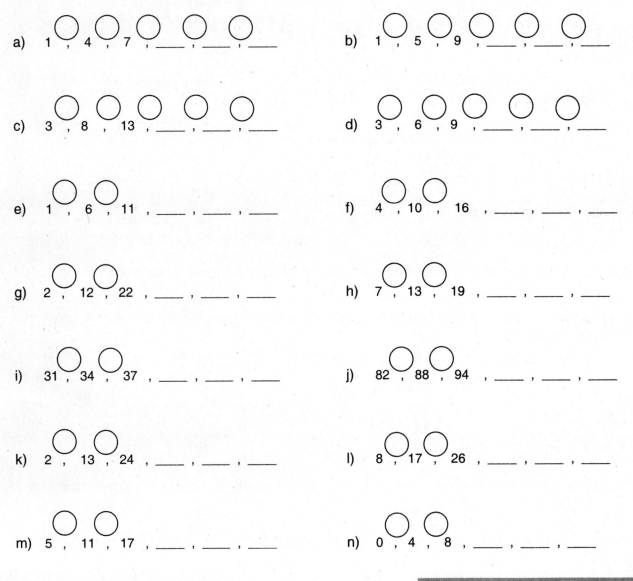

a) 1 , 4 , 7 , ___ , ___ , ___

b) 1 , 5 , 9 , ___ , ___ , ___

c) 3 , 8 , 13 , ___ , ___ , ___

d) 3 , 6 , 9 , ___ , ___ , ___

e) 1 , 6 , 11 , ___ , ___ , ___

f) 4 , 10 , 16 , ___ , ___ , ___

g) 2 , 12 , 22 , ___ , ___ , ___

h) 7 , 13 , 19 , ___ , ___ , ___

i) 31 , 34 , 37 , ___ , ___ , ___

j) 82 , 88 , 94 , ___ , ___ , ___

k) 2 , 13 , 24 , ___ , ___ , ___

l) 8 , 17 , 26 , ___ , ___ , ___

m) 5 , 11 , 17 , ___ , ___ , ___

n) 0 , 4 , 8 , ___ , ___ , ___

PA5-3: Counting Backwards

What number must you subtract from 43 to get 39?

43 – ? = 39

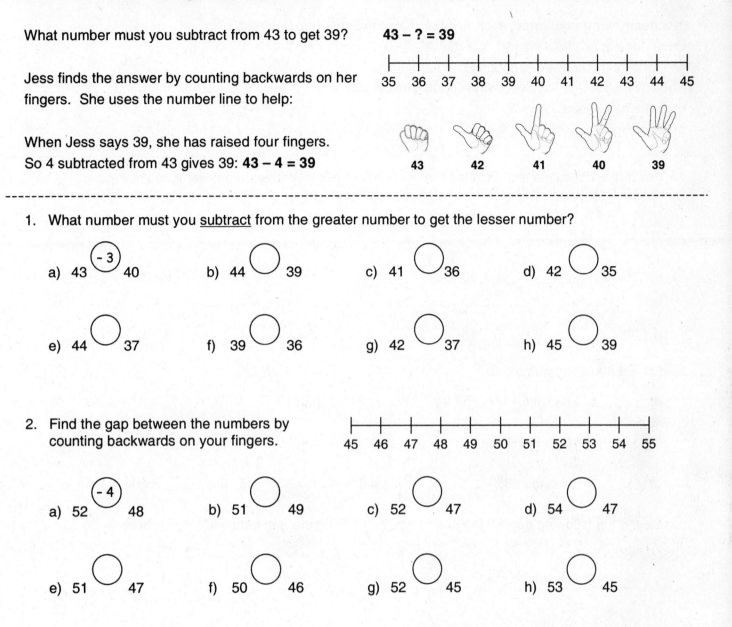

Jess finds the answer by counting backwards on her fingers. She uses the number line to help:

When Jess says 39, she has raised four fingers.
So 4 subtracted from 43 gives 39: **43 – 4 = 39**

----

1. What number must you <u>subtract</u> from the greater number to get the lesser number?

   a) 43 (– 3) 40   b) 44 ◯ 39   c) 41 ◯ 36   d) 42 ◯ 35

   e) 44 ◯ 37   f) 39 ◯ 36   g) 42 ◯ 37   h) 45 ◯ 39

2. Find the gap between the numbers by counting backwards on your fingers.

   a) 52 (– 4) 48   b) 51 ◯ 49   c) 52 ◯ 47   d) 54 ◯ 47

   e) 51 ◯ 47   f) 50 ◯ 46   g) 52 ◯ 45   h) 53 ◯ 45

3. Find the gap between the numbers by counting backwards on your fingers (or by using your subtraction facts):

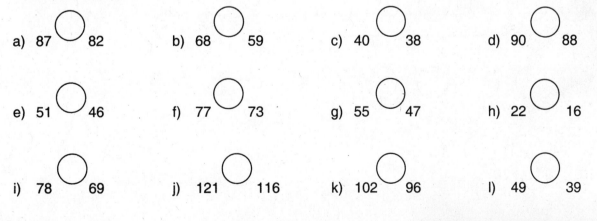

   a) 87 ◯ 82   b) 68 ◯ 59   c) 40 ◯ 38   d) 90 ◯ 88

   e) 51 ◯ 46   f) 77 ◯ 73   g) 55 ◯ 47   h) 22 ◯ 16

   i) 78 ◯ 69   j) 121 ◯ 116   k) 102 ◯ 96   l) 49 ◯ 39

Patterns & Algebra 1

PA5-4: Decreasing Sequences

In a **decreasing sequence**, each number is less than the one before it.

What number is 3 less than 9?   (Or: $9 - 3 = ?$)

Jenna finds the answer by counting on her fingers.

She says 9 with her fist closed and counts backwards

until she has raised 3 fingers:

The number 6 is 3 <u>less than</u> 9:   **$9 - 3 = 6$**

9   8   7   6

----

1. Follow the directions to the circle from the number given. Write your answer in the blank:

a) 7 $\overset{-3}{\bigcirc}$ _____   b) 13 $\overset{-3}{\bigcirc}$ _____   c) 9 $\overset{-4}{\bigcirc}$ _____   d) 17 $\overset{-1}{\bigcirc}$ _____

e) 16 $\overset{-5}{\bigcirc}$ _____   f) 19 $\overset{-4}{\bigcirc}$ _____   g) 25 $\overset{-1}{\bigcirc}$ _____   h) 29 $\overset{-2}{\bigcirc}$ _____

i) 38 $\overset{-4}{\bigcirc}$ _____   j) 45 $\overset{-6}{\bigcirc}$ _____   k) 63 $\overset{-8}{\bigcirc}$ _____   l) 72 $\overset{-4}{\bigcirc}$ _____

2. Fill in the missing numbers:

a) _____ is 5 less than 17   b) _____ is 3 less than 19   c) _____ is 2 less than 18

d) _____ is 6 less than 26   e) _____ is 8 less than 20   f) _____ is 4 less than 29

g) _____ is 7 less than 35   h) _____ is 9 less than 42   i) _____ is 8 less than 90

3. Extend the following <u>decreasing</u> patterns by first finding the gap between the numbers.

a) 13 , 11 , 9 , ____ , ____ , ____

b) 33 , 28 , 23 , ____ , ____ , ____

c) 64 , 61 , 58 , ____ , ____ , ____

d) 55 , 46 , 37 , ____ , ____ , ____

e) 110 , 90 , 70 , ____ , ____ , ____

Example:

11 , 9 , 7 , ____ , ____ , ____

Step 1: $\overset{-2}{\bigcirc}$ $\overset{-2}{\bigcirc}$ $\overset{-2}{\bigcirc}$ $\overset{-2}{\bigcirc}$ $\overset{-2}{\bigcirc}$
11 , 9 , 7 , ____ , ____ , ____

Step 2: $\overset{-2}{\bigcirc}$ $\overset{-2}{\bigcirc}$ $\overset{-2}{\bigcirc}$ $\overset{-2}{\bigcirc}$ $\overset{-2}{\bigcirc}$
11 , 9 , 7 , 5 , 3 , 1

PA5-5: Increasing and Decreasing Sequences

1. Extend the following patterns, using the "gap" provided:

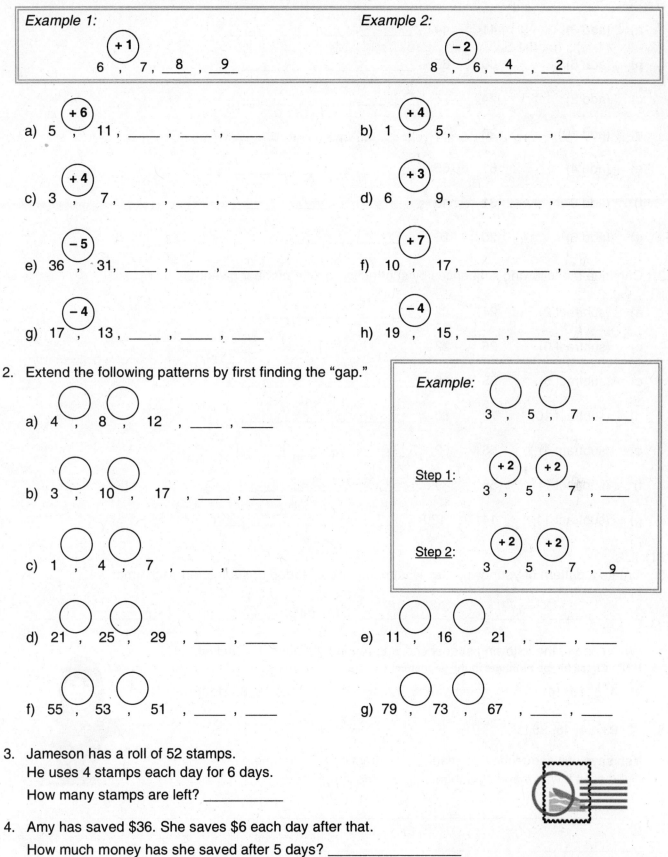

Example 1:

⊕+1
6 , 7, __8__ , __9__

Example 2:

⊖−2
8 , 6, __4__ , __2__

a) 5 (+6) 11 , ____ , ____ , ____

b) 1 (+4) 5 , ____ , ____ , ____

c) 3 (+4) 7 , ____ , ____ , ____

d) 6 (+3) 9 , ____ , ____ , ____

e) 36 (−5) 31 , ____ , ____ , ____

f) 10 (+7) 17 , ____ , ____ , ____

g) 17 (−4) 13 , ____ , ____ , ____

h) 19 (−4) 15 , ____ , ____ , ____

2. Extend the following patterns by first finding the "gap."

a) 4 ◯ 8 ◯ 12 , ____ , ____

b) 3 ◯ 10 ◯ 17 , ____ , ____

c) 1 , 4 , 7 , ____ , ____

d) 21 , 25 , 29 , ____ , ____

e) 11 , 16 , 21 , ____ , ____

f) 55 , 53 , 51 , ____ , ____

g) 79 , 73 , 67 , ____ , ____

Example:

3 ◯ 5 ◯ 7 , ____

Step 1: 3 (+2) 5 (+2) 7 , ____

Step 2: 3 (+2) 5 (+2) 7 , __9__

3. Jameson has a roll of 52 stamps.
   He uses 4 stamps each day for 6 days.
   How many stamps are left? _____

4. Amy has saved $36. She saves $6 each day after that.
   How much money has she saved after 5 days? _____

Patterns & Algebra 1

PA5-6: Extending a Pattern Using a Rule

1. Continue the following sequences by <u>adding</u> the number given:

   a) (add 3)   41 , 44 , _____, _____, _____

   b) (add 5)   60 , 65 , _____, _____, _____

   c) (add 2)   74 , 76 , _____, _____, _____

   d) (add 10)   20 , 30 , _____, _____, _____

   e) (add 4)   61 , 65 , _____, _____, _____

   f) (add 9)   31 , 40 , _____, _____, _____

   g) (add 6)   20 , 26 , _____, _____, _____

2. Continue the following sequences by <u>subtracting</u> by the number given:

   a) (subtract 2)   24 , 22 , _____, _____, _____

   b) (subtract 3)   25 , 22 , _____, _____, _____

   c) (subtract 5)   85 , 80 , _____, _____, _____

   d) (subtract 10)   70 , 60 , _____, _____, _____

   e) (subtract 4)   56 , 52 , _____, _____, _____

   f) (subtract 7)   56 , 49 , _____, _____, _____

   g) (subtract 11)   141 , 130 , _____, _____, _____

BONUS
3. Create a pattern of your own. Say what number you added or subtracted each time:

   _____ , _____ , _____ , _____ , _____   My rule: _____

4. Which one of the following sequences was made by adding 4? Circle it.
   HINT: Check all the numbers in the sequence.

   a) 4, 8, 10, 14   b) 4, 8, 12, 16   c) 3, 9, 11, 15

5. **72, 63, 54, 45, 36, ...**

   Yen says this sequence was made by subtracting 8 each time.
   Hyun says it was made by subtracting 9. Who is right?

   _____

   _____

Patterns & Algebra 1

PA5-7: Identifying Pattern Rules

1. What number was added each time to make the pattern?

    a) 2, 6, 10, 14   add ____   b) 2, 5, 8, 11   add ____

    c) 18, 24, 30, 36   add ____   d) 40, 47, 54, 61   add ____

    e) 81, 86, 91, 96   add ____   f) 69, 72, 75, 78   add ____

2. What number was subtracted each time to make each pattern?

    a) 38, 36, 34, 32   subtract ____   b) 65, 60, 55, 50   subtract ____

    c) 200, 199, 198, 197   subtract ____   d) 91, 88, 85, 82   subtract ____

    e) 67, 64, 61, 58   subtract ____   f) 399, 397, 395, 393   subtract ____

3. State the rule for the following patterns:

    a) 219, 212, 205, 198, 191   subtract ____   b) 11, 19, 27, 35, 43, 51   add _____

    c) 301, 305, 309, 313   _____   d) 210, 198, 186, 174   _____

    e) 633, 622, 611, 600, 589   _____   f) 821, 830, 839, 848, 857   _____

    g) 407, 415, 423, 431   _____   h) 731, 725, 719, 713   _____

4. Find the rule for the pattern. Then continue the pattern:

    a) 22, 27, 32, __37__, __42__, __47__   The rule is: ___Start at 22 and add 5 each time___

    b) 38, 45, 52, _____, _____, _____   The rule is: _____

    c) 124, 136, 148, _____, _____, _____   The rule is: _____

5.   **5, 9, 13, 17, 21, ...**

    Jonah says the pattern rule is: "Start at 5 and subtract 4 each time."
    Pria says the rule is: "Start at 5 and add 5 each time."
    Genevieve says the rule is: "Start at 5 and add 4 each time."

    a) Whose rule is correct? _____

    b) What mistakes did the others make? _____

    _____

    _____

PA5-8: Introduction to T-tables

Claude makes a **growing pattern** with squares.
He records the number of squares in each figure in a chart or T-table.

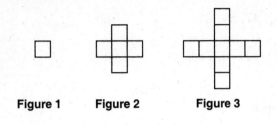

| Figure 1 | Figure 2 | Figure 3 |

Figure	# of Squares
1	1
2	5
3	9

④ ← Number of squares
④ ← <u>added</u> each time.

The number of squares in the figures are 1, 5, 9, …
Claude writes a rule for this number pattern:

RULE: Start at 1 and add 4 each time.

---

1. Claude makes other growing patterns with squares.
   How many squares does he add to make each new figure?
   Write your answer in the circles provided. Then write a rule for the pattern:

a)

Figure	Number of Squares
1	2
2	7
3	12

Rule:
Start at 2 and
add 5 each time

b)

Figure	Number of Squares
1	2
2	9
3	16

Rule:

c)

Figure	Number of Squares
1	1
2	4
3	7

Rule:

d)

Figure	Number of Squares
1	1
2	7
3	13

Rule:

e)

Figure	Number of Squares
1	5
2	12
3	19

Rule:

f)

Figure	Number of Squares
1	13
2	21
3	29

Rule:

Patterns & Algebra 1

g)

Figure	Number of Squares
1	3
2	11
3	19

Rule:

h)

Figure	Number of Squares
1	7
2	11
3	15

Rule:

i)

Figure	Number of Squares
1	8
2	14
3	20

Rule:

2. Extend the number pattern. How many squares would be used in Figure 6?

a)

Figure	Number of Squares
1	2
2	9
3	16

b)

Figure	Number of Squares
1	2
2	6
3	10

c)

Figure	Number of Squares
1	6
2	11
3	16

3. Trina makes the following growing patterns with squares.
After making Figure 3, she only has 16 squares left.
Does she have enough squares to complete Figure 4?

a)

Figure	Number of Squares
1	4
2	9
3	14

YES   NO

b)

Figure	Number of Squares
1	5
2	9
3	13

YES   NO

c)

Figure	Number of Squares
1	3
2	7
3	11

YES   NO

4. Make a chart to show how many shapes will be needed to make the fifth figure in each pattern.

a)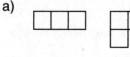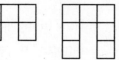

b)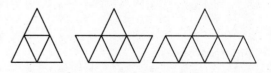

1. Count the number of line segments (lines that join pairs of dots) in each figure.
   HINT: Count around the outside of the figure first, marking line segments as you go.

Example:
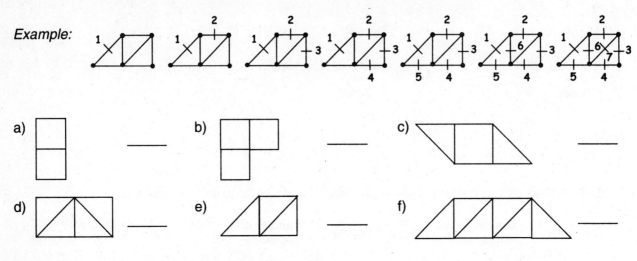

a) [square divided into two] ___

b) [L-shaped figure] ___

c) [parallelogram with line] ___

d) [rectangle with triangles] ___

e) [triangle figure] ___

f) [row of triangles] ___

2. Continue the pattern below, then complete the chart:

Figure 1

Figure 2

Figure 3

Figure 4

Figure	Number of Line Segments
1	
2	
3	
4	

How many line segments would Figure 5 have? _____

3. Continue the pattern below, then complete the chart:

Figure 1

Figure 2

Figure 3

Figure 4

Figure	Number of Line Segments
1	
2	
3	
4	

How many line segments would Figure 7 have? _____

Patterns & Algebra 1

Continue the patterns below, then complete the charts.

4.

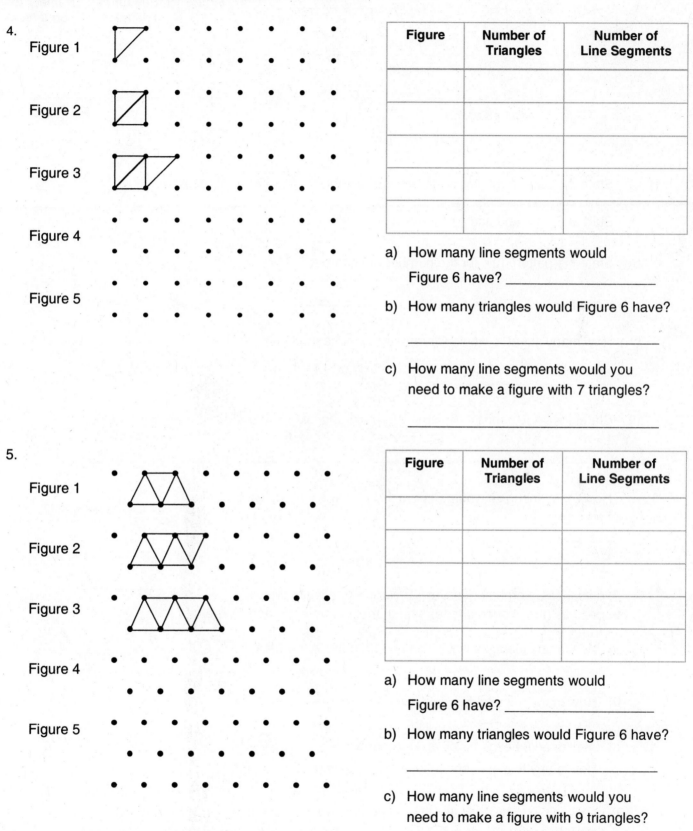

Figure 1

Figure 2

Figure 3

Figure 4

Figure 5

Figure	Number of Triangles	Number of Line Segments

a) How many line segments would Figure 6 have? _____

b) How many triangles would Figure 6 have?

_____

c) How many line segments would you need to make a figure with 7 triangles?

_____

5.

Figure 1

Figure 2

Figure 3

Figure 4

Figure 5

Figure	Number of Triangles	Number of Line Segments

a) How many line segments would Figure 6 have? _____

b) How many triangles would Figure 6 have?

_____

c) How many line segments would you need to make a figure with 9 triangles?

_____

6.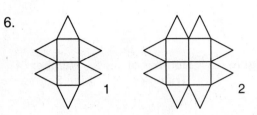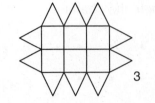

Clare's pattern

Figure	Number of Triangles	Number of Squares

a) State the pattern rule for the number of triangles:

Start at _____ and add _____ each time.

b) State the pattern rule for the number of squares:

_____

c) How many squares would Clare need to make the fifth figure?

_____

d) Clare says she needs 17 triangles to make the sixth figure. Is she correct?

_____

e) How many triangles would Clare need to make a figure with 10 squares?

_____

7. Avril makes an ornament using a hexagon (the white shape), trapezoids (the shaded shape), and triangles (the patterned shapes):

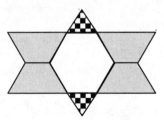

a) How many triangles would Avril need to make 9 ornaments?

b) How many trapezoids would Avril need to make 5 ornaments?

c) Avril used 6 hexagons to make ornaments.
   How many triangles and how many trapezoids did she use?

d) How many trapezoids would Avril need to make ornaments with 14 triangles?
   HINT: Use skip counting or division to find out how many ornaments 14 triangles would make.

Patterns & Algebra 1

1. Sarah's fish tank is leaking.

    At 6 pm, there are 21 L of water in the tank.

    At 7 pm, there are 18 L.

    At 8 pm, there are 15 L.

Hour	Amount of water in the tank
6 pm	21 L
7 pm	18 L
8 pm	15 L
9 pm	
10 pm	

a) How many litres of water leak out each hour?

    _____

b) How many litres will be left in the tank at 10 pm?

    _____

c) How many hours will it take for all the water to leak out?

    _____

2. Maral has $28 in his savings account at the end of March.
    He saves $7 each month.
    How much does he have in his account at the end of June?

Month	Savings
March	$28

3. Reema has $42 in her savings account at the end of October.
    She spends $7 each month.
    How much does she have at the end of January?

Month	Savings
October	$42

4. Jane plants a 30 cm tall rose bush on May 1st.
    It grows 25 cm every month.
    What is its height on August 1st?

Date	Height
May 1st	30 cm

5. A white cedar tree seedling grows about 9 cm in a year.
    How tall will it be after 3 years?

Years	Height
0	0 cm

Patterns & Algebra 1

The **terms** of a sequence are the numbers or items in the sequence.

A **term number** gives the position of each item.

This is **term number 4** since
it is in the fourth position.

↓

4, 7, 10, 13, 16

----

1. Extend the T-table to find the 5th term in the sequence:

   3, 5, 7, …

Term Number	Term
1	3
2	5
3	7
4	
5	

2. Draw a T-table for each sequence to find the given term:

   a) Find the 6th term: 2, 5, 8, 11, …

   b) Find the 7th term: 21, 26, 31, 36, …

3. Travis says that the 6th term of the sequence 5, 7, 9, … is 17. Is he correct? Explain.

4. Using blocks or other shapes, make a model of a sequence of figures that could go with each T-table:

a)

Term Number	Term
1	2
2	5
3	8
4	11

b)

Term Number	Term
1	1
2	5
3	9
4	13

5. A marina rents sailboats at $6 for the first hour and $5 for every hour after that. How much does it cost to rent a sailboat for 6 hours?

6. Zoe saves $65 in August. She saves $6 each month after that.
   Adrian saves $62 in August. He saves $7 each month after that.
   Who has saved more money by the end of January?

7. A newborn elephant weighs about 77 kg.
   It drinks about 11 litres of milk a day and gains about 1 kg every day.

   a) How much weight does the baby gain in a week?

   b) How many litres of milk does the baby drink in a week?

   c) How many days does it take for the baby to double its weight?

Marco makes a **repeating** pattern using blocks:

This is the **core** of Marco's pattern.

The **core** of a pattern is the part that repeats.

---

1. Circle the core of the following patterns. The first one is done for you:

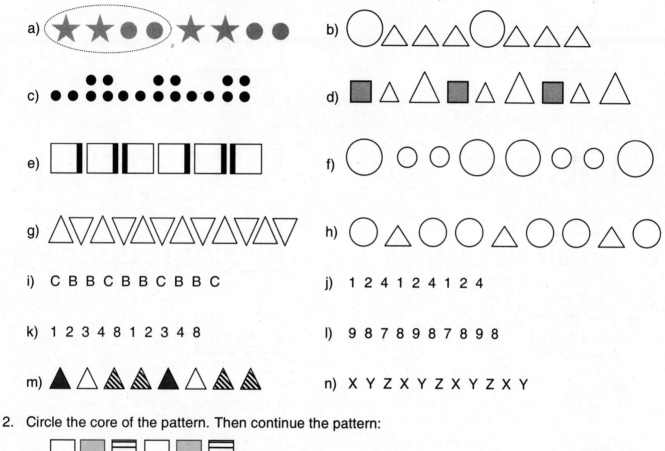

i) C B B C B B C B B C

j) 1 2 4 1 2 4 1 2 4

k) 1 2 3 4 8 1 2 3 4 8

l) 9 8 7 8 9 8 7 8 9 8

m) ▲△▲▲△▲△▲▲

n) X Y Z X Y Z X Y Z X Y

2. Circle the core of the pattern. Then continue the pattern:

a) ☐ ☐ ☰ ☐ ☐ ☰ ____ ____ ____ ____

b) ■ △ ■ ■ △ ■ ____ ____ ____ ____

c) A B C A B C A ___ ___ ___ ___

d) 2 8 9 6 2 8 9 6 ___ ___ ___ ___

e) 3 0 0 4 3 0 0 4 3 0 ___ ___ ___ ___

3. In a notebook (or using blocks), make several repeating patterns of your own. Have a parent guess the core of your pattern.

Patterns & Algebra 1

PA5-13: Extending Patterns & Predicting Positions

1. Angela makes a repeating pattern using blue (**B**) and yellow (**Y**) blocks.
   The box shows the core of her pattern. Continue the pattern by writing Bs and Ys:

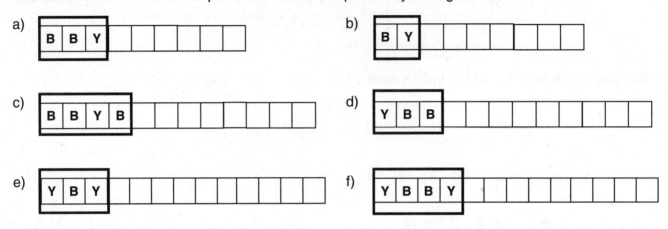

a) B B Y

b) B Y

c) B B Y B

d) Y B B

e) Y B Y

f) Y B B Y

2. Barry tried to continue the pattern in the box. Did he continue the pattern correctly?
   HINT: Shade the yellows (Y) if it helps.

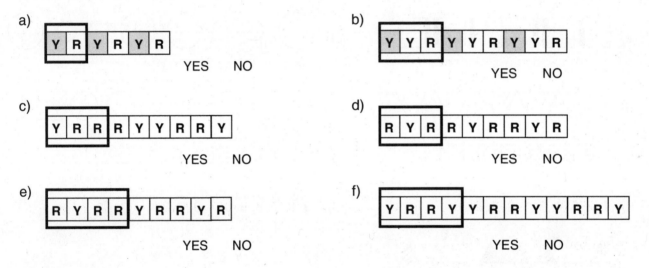

a) Y R Y R Y R   YES   NO

b) Y Y R Y Y R Y Y R   YES   NO

c) Y R R R Y Y R R Y   YES   NO

d) R Y R R Y R R Y R   YES   NO

e) R Y R R Y R R Y R   YES   NO

f) Y R R Y Y R R Y Y R R Y   YES   NO

3. For each pattern below, say whether the blocks in the rectangle are the <u>core</u> of the pattern:

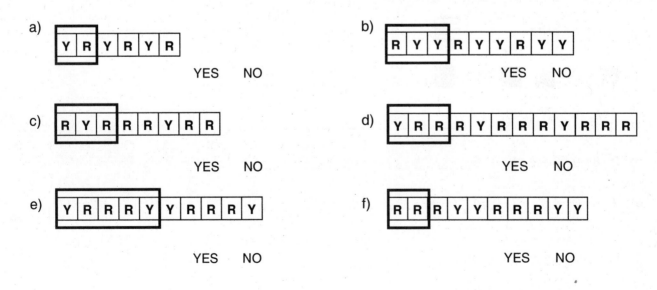

a) Y R Y R Y R   YES   NO

b) R Y Y R Y Y R Y Y   YES   NO

c) R Y R R R Y R R   YES   NO

d) Y R R R Y R R R Y R R R   YES   NO

e) Y R R R Y Y R R R Y   YES   NO

f) R R R Y Y R R R Y Y   YES   NO

Patterns & Algebra 1

Sally wants to predict the colour of the 17th block in the pattern. First she finds the core of the pattern:

R	R	Y	R	R	Y	R	R	Y	R	R	Y

The core is 3 blocks long. Sally marks every <u>third</u> number on a hundreds chart.

Each X shows the position of a block where the core ends:

1	2	✗3	4	5	✗6	7	8	✗9	10
11	✗12	13	14	✗15	16 R	17 R	18 Y	19	20

The core ends on the 15th block.

Sally writes the letters of the core on the chart, starting at 16.

The 17th block is red.

----

4. In the patterns below, put a rectangle around the blocks that make up the core:

a)
Y	R	R	Y	R	R	Y	R	R

b)
R	Y	R	Y	R	Y	R	Y

c)
Y	Y	R	R	Y	Y	R	R	Y	Y	R	R

d)
Y	R	R	Y	Y	R	R	Y	Y

e)
R	Y	R	Y	Y	Y	R	Y	R	Y	Y	Y

f)
R	R	R	Y	R	R	R	Y	R	R

5. Predict the colour of the 18th block using Sally's method:
   NOTE: Start by finding the core of the pattern.

R	Y	Y	Y	R	Y	Y	Y

Colour: _____

1	2	3	4	5	6	7	8	9	10
11	12	13	14	15	16	17	18	19	20

6. Predict the colour of the 19th block:

R	R	Y	Y	R	R	Y	Y

Colour: _____

1	2	3	4	5	6	7	8	9	10
11	12	13	14	15	16	17	18	19	20

7. Predict the colour of the 17th block:

R	R	Y	Y	Y	R	R	Y	Y	Y

Colour: _____

1	2	3	4	5	6	7	8	9	10
11	12	13	14	15	16	17	18	19	20

Patterns & Algebra 1

PA5-13: Extending Patterns & Predicting Positions (continued)   page 18

8. Draw a box around the core of the pattern. Then predict the colour of the 35th block:

Y	R	Y	Y	R	Y	Y	R	Y

Colour: _____

1	2	3	4	5	6	7	8	9	10
11	12	13	14	15	16	17	18	19	20
21	22	23	24	25	26	27	28	29	30
31	32	33	34	35	36	37	38	39	40

9. Carl makes a pattern with red, green, and yellow beads:

What colour will the 43rd bead be?

10. Megan plants a row of daisies and pansies in the pattern shown:

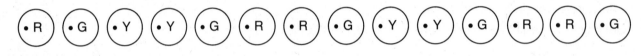

D   P   P   D   P   P   D

Is the 37th flower a daisy or a pansy?

11. Explain how you could find the colour of the 48th block in this pattern without using a hundreds chart.

R	R	Y	Y	Y	R	R	Y	Y	Y

12. Design a repeating pattern that has a core that is ten squares long.
    What is the colour of the 97th square? How do you know?

13. a) What is the 15th coin in this pattern? Explain how you know.

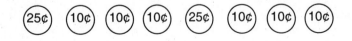

    BONUS
    b) What is the total value of the first 20 coins?

On Monday morning, Olivia is 600 kilometres from Winnipeg.

Her solar-powered car can travel 150 km per day.

How far from Winnipeg will she be by Wednesday evening?

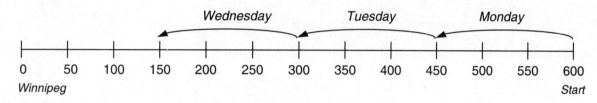

On Wednesday evening, Olivia will be 150 km from Winnipeg.

- -

1. On Thursday morning, Eduardo's campsite is 19 km from Great Bear Lake.
    He plans to hike 6 km towards the lake each day.

    How far from the lake will he be on Saturday evening? _____

```
|—+—+—+—+—+—+—+—+—+—+—+—+—+—+—+—+—+—+—+—|
0   1   2   3   4   5   6   7   8   9  10  11  12  13  14  15  16  17  18  19  20
```

2. On Sunday morning, Nandita is on a bicycle tour 400 km from her home.
    She can cycle 75 km each day.

    How far from home will she be on Wednesday evening? _____

```
|—+—+—+—+—+—+—+—+—+—+—+—+—+—+—+—|
0   25  50  75 100 125 150 175 200 225 250 275 300 325 350 375 400
```

Draw and label a number line in the grid to solve.

3. Helen is 14 blocks from home. She can run 2 blocks in a minute.

    How far from home will she be in 3 minutes?

    ```
    |—|—|
    0   1   2
    ```

4. Ravi is 15 blocks from the store. He can cycle 4 blocks in a minute.

    How far from the store will he be after 3 minutes?

Patterns & Algebra 1

PA5-15: Number Lines (Advanced)

In each of the problems below you will have to decide on a scale for your number line.

1.  Kristal has entered a 250 km bike race. He can cycle 75 km each day.
   How far from the finish will he be after 3 days?

   0   25   50   75

2. Wendy has to climb 5 walls in an obstacle course.
   The first wall is 100 metres from the start.
   After that, each wall is 75 metres farther than the last.
   How far from the start is the 3rd wall?

3. Six telephone poles are placed 50 m apart.
   Alan wants to string a wire between the first and last pole.
   What length of wire will he need?

4. Peter plants 4 rosebushes in a row.
   The nearest bush is 8 metres from his house.
   The bushes are 3 metres apart.
   How far away from Peter's house is the last rosebush?
   HINT: Put Peter's house at zero on the number line.

5. Jill's house is 20 metres from the sidewalk.
   A dog is tied to a tree halfway between the house and the sidewalk.
   The dog's leash is 8 m long.
   How close to the sidewalk can the dog come?

Patterns & Algebra 1

PA5-16: 2-Dimensional Patterns

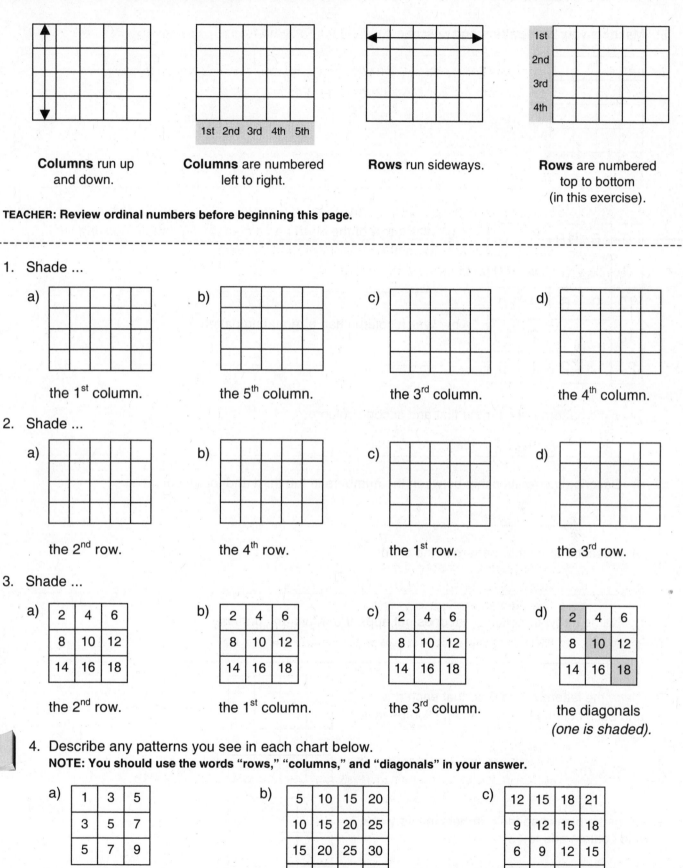

Columns run up and down.

Columns are numbered left to right.

1st 2nd 3rd 4th 5th

Rows run sideways.

Rows are numbered top to bottom (in this exercise).

1st 2nd 3rd 4th

TEACHER: Review ordinal numbers before beginning this page.

1. Shade ...

   a) the 1st column.

   b) the 5th column.

   c) the 3rd column.

   d) the 4th column.

2. Shade ...

   a) the 2nd row.

   b) the 4th row.

   c) the 1st row.

   d) the 3rd row.

3. Shade ...

   a)
2	4	6
8	10	12
14	16	18

   the 2nd row.

   b)
2	4	6
8	10	12
14	16	18

   the 1st column.

   c)
2	4	6
8	10	12
14	16	18

   the 3rd column.

   d)
2	4	6
8	10	12
14	16	18

   the diagonals *(one is shaded).*

4. Describe any patterns you see in each chart below.
   NOTE: You should use the words "rows," "columns," and "diagonals" in your answer.

   a)
1	3	5
3	5	7
5	7	9

   b)
5	10	15	20
10	15	20	25
15	20	25	30
20	25	30	35

   c)
12	15	18	21
9	12	15	18
6	9	12	15
3	6	9	12

No unauthorized copying

Patterns & Algebra 1

5. Make up your own pattern and describe it.

6.

0	5	10	5	0
6	7	8	4	10
12	9	6	3	0
18	11	4	2	10
24	13	2	1	0

a) Which row of the chart has a decreasing pattern (looking left to right)?

_____

b) Which column has a repeating pattern?

_____

c) Write pattern rules for the first and second column.

_____

d) Describe the relationship between the numbers in the third and fourth columns.

_____

e) Describe one other pattern in the chart.

_____

f) Name a row or column that does not appear to have any pattern.

_____

7. Place the letters A and B so that each row and each column has two As and two Bs in it:

8. Fill in the blanks so the numbers in every row and column add to 15:

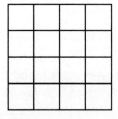

Patterns & Algebra 1

1. a)

1	2	3	4	5	6	7	8	9	10
11	12	13	14	15	16	17	18	19	20

Look at the ones digit in the multiples of 2.

How can you tell whether a number is a multiple of two?

b) The multiples of two (including zero) are called <u>even</u> numbers. Circle the even numbers:

17   3   418   132   64   76   234   89   94   167   506

2. a) Write out the first 12 multiples of 5 greater than zero:

____5____ , ____10____ , ____ , ____ , ____ , ____ , ____ , ____ , ____ , ____ , ____ , ____

b) How can you tell whether a number is a multiple of five?

c) Without counting up, circle the numbers that are multiples of 5:

83   17   45   37   150   64   190   65   71   235   618   1645

3.

1	2	3
11	12	13
21	22	23

Example

Shade all the multiples of 3 on a hundreds chart.

You should find that the shaded squares lie in diagonal lines.

Now add the ones digit and the tens digit of each number along any diagonal line.

Describe what you notice below. (Try this for each shaded diagonal.)

4. A number is a multiple of 3 if the sum of its digits is a multiple of 3. Fill in the chart below:

Number	28	37	42	61	63	87	93	123
Sum of digits	2 + 8 = 10							
Multiple of 3?	No							

Patterns & Algebra 1

PA5-18: Patterns in the Eight Times Table

1. On a hundreds chart, shade every eighth number (i.e., shade the numbers you would say when counting by eights: 8, 16, 24, ...).

   The numbers you shaded are the <u>multiples</u> of eight (up to 100).

2. Complete the following:

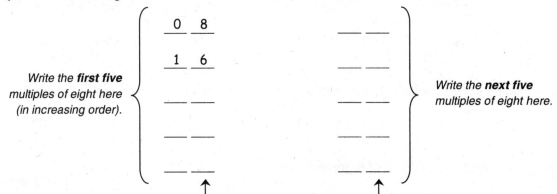

   Write the **first five** multiples of eight here (in increasing order).

   Write the **next five** multiples of eight here.

   Look down the columns marked by the arrows. What pattern do you see in the <u>ones</u> digits?

3. What pattern do you see in the number of tens?

PARENT:
Review the answers to Questions 2 and 3 before allowing your child to go further.

4. Use the pattern you found in Questions 2 and 3 to write out the multiples of 8 from 88 to 160:

Patterns & Algebra 1

PARENT:
Review Venn diagrams with your child before assigning the questions below.

1. a) Sort the numbers below into the Venn diagram.
   The first number has been done for you:

10	20	15	27	74	39	5	27	34
70	4	19	63	60	50	75	6	66

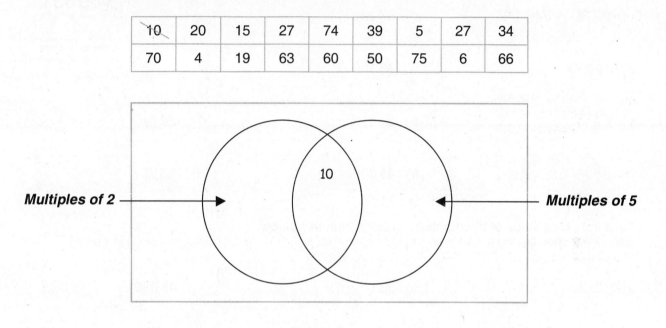

   b) Think of two numbers from 50 to 100 that would go in the middle of the diagram: _____, _____

   c) Think of two numbers from 50 to 100 that could not be placed in either circle: _____, _____

2. Sort the numbers below into the Venn diagram.
   REMEMBER: A number is a multiple of 3 if the sum of its digits is a multiple of 3.

24	30	47	21	26	60	80	13	11
48	35	56	72	10	75	16	40	6

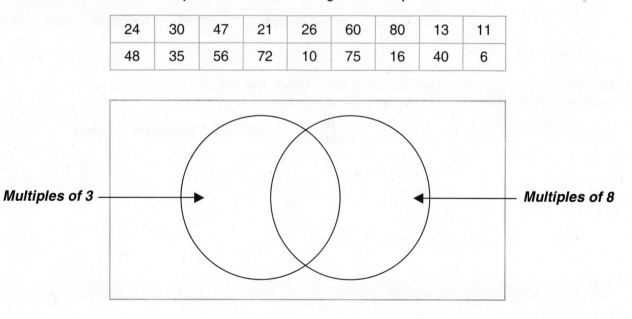

NS5-1: Place Value

1. Write the place value of the underlined digit.

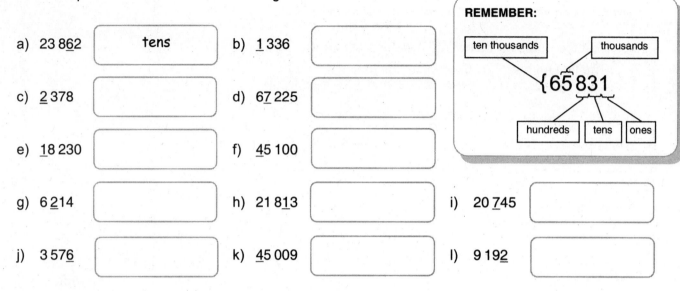

a) 23 8<u>6</u>2   **tens**

b) <u>1</u> 336

c) <u>2</u> 378

d) 6<u>7</u> 225

e) <u>1</u>8 230

f) <u>4</u>5 100

g) 6<u>2</u>14

h) 21 8<u>1</u>3

i) 20 <u>7</u>45

j) 3 57<u>6</u>

k) <u>4</u>5 009

l) 9 19<u>2</u>

2. Give the place value of the number 5 in each number below.
   HINT: First underline the 5.

a) 15 640

b) 358

c) 45 636

d) 2 415

e) 51 188

f) 451

g) 1 512

h) 125

i) 35 380

3. You can also write numbers using a place value chart.

   Example:

   In a place value chart, the number 52 953 is:

ten thousands	thousands	hundreds	tens	ones
5	2	9	5	3

Write the following numbers into the place value chart. The first one has been done for you.

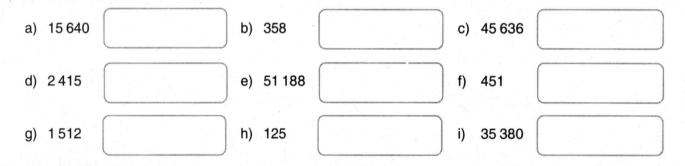

	ten thousands	thousands	hundreds	tens	ones
a) 12 305	1	2	3	0	5
b) 45 001					
c) 3 699					
d) 19 053					
e) 546					
f) 20 127					

Number Sense 1

NS5-1: Place Value (continued)

The number 23 967 is a **5-digit number.**

- The **digit** 2 stands for 20 000 – the **value** of the digit 2 is 20 000.

- The **digit** 3 stands for 3 000 – the **value** of the digit 3 is 3 000.

- The **digit** 9 stands for 900 – the **value** of the digit 9 is 900.

- The **digit** 6 stands for 60 – the **value** of the digit 6 is 60.

- The **digit** 7 stands for 7 – the **value** of the digit 7 is 7.

----

4. Write the **value** of each digit.

5	4	3	6	2

2	8	5	3	7

1	3	2	7	5

5. What does the digit 4 stand for in the number? The first one is done for you.

a) 847

40

b) 5 243

c) 16 423

d) 43 228

e) 4 207

f) 3 742

g) 43 092

h) 54 283

6. Fill in the blank.

a) In the number 36 572, the **digit** 5 stands for _____ .

b) In the number 24 236, the **digit** 3 stands for _____ .

c) In the number 62 357, the **digit** 6 stands for _____ .

d) In the number 8 021, the **value** of the digit 8 is _____ .

e) In the number 26 539, the **value** of the digit 2 is _____ .

f) In the number 7 253, the digit _____ is in the **thousands place.**

g) In the number 57 320, the digit _____ is in the **ten thousands place.**

NS5-2: Representation with Base Ten Materials

1. Write the number in expanded word form (numerals and words).

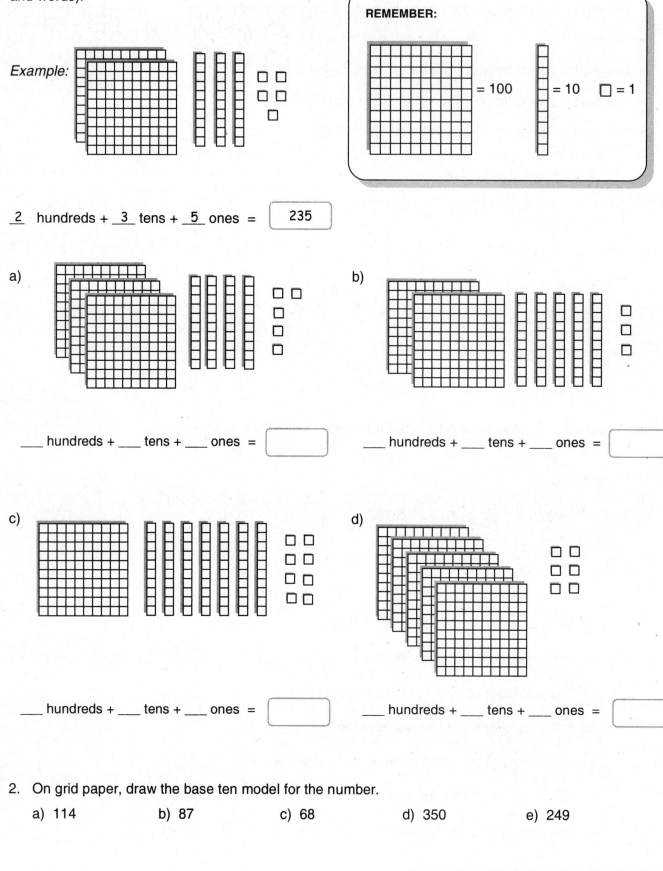

REMEMBER:

= 100   = 10   □ = 1

Example:

_2_ hundreds + _3_ tens + _5_ ones = [235]

a)

___ hundreds + ___ tens + ___ ones = [   ]

b)

___ hundreds + ___ tens + ___ ones = [   ]

c)

___ hundreds + ___ tens + ___ ones = [   ]

d)

___ hundreds + ___ tens + ___ ones = [   ]

2. On grid paper, draw the base ten model for the number.

  a) 114   b) 87   c) 68   d) 350   e) 249

3. Write the number in expanded word form
   (numerals and words) and then as a numeral.

REMEMBER:

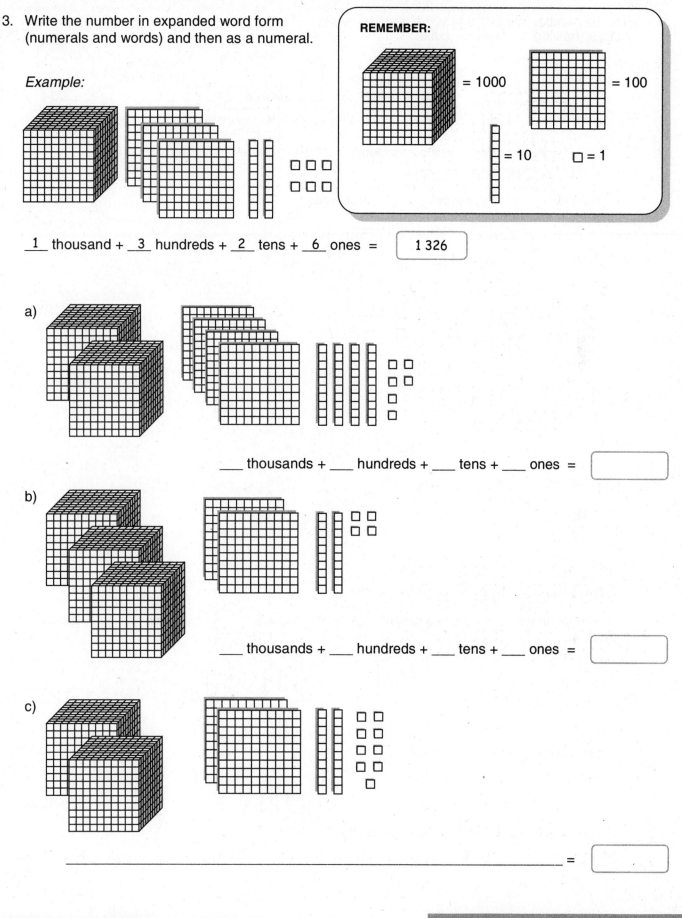

= 1000

= 100

= 10

☐ = 1

Example:

_1_ thousand + _3_ hundreds + _2_ tens + _6_ ones = | 1 326 |

a) ___ thousands + ___ hundreds + ___ tens + ___ ones =   [   ]

b) ___ thousands + ___ hundreds + ___ tens + ___ ones =   [   ]

c) _____ =   [   ]

Steps for drawing a thousands cube:

Step 1:
Draw a square.

Step 2:
Draw lines from
its 3 vertices.

Step 3:
Join the lines.

4. Represent the given numbers using base ten blocks in the place value chart.
   The first one has been started for you.

	Number	Thousands	Hundreds	Tens	Ones
a)	2 435				
b)	2 124				
c)	3 302				

5. Write the number for the given base ten blocks.

	Thousands	Hundreds	Tens	Ones	Number
a)					_____
b)					_____

NS5-3: Representation in Expanded Form

1. Expand the number using **numerals** and **words**. The first one is done for you.

   a) 43 427 = __4__ ten thousands + __3__ thousands + __4__ hundreds + __2__ tens + __7__ ones

   b) 25 312 = ____ ten thousands + ____ thousands + ____ hundreds + ____ tens + ____ ones

   c) 28 547 = _____

   _____

2. Write the number in expanded form (using **numerals**). The first one is done for you.

   a) 2 613 = _____2 000 + 600 + 10 + 3_____   b) 27 = _____

   c) 48 = _____   d) 1 232 = _____

   e) 36 273 = _____

   f) 19 384 = _____

   g) 49 805 = _____

3. Write the number for the sum.

   a) 4 000 + 900 + 50 + 3 = _____   b) 2 000 + 30 + 2 = _____

   c) 60 000 + 3 000 + 900 + 90 + 7 = _____

   d) 50 000 + 30 + 4 = _____

   BONUS

   e) 500 + 2 000 + 80 + 90 000 + 8 = _____

   f) 40 000 + 500 +1 000 = _____   g) 10 000 + 3 000 + 7 + 600 = _____

   h) 300 + 80 000 + 2 = _____   i) 90 + 400 + 70 000 + 6 = _____

   j) 90 000 + 5 = _____   k) 80 000 + 8 + 800 = _____

   l) 30 000 + 1 + 5 000 = _____   m) 3 000 + 20 000 = _____

Number Sense 1

4. Find the missing numbers.

   a) 4 000 + 800 + _____ + 7 = 4 827

   b) 3 000 + 200 + _____ + 5 = 3 275

   c) 70 000 + 9 000 + _____ + 20 + 5 = 79 825

   d) 60 000 + 5 000 + _____ + 60 + 3 = 65 263

   e) 10 000 + 7 000 + 200 + 10 + _____ = 17 212

   f) 20 000 + 6 000 + 300 + _____ + 8 = 26 328

   BONUS

   g) _____ + 300 = 7 300

   h) 6 000 + _____ = 6 080

   i) 30 000 + 9 000 + _____ + _____ = 39 260

   j) 60 000 + _____ + _____ = 67 003

5. Write the number in expanded form. Then draw a base ten model for the number.

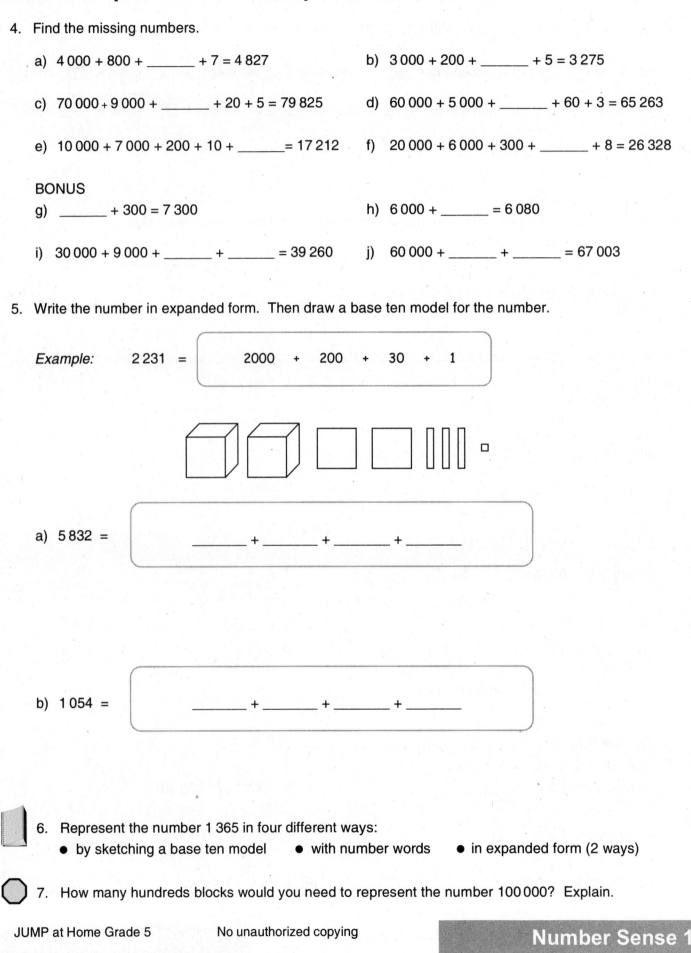

   Example:　2 231　=　　2000　+　200　+　30　+　1

   a) 5 832 = _____ + _____ + _____ + _____

   b) 1 054 = _____ + _____ + _____ + _____

6. Represent the number 1 365 in four different ways:
   - by sketching a base ten model
   - with number words
   - in expanded form (2 ways)

7. How many hundreds blocks would you need to represent the number 100 000? Explain.

1. Write the **value** of each digit. Then complete the sentence.

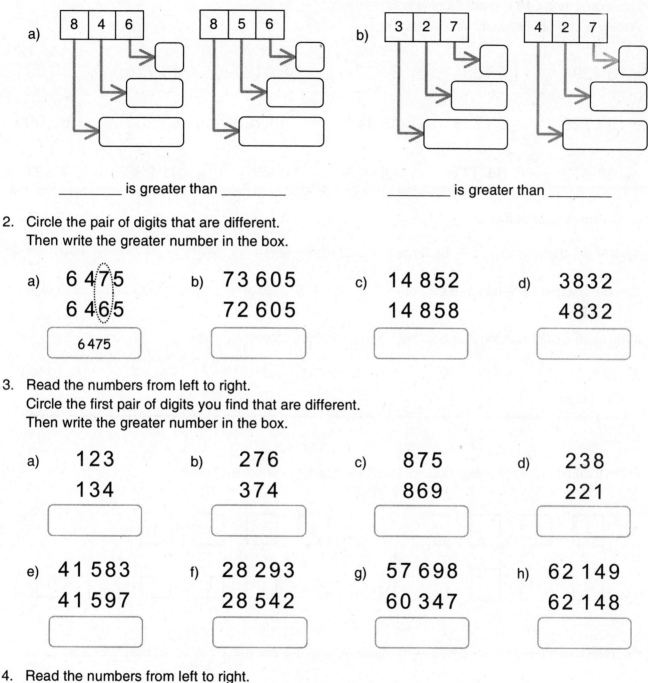

a)

| 8 | 4 | 6 |

| 8 | 5 | 6 |

b)

| 3 | 2 | 7 |

| 4 | 2 | 7 |

_____ is greater than _____   _____ is greater than _____

2. Circle the pair of digits that are different.
   Then write the greater number in the box.

a)　6 4 7 5
　　6 4 6 5

　　6 475

b)　73 605
　　72 605

c)　14 852
　　14 858

d)　3832
　　4832

3. Read the numbers from left to right.
   Circle the first pair of digits you find that are different.
   Then write the greater number in the box.

a)　123
　　134

b)　276
　　374

c)　875
　　869

d)　238
　　221

e)　41 583
　　41 597

f)　28 293
　　28 542

g)　57 698
　　60 347

h)　62 149
　　62 148

4. Read the numbers from left to right.
   Underline the first pair of digits you find that are different.
   Then circle the greater number.

a) 32 5_4_7　(32 5_6_2)

b) 71 254　81 254

c) 37 123　37 321

d) 61 201　61 275

e) 63 235　63 233

f) 81 234　84 214

g) 32 153　31 278

h) 60 154　66 254

i) 96 567　96 528

NS5-4: Comparing and Ordering Numbers *(continued)*

5. The inequality sign **>** in **7 > 5** is read "seven is greater than five."
   The sign **<** in **8 < 10** is read "eight is less than ten."
   Write the correct inequality sign in the box.

   a) 3 129 ☐ 4 703   b) 5 332 ☐ 6 012   c) 16 726 ☐ 16 591

   d) 23 728 ☐ 23 729   e) 48 175 ☐ 48 123   f) 59 239 ☐ 60 009

   g) 64 872 ☐ 64 871   h) 48 025 ☐ 4 952   i) 91 232 ☐ 9 327

6. Circle the greater number.

   a) 32 or thirty-five   b) three hundred eighty-seven or 392   c) twenty-seven or 81

   d) one thousand one hundred six or 1 232   e) 50 273 or fifty thousand three hundred eighty-five

7. Mark each number on the number line. Then circle the greatest number.

   A 23 800   **B** 23 400   **C** 23 600

   23 000   24 000

8. Fill in the boxes with any digit that will make the number statement true.

   a) ☐ 5 ☐ ☐ < 4 ☐ ☐ 1

   b) 3 ☐ ☐ ☐ 1 > ☐ 8 ☐ ☐ 9

9. Which number must be greater (no matter what digits are placed in the boxes)? Explain.

   ☐ 2 3 5 OR ☐☐ 1 2 3

10. How many numbers are greater than 59 990 and less than 60 000?

11. Buenos Aires, Argentina, is 9001 km away from Ottawa.
    Concepcion, Chile, is 9106 km away.

    Which city is farther from Ottawa?

    Explain how you know.

1. Write "10 more," "10 less," "100 more," or "100 less" in the blank.

   a) 90 is _____ than 80

   b) 400 is _____ than 500

   c) 10 is _____ than 20

   d) 100 is _____ than 90

   e) 400 is _____ than 300

   f) 60 is _____ than 70

2. Write "100 more," "100 less," "1 000 more," or "1 000 less" in the blank.

   a) 6 000 is _____ than 5 000

   b) 12 000 is _____ than 13 000

   c) 4 000 is _____ than 5 000

   d) 800 is _____ than 900

   e) 600 is _____ than 500

   f) 9 000 is _____ than 8 000

3. Write "1 000 more," "1 000 less," "10 000 more," or "10 000 less" in the blank.

   a) 6 000 is _____ than 5 000

   b) 12 000 is _____ than 13 000

   c) 30 000 is _____ than 40 000

   d) 50 000 is _____ than 40 000

   e) 6 000 is _____ than 7 000

   f) 10 000 is _____ than 20 000

   g) 80 000 is _____ than 70 000

   h) 9 000 is _____ than 10 000

4. Circle the pair of digits that are different. Then fill in the blank.

   a) 72 652
      72 752

      72 652 is ___100 less___
      than 72 752

   b) 91 385
      91 485

      91 385 is _____
      than 91 485

   c) 43 750
      33 750

      43 750 is _____
      than 33 750

   d) 62 250
      63 250

      62 250 is _____
      than 63 250

   e) 38 405
      38 415

      38 405 is _____
      than 38 415

   f) 85 871
      85 872

      85 871 is _____
      than 85 872

5. Fill in the blank.

a) _____ is 10 more than 325

b) _____ is 10 less than 1 562

c) _____ is 100 more than 592

d) _____ is 100 less than 4 135

e) _____ is 100 more than 6 821

f) _____ is 100 less than 3 295

g) _____ is 1 000 less than 8 305

h) _____ is 1 000 more than 4 253

i) _____ is 10 000 less than 73 528

j) _____ is 1 000 less than 62 381

6. Fill in the blank.

a) $234 + 10 =$ _____

b) $2382 + 10 =$ _____

c) $19035 + 10 =$ _____

d) $21270 + 100 =$ _____

e) $3283 + 100 =$ _____

f) $7325 + 1000 =$ _____

g) $357 - 10 =$ _____

h) $683 - 10 =$ _____

i) $837 - 100 =$ _____

j) $2487 - 100 =$ _____

k) $1901 - 100 =$ _____

l) $4316 - 1000 =$ _____

m) $3301 - 10 =$ _____

n) $12507 - 10000 =$ _____

o) $39397 + 10 =$ _____

7. Fill in the blank.

a) $385 +$ _____ $= 395$

b) $608 +$ _____ $= 708$

c) $1483 +$ _____ $= 1493$

d) $2617 +$ _____ $= 2717$

e) $43210 +$ _____ $= 44210$

f) $26287 +$ _____ $= 26387$

g) $1287 -$ _____ $= 1187$

h) $325 -$ _____ $= 315$

i) $14392 -$ _____ $= 14292$

j) $87001 -$ _____ $= 86001$

k) $86043 -$ _____ $= 85943$

l) $61263 -$ _____ $= 51263$

8. Continue the number pattern.

a) 8 508, 8 518, 8 528, _____, _____

b) 35 730, 36 730, 37 730, _____, _____

c) 41 482, 41 492, _____, 41 512, _____

d) 28 363, _____, _____, 28 393, 28 403

9. Circle the pair of digits that are different. Then fill in the blanks.

a) 45241
   45231

b) 82350
   92350

c) 68254
   69254

   _45 231_ is _10_   _____ is _____   _____ is _____

less than _45 241_   more than _____   less than _____

1. Write the number represented by the base ten materials in each box. Then circle the greater number.

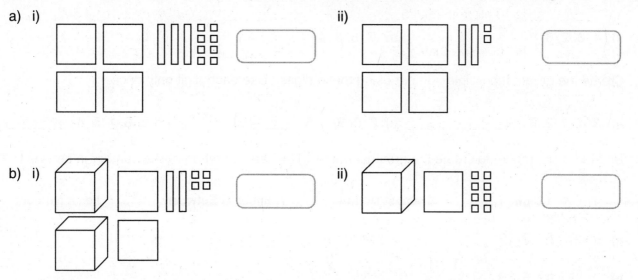

   a) i)

   ii)

   b) i)

   ii)

2. List all the two-digit numbers you can make using the digits provided. Then circle the greatest number.

   a) 7, 8, and 9

   b) 3, 4, and 0

3. What is the greatest number less than 1000 whose digits are all the same? _____

4. What is the greatest possible number you can create with:

   a) three digits _____   b) four digits _____   c) five digits _____

5. Identify the greater number by writing > or <.

   a) 37 432 ☐ 37 512

   b) 87 386 ☐ 87 384

   c) 17 329 ☐ 8 338

   d) 63 923 ☐ 62 857

Number Sense 1

6. Create the greatest possible **four-digit** number using the digits given.

    a) 4, 3, 2, 6 [   ]   b) 7, 8, 9, 4 [   ]   c) 0, 4, 1, 2 [   ]

7. Create the greatest possible number using these digits. Use each digit only once.

    a) 3, 4, 1, 2, 8 _____   b) 2, 8, 9, 1, 5 _____   c) 3, 6, 1, 5, 4 _____

8. Use the digits (once) to create the greatest number, the least number, and a number in between.

	Digits	Greatest Number	Number in Between	Least Number
a)	8 5 7 2 1			
b)	2 1 5 3 9			
c)	3 0 1 5 3			

9. Arrange the numbers in order, starting with the **least** number.

    a) 3 257, 3 352, 3 183

    _____ , _____ , _____

    b) 17 251, 17 385, 17 256

    _____ , _____ , _____

    c) 87 500, 87 498, 87 499

    _____ , _____ , _____

    d) 36 725, 3 281, 93 859

    _____ , _____ , _____

    e) 60 052, 60 001, 60 021

    _____ , _____ , _____

    f) 273, 5 891, 17

    _____ , _____ , _____

10. Using the digits 0, 1, 2, 3, and 4, create a number greater than 32 000 and less than 34 000.

    _____

11. Using the digits 3, 5, 6, 7, and 8, create an even number greater than 85 000 and less than 87 000.

    _____

12. What digit can be substituted for [   ] to make the statement true?

    a) 32[   ]56 is between 32 675 and 32 854   b) 68[   ]32 is between 68 379 and 68 464

Gwendolyne has 2 hundreds blocks, 16 tens blocks, and 9 ones blocks.
She regroups 10 tens blocks as 1 hundreds block.

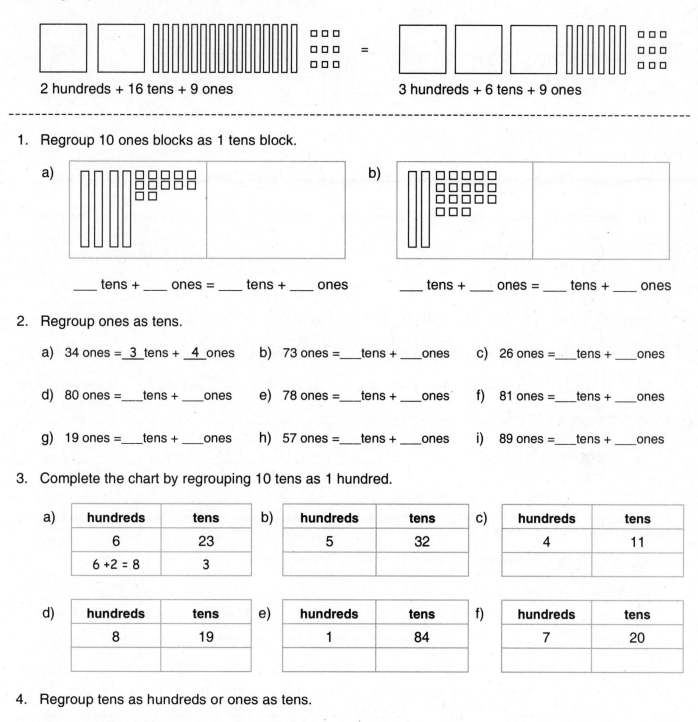

2 hundreds + 16 tens + 9 ones   3 hundreds + 6 tens + 9 ones

----

1. Regroup 10 ones blocks as 1 tens block.

a)

___ tens + ___ ones = ___ tens + ___ ones

b)

___ tens + ___ ones = ___ tens + ___ ones

2. Regroup ones as tens.

a) 34 ones = _3_ tens + _4_ ones   b) 73 ones =___tens + ___ones   c) 26 ones =___tens + ___ones

d) 80 ones =___tens + ___ones   e) 78 ones =___tens + ___ones   f) 81 ones =___tens + ___ones

g) 19 ones =___tens + ___ones   h) 57 ones =___tens + ___ones   i) 89 ones =___tens + ___ones

3. Complete the chart by regrouping 10 tens as 1 hundred.

a)

hundreds	tens
6	23
6 +2 = 8	3

b)

hundreds	tens
5	32

c)

hundreds	tens
4	11

d)

hundreds	tens
8	19

e)

hundreds	tens
1	84

f)

hundreds	tens
7	20

4. Regroup tens as hundreds or ones as tens.

a) 5 hundreds + 4 tens + 24 ones = ___5 hundreds + 6 tens + 4 ones_____

b) 7 hundreds + 0 tens + 47 ones = _____

c) 3 hundreds + 57 tens + 8 ones = _____

Ara has 1 thousands block, 12 hundreds blocks, 1 tens block, and 2 ones blocks.
She regroups 10 hundreds blocks as 1 thousands block.

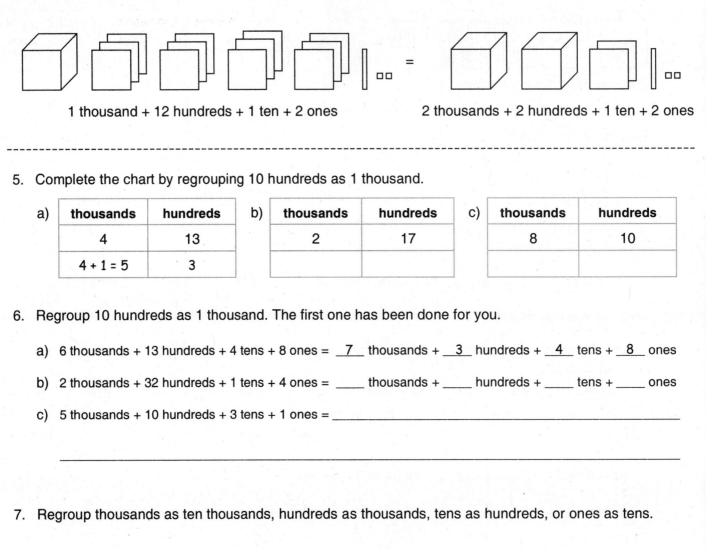

1 thousand + 12 hundreds + 1 ten + 2 ones   2 thousands + 2 hundreds + 1 ten + 2 ones

---

5. Complete the chart by regrouping 10 hundreds as 1 thousand.

a)

thousands	hundreds
4	13
4 + 1 = 5	3

b)

thousands	hundreds
2	17

c)

thousands	hundreds
8	10

6. Regroup 10 hundreds as 1 thousand. The first one has been done for you.

   a) 6 thousands + 13 hundreds + 4 tens + 8 ones = __7__ thousands + __3__ hundreds + __4__ tens + __8__ ones

   b) 2 thousands + 32 hundreds + 1 tens + 4 ones = ____ thousands + ____ hundreds + ____ tens + ____ ones

   c) 5 thousands + 10 hundreds + 3 tens + 1 ones = _____

   _____

7. Regroup thousands as ten thousands, hundreds as thousands, tens as hundreds, or ones as tens.

   a) 2 thousands + 25 hundreds + 4 tens + 2 ones = ____ thousands + ____ hundreds + ____ tens + ____ ones

   b) 3 thousands + 7 hundreds + 24 tens + 5 ones = _____

   _____

   c) 4 ten thousands + 25 thousands + 6 hundreds + 1 ten + 45 ones = _____

   _____

8. Karim wants to build a model of four thousand three hundred forty-six.

   He has 3 thousands blocks, 13 hundreds blocks, and 50 ones blocks.

   Can he build the model? Explain.

1. Add the numbers by drawing a picture and by adding the digits.

a) **14 + 37**

with base ten materials		with numerals	
tens	ones	tens	ones
14		1	4
37		3	7
sum (regroup 10 ones as a ten)		4	11
(after regrouping)		5	1

b) **35 + 27**

with base ten materials		with numerals	
tens	ones	tens	ones

2. Add the ones digits. Show how you would regroup 10 ones as 1 ten.

a)
```
    1
    1   4
  + 1   9
    3
```
tens go here / ones go here

b)
```
    3   6
  + 4   9
```

c)
```
    6   4
  + 2   8
```

d)
```
    3   5
  + 4   5
```

e)
```
    2   6
  + 1   9
```

3. Add the numbers by regrouping.

a)
```
  1
    2   5
  + 1   6
    4   1
```

b)
```
    1   9
  + 3   2
```

c)
```
    6   4
  + 2   9
```

d)
```
    7   7
  + 1   8
```

e)
```
    3   6
  + 3   6
```

f)
```
    8   5
  +     6
```

g)
```
    2   9
  + 3   2
```

h)
```
    4   3
  + 1   8
```

i)
```
    2   1
  + 5   9
```

j)
```
    7   8
  + 2   8
```

Allen adds 243 + 381 using base ten materials.

243	=	2 hundred	+	4 tens	+	3 ones

+ 381	=	3 hundreds	+	8 tens	+	1 one

	=	5 hundreds	+	12 tens	+	4 ones

Then, to get the final answer, Allen regroups 10 tens as 1 hundred.

	=	6 hundreds	+	2 tens	+	4 ones

1. Add the numbers using base ten materials or a picture (and record your work).

$$572 \; = \; \underline{\quad} \text{ hundreds} + \underline{\quad} \text{ tens} + \underline{\quad} \text{ ones}$$

$$+\,251 \; = \; \underline{\quad} \text{ hundreds} + \underline{\quad} \text{ tens} + \underline{\quad} \text{ ones}$$

$$= \; \underline{\quad} \text{ hundreds} + \underline{\quad} \text{ tens} + \underline{\quad} \text{ ones}$$

after regrouping $= \; \underline{\quad} \text{ hundreds} + \underline{\quad} \text{ tens} + \underline{\quad} \text{ ones}$

2. Add. You will need to regroup. The first one is started for you.

a)
```
   1
   2 5 8
 + 3 7 1
 ───────
     2 9
```

b)
```
   3 6 1
 + 4 9 6
 ───────
```

c)
```
   8 2 3
 +   9 6
 ───────
```

d)
```
   9 5 0
 + 5 9 9
 ───────
```

e)
```
   6 4 3
 + 2 6 4
 ───────
```

3. Add, regrouping where necessary.

a)
```
   2 8 2
 + 3 7 1
 ───────
```

b)
```
   1 5 6
 + 5 5 7
 ───────
```

c)
```
   6 4 2
 + 1 8 9
 ───────
```

d)
```
   3 9 0
 + 2 5 9
 ───────
```

e)
```
   8 5 6
 + 1 0 6
 ───────
```

f)
```
   2 8 9
 + 4 4 4
 ───────
```

4. Add by lining the numbers up correctly in the grid. The first one has been started for you.

a) 643 + 182

	6	4	3
+	1	8	2

b) 547 + 236

c) 405 + 368

d) 256 + 92

Louisa adds 2 862 + 2 313 using base ten materials.

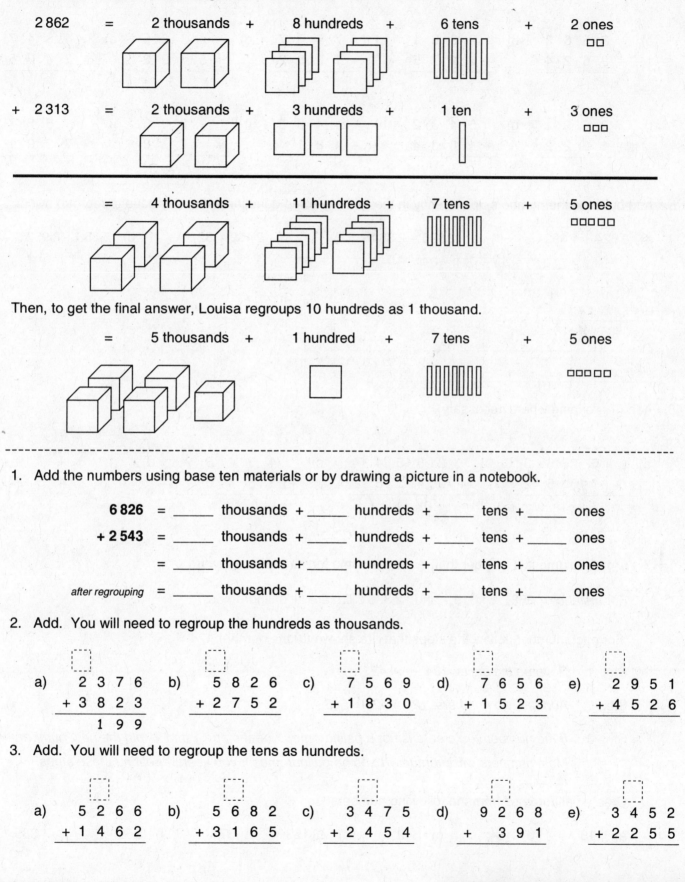

2 862 = 2 thousands + 8 hundreds + 6 tens + 2 ones

+ 2 313 = 2 thousands + 3 hundreds + 1 ten + 3 ones

= 4 thousands + 11 hundreds + 7 tens + 5 ones

Then, to get the final answer, Louisa regroups 10 hundreds as 1 thousand.

= 5 thousands + 1 hundred + 7 tens + 5 ones

1. Add the numbers using base ten materials or by drawing a picture in a notebook.

6 826 = _____ thousands + _____ hundreds + _____ tens + _____ ones

+ 2 543 = _____ thousands + _____ hundreds + _____ tens + _____ ones

= _____ thousands + _____ hundreds + _____ tens + _____ ones

after regrouping = _____ thousands + _____ hundreds + _____ tens + _____ ones

2. Add. You will need to regroup the hundreds as thousands.

a)   2 3 7 6
   + 3 8 2 3
   _____
       1 9 9

b)   5 8 2 6
   + 2 7 5 2

c)   7 5 6 9
   + 1 8 3 0

d)   7 6 5 6
   + 1 5 2 3

e)   2 9 5 1
   + 4 5 2 6

3. Add. You will need to regroup the tens as hundreds.

a)   5 2 6 6
   + 1 4 6 2

b)   5 6 8 2
   + 3 1 6 5

c)   3 4 7 5
   + 2 4 5 4

d)   9 2 6 8
   +   3 9 1

e)   3 4 5 2
   + 2 2 5 5

4. Add (regrouping when necessary).

a)   3 5 6 2   b)   2 2 6 1   c)   7 5 6 7   d)   2 3 6 5   e)   4 8 4 7
   + 3 6 2 4   + 6 9 2 5   + 1 3 8 2   + 5 4 9 2   + 2 0 0 5

f)   8 6 9 1   g)   5 4 3 2   h)   4 4 8 5   i)   9 2 0 5   j)   1 5 6 7
   + 1 2 2 2   + 1 8 3 4   + 4 8 1 4   +   7 5 8   + 7 2 9 1

5. Add by lining the numbers up correctly in the grid. In some questions you may have to regroup twice.

a) 8 624 + 1 192   b) 2 895 + 2 384   c) 2 469 + 62   d) 5 263 + 3 953

6. Add (regrouping where necessary).

a)   5 2 6 3   b)   2 8 5 4 7   c)   4 5 4 8 9   d)   3 6 1 7 9
   + 1 5 5 2   + 3 4 2 8 2   + 2 6 4 0 1   + 3 3 4 5 2

7. A **palindrome** is a number that reads the same forward and backward.

For instance: 363, 51 815, and 2 375 732 are all palindromes.

For each number, follow the steps that are shown for the number 124.

Step 1:   *Reverse the digits: 124 —> 421*

Step 2:   *Add the two numbers: 124 + 421 = 545*

Step 3:   *If the number you create is not a palindrome, repeat steps 1 and 2 with the new number.*
         Most numbers will eventually become palindromes if you keep repeating these steps.

Create palindromes from the following numbers.

a) 216   b) 154   c) 342   d) 23 153   e) 371   f) 258   g) 1 385

NS5-11: Subtraction

Ken subtracts 34 – 16 using base ten blocks.

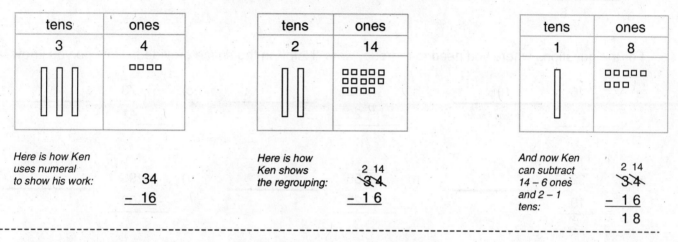

Step 1:
Ken represents 34 with base ten materials.

tens	ones
3	4

Here is how Ken uses numeral to show his work:

```
  34
- 16
```

Step 2:
6 (the ones digit of 16) is greater than 4 (the ones digit of 34) so Ken exchanges a tens block for 10 ones.

tens	ones
2	14

Here is how Ken shows the regrouping:

```
  2 14
  3̶4̶
- 1 6
```

Step 3:
Ken subtracts 16 (he takes away 1 tens block and 6 ones).

tens	ones
1	8

And now Ken can subtract 14 – 6 ones and 2 – 1 tens:

```
  2 14
  3̶4̶
- 1 6
  1 8
```

----

1. Show how Ken can subtract by regrouping a tens block as 10 ones.

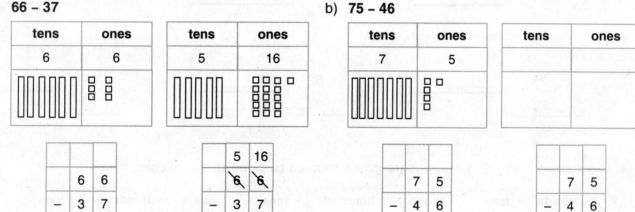

a) **66 – 37**

tens	ones
6	6

tens	ones
5	16

```
    6 6
  - 3 7
```

```
  5 16
  6̶ 6̶
- 3 7
```

b) **75 – 46**

tens	ones
7	5

tens	ones

```
    7 5
  - 4 6
```

```
    7 5
  - 4 6
```

c) **34 – 16**

tens	ones
3	4

tens	ones

```
    3 4
  - 1 6
```

```
    3 4
  - 1 6
```

d) **77 – 29**

tens	ones
7	7

tens	ones

```
    7 7
  - 2 9
```

```
    7 7
  - 2 9
```

No unauthorized copying

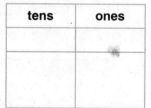

Number Sense 1

2. Subtract by regrouping.

a)
	4	16
	5̶	6̶
−	1	8
	3	8

b)
	7	8
−	3	9

c)
	5	3
−	2	9

d)
	8	2
−	4	3

e)
	6	6
−	4	8

3. For the questions where you need to regroup, write "Help!" in the space provided. How do you know?

a)   46
    − 28   _Help!_
             6 is less than 8

b)   52
    − 26   _____

c)   73
    − 41   _____

d)   32
    − 19   _____

e)   56
    − 22   _____

f)   95
    − 58   _____

g)   66
    − 13   _____

h)   24
    −   9   _____

i)   84
    − 26   _____

j)   79
    − 27   _____

k)   52
    − 43   _____

l)   41
    − 17   _____

4. To subtract 456 − 283, Laura regroups 1 hundreds block as 10 tens blocks.

hundreds	tens	ones
4	5	6

hundreds	tens	ones
3	15	6

hundreds	tens	ones
1	7	3

Subtract by regrouping **hundreds** as tens. The first one has been started for you.

a)
	5	15	
	6̶	5̶	2
−	3	8	1

b)
	6	7	9
−	1	9	4

c)
	8	1	6
−	2	9	6

d)
	9	5	8
−	7	6	5

5. Subtract by regrouping the **tens**. The first one has been started for you.

a)
```
        4  13
     6  5̶  3̶
  -  5  2  6
  _____
```

b)
```
     5  7  2
  -  4  3  9
  _____
```

c)
```
     9  6  4
  -  6  3  8
  _____
```

d)
```
     8  9  0
  -  4  1  6
  _____
```

6. For the following questions, you will have to regroup **twice**.

Example:

Step 1:
```
       3 12
     7 4̶ 2̶
  -  2 7 4
  _____
```

Step 2:
```
       3 12
     7 4̶ 2̶
  -  2 7 4
  _____
           8
```

Step 3:
```
      13
    6 3̶ 12
    7̶ 4̶ 2̶
  - 2 7 4
  _____
          8
```

Step 4:
```
      13
    6 3̶ 12
    7̶ 4̶ 2̶
  - 2 7 4
  _____
       6  8
```

Step 5:
```
      13
    6 3̶ 12
    7̶ 4̶ 2̶
  - 2 7 4
  _____
     4 6 8
```

a)
```
     7  5  2
  -  3  6  3
  _____
```

b)
```
     8  2  3
  -  1  7  5
  _____
```

c)
```
     3  0  4
  -     2  7
  _____
```

d)
```
     9  8  3
  -  5  8  4
  _____
```

7. To subtract 4 135 – 2 314, Laura exchanges 1 thousands block for 10 hundreds blocks.

thousands	hundreds	tens	ones
4	1	3	5

thousands	hundreds	tens	ones
3	11	3	5

thousands	hundreds	tens	ones
1	8	2	1

Subtract by regrouping thousands as hundreds. The first one has been done for you.

a)
```
        5 15
     6̶  5̶  2  6
  -  2  7  1  4
  _____
     3  8  1  2
```

b)
```
     4  2  8  5
  -  1  8  5  3
  _____
```

c)
```
     9  6  4  3
  -  5  7  2  2
  _____
```

d)
```
     6  5  7  9
  -  3  8  5  7
  _____
```

8. In some of the following questions, you will need to regroup twice.

a)
	2	5	8	7
−	1	2	5	9

b)
	8	5	3	7
−	6	7	2	5

c)
	9	6	2	8
−	5	4	3	4

d)
	3	5	6	0
−	1	9	6	0

e)
	5	6	2	7	3
−	4	2	0	1	6

f)
	8	2	5	2	9
−	3	7	2	5	1

g)
	9	0	5	2	3
−	1	8	2	1	9

9. In the following questions, you will have to regroup three times.

Step 1:
```
    2  16
8 4 3̶ 6̶
- 2 5 6 8
_____
          8
```

Step 2:
```
    2  16
8 4 3̶ 6̶
- 2 5 6 8
_____
```

Step 3:
```
      12
    3̶ 2̶  16
8 4̶ 3̶ 6̶
- 2 5 6 8
_____
        6 8
```

Step 4:
```
  7 13 12
  4̶ 3̶ 2̶ 16
8̶ 4̶ 3̶ 6̶
- 2 5 6 8
_____
      8 6 8
```

Step 5:
```
  7 13 12
  4̶ 3̶ 2̶ 16
8̶ 4̶ 3̶ 6̶
- 2 5 6 8
_____
    5 8 6 8
```

a)
	7	6	5	2
−	1	8	9	5

b)
	8	3	2	4
−	3	8	6	5

c)
	4	5	7	1
−	1	8	8	4

d)
	9	0	6	8
−	1	5	7	9

10. In the following questions, you will have to regroup two or three times.

Step 1:
```
  0  10
1̶ 0̶ 0 0
-   5 3 2
```

Step 2:
```
    9
  0 1̶0 10
1̶ 0̶ 0̶ 0
-   5 3 2
```

Step 3:
```
    9 9
  0 1̶0 1̶0 10
1̶ 0̶ 0̶ 0̶
-   5 3 2
```

Step 4:
```
    9 9
  0 1̶0 1̶0 10
1̶ 0̶ 0̶ 0̶
-   5 3 2
_____
    4 6 8
```

a)
	1	0	0	0
−		3	5	8

b)
	1	0	0
−		4	8

c)
	1	0	0	0
−		7	6	2

d)
	1	0	0	0
−		2	5	9

NS5-12: Larger Numbers

Answer the following questions in a notebook.

1. Alex has $57 and Borana has $12.
   How much money do they have altogether?

2. Camile cycled 2 375 km one year and 5 753 the next. How many km did she cycle altogether?

3. The maximum depth of Lake Ontario is 244 m. The maximum depth of Lake Superior is 406 m.

   How much deeper is Lake Superior than Lake Ontario?

4. Mount Kilimanjaro in Tanzania is 5 895 m high and Mount Fuji in Japan is 3 776 m high.

   How much higher is Mount Kilimanjaro than Mount Fuji?

5. In space, the Apollo 10 command module travelled 39 666 km per hour.

   How far did it travel in 2 hours?

6. Two nearby towns have populations of 12 475 and 14 832 people.

   What is the total population of both towns?

7. Canada was founded in 1867.
   How many years ago was Canada founded?

8. In the number 432:

   The 100s digit is 1 more than the 10s digit.
   The 10s digit is 1 more than the 1s digit.

   Make up your own number with this property.

   _____ _____ _____

   Now write the number backward.

   _____ _____ _____

   Write your two numbers in the grid and subtract (put the greater number on top).

   Try this again with several other numbers.
   You will always get 198!

   BONUS
   Can you explain why this works?

9. Sahar had 20 stickers.
   She put 5 in a book and gave 4 to her friend Nina.
   How many were left over?

10. John has 26 marbles.
    David has 15 fewer marbles than John.
    Claude has 10 more marbles than John.

    How many marbles do David and Claude have altogether?

Answer the following questions in a notebook.

1. The chart gives the area of some of the largest lakes in North America.

   a) How much more area does Lake Michigan cover than Lake Erie?

   b) How much more area does the largest lake cover than the smallest lake?

   c) Write the areas of the lakes in order from least to greatest.

   d) The largest lake in the world is the Caspian Sea in Asia. Its area is 370 990 km^2.

      How much greater than the area of Lake Superior is the area of the Caspian Sea?

Lake	Area (in km^2)
Erie	25 690
Great Slave	28 570
Michigan	58 020
Great Bear	31 340
Superior	82 100

2. A clothing store had 500 shirts. In one week, they sold:

   • 20 red shirts   • 50 blue shirts   • 100 green shirts

   How many shirts were left?

3. Use the digits 1, 2, 3, 4, 5, 6, 7, and 8 once each to fill in the boxes.

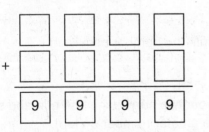

4. Use each of the digits 4, 5, 6, 7, and 8 once to create:

   a) The greatest odd number possible.

   b) A number between 56 700 and 57 000.

   c) An odd number whose tens digit and hundreds digit add to 12.

   d) An odd number whose thousands digit is twice its hundreds digit.

5. Design your own problem using the numbers in the chart in Question 1.

6. What is the greatest number you can add to 74 253 without having to regroup?

When you multiply a pair of numbers, the result is called the **product** of the numbers.

In the **array** shown, there are 3 **rows** of dots. There are 5 dots **in each row**.

row

5
10
15

Carmelle counts the dots by skip counting by 5s.

Carmelle writes a multiplication statement for the array: **3 × 5 = 15**   (3 rows of 5 dots is 15 dots)

The numbers **3** and **5** are called **factors** of 15.

---

1. How many rows? How many dots in each row? Write a multiplication statement.

a)

____2____ rows

____4____ dots in each row

____2 □ 4 = 8____

b)

_____ rows

_____ dots in each row

_____

c)

_____

_____

_____

2. Write a product for the array.

a)

____4 × 3____
↑ rows   ↑ dots in each row

b)

_____

c)

_____

d)

_____

3. Draw an array and write a multiplication statement to find the answer.

a) In a garden, there are 6 rows of plants. There are 5 plants in each row. How many plants are there altogether?

b) Paul lines up 7 chairs in each row. There are 3 rows of chairs. How many chairs are there altogether?

4. a) Draw arrays for the products 4 × 3 and 3 × 4. Are the products the same or different?

b) Is 6 × 4 equal to 4 × 6? Explain.

5. Jen finds all the factors of 4 by drawing arrays.

Factors of 4:   1,   2,   4

1 × 4

2 × 2

4 × 1

Draw arrays to find all the factors of:

a) 6   b) 10   c) 11   d) 12

Amy finds the product of **3** and **5** by skip
counting on a number line. She counts off
three 5s. From the picture, Amy can see
that the **product** of 3 and 5 is 15.

$$3 \times 5 = \quad 5 \quad + \quad 5 \quad + \quad 5 \quad = 15$$

0 1 2 3 4 5 6 7 8 9 10 11 12 13 14 15

----

1. Draw arrows to find the product by skip counting.

   a) **4 x 2 =**

   0 1 2 3 4 5 6 7 8 9 10 11 12 13 14 15

   b) **3 x 4 =**

   0 1 2 3 4 5 6 7 8 9 10 11 12 13 14 15

2. Use the number line to skip count by 4s, 6s, and 7s. Fill in the boxes as you count.

0 1 2 3 4 5 6 7 8 9 **10** 11 12 13 14 15 16 17 18 19 **20** 21 22 23 24 25 26 27 28 29 **30** 31 32 33 34 35 36 37 38 39 **40** 41 42

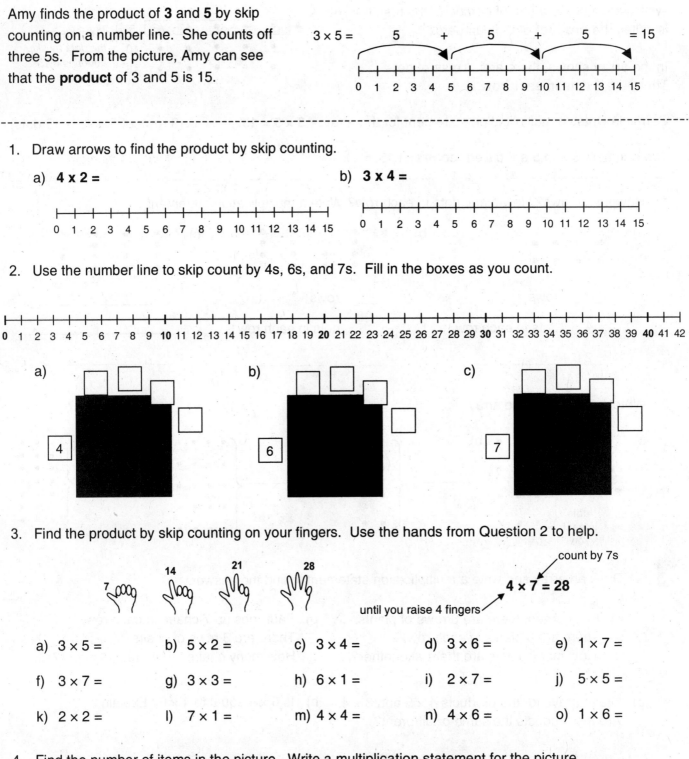

   a) 4

   b) 6

   c) 7

3. Find the product by skip counting on your fingers. Use the hands from Question 2 to help.

count by 7s

4 × 7 = 28

until you raise 4 fingers

7   14   21   28

   a) $3 \times 5 =$ b) $5 \times 2 =$ c) $3 \times 4 =$ d) $3 \times 6 =$ e) $1 \times 7 =$

   f) $3 \times 7 =$ g) $3 \times 3 =$ h) $6 \times 1 =$ i) $2 \times 7 =$ j) $5 \times 5 =$

   k) $2 \times 2 =$ l) $7 \times 1 =$ m) $4 \times 4 =$ n) $4 \times 6 =$ o) $1 \times 6 =$

4. Find the number of items in the picture. Write a multiplication statement for the picture.

   a)   b)

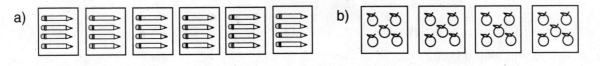

_____   _____

To multiply **4 × 20**, Allen makes 4 groups containing 2 **tens** blocks (20 = 2 tens):

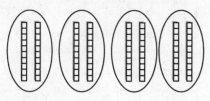

$4 × 20 = 4 × 2$ tens $= 8$ tens $= 80$

To multiply **4 × 200**, Allen makes 4 groups containing 2 **hundreds** blocks (200 = 2 hundreds).

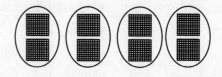

$4 × 200 = 4 × 2$ hundreds $= 8$ hundreds $= 800$

Allen notices a pattern: **4 × 2 = 8**   **4 × 20 = 80**   **4 × 200 = 800**

----

1. Draw a model for the multiplication statement, then calculate the answer. The first one is started.

   a) 4 × 30

   b) 2 × 20

   $4 × 30 = 4 ×$ ____ tens $=$ ____ tens $=$ ____ $2 × 20 = 2 ×$ ____ tens $=$ ____ tens $=$ ____

2. Regroup to find the answer. The first one is done for you.

   a) $3 × 70 = 3 ×$ ___7___ tens $=$ ___21___ tens $=$ ___210___

   b) $4 × 50 = 4 ×$ _____ tens $=$ _____ tens $=$ _____

   c) $3 × 40 = 3 ×$ _____ tens $=$ _____ tens $=$ _____

   d) $6 × 30 = 6 ×$ _____ tens $=$ _____ tens $=$ _____

3. Complete the pattern by multiplying.

   a) $2 × 3 =$ _____   b) $5 × 1 =$ _____   c) $5 × 4 =$ _____   d) $4 × 2 =$ _____

   $2 × 30 =$ _____ $5 × 10 =$ _____ $5 × 40 =$ _____ $4 × 20 =$ _____

   $2 × 300 =$ _____ $5 × 100 =$ _____ $5 × 400 =$ _____ $4 × 200 =$ _____

4. Multiply.

   a) $5 × 30 =$ _____   b) $30 × 4 =$ _____   c) $4 × 40 =$ _____   d) $50 × 3 =$ _____

   e) $3 × 500 =$ _____   f) $500 × 6 =$ _____   g) $3 × 80 =$ _____   h) $500 × 5 =$ _____

   i) $2 × 900 =$ _____   j) $70 × 6 =$ _____   k) $8 × 40 =$ _____   l) $900 × 3 =$ _____

5. Draw a base ten model (using cubes to represent thousands) to show: $6 × 1\,000 = 6000$.

6. Knowing that $4 × 2 = 8$, how can you use this fact to multiply $4 × 2\,000$? Explain.

NS5-17: Advanced Arrays

1. Write a multiplication statement for the array.

a)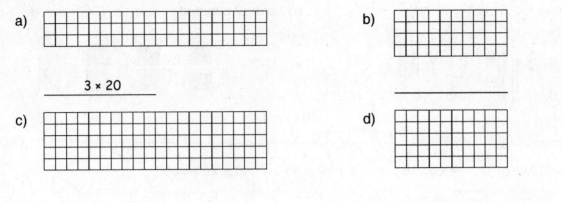

3 × 20

b)

c)

d)

2. Write a multiplication statement for the whole array and each part of the array, as shown in a).

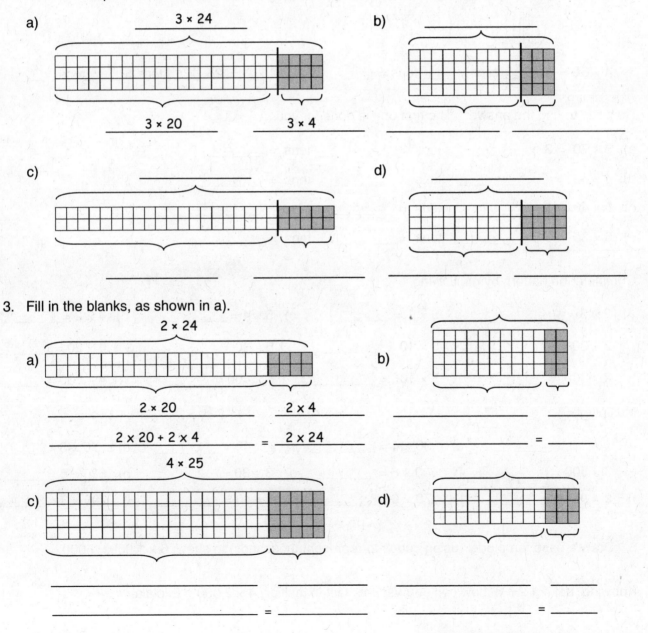

a) 3 × 24

3 × 20   3 × 4

b)

c)

d)

3. Fill in the blanks, as shown in a).

a) 2 × 24

2 × 20   2 × 4

2 × 20 + 2 × 4 = 2 × 24

b)

_____ = _____

c) 4 × 25

d)

_____ = _____   _____ = _____

NS5-18: Mental Math

To multiply 4 × 23, Anya rewrites 23 as a sum:

23 = 20 + 3

She multiplies 20 by 4:   **4 × 20 = 80**

Then she multiplies 4 × 3:   **4 × 3 = 12**

Finally she adds the result: **80 + 12 = 92**

The picture shows why Anya's method works.   **4 × 23 = 4 × 20 + 4 × 3 = 80 + 12 = 92**

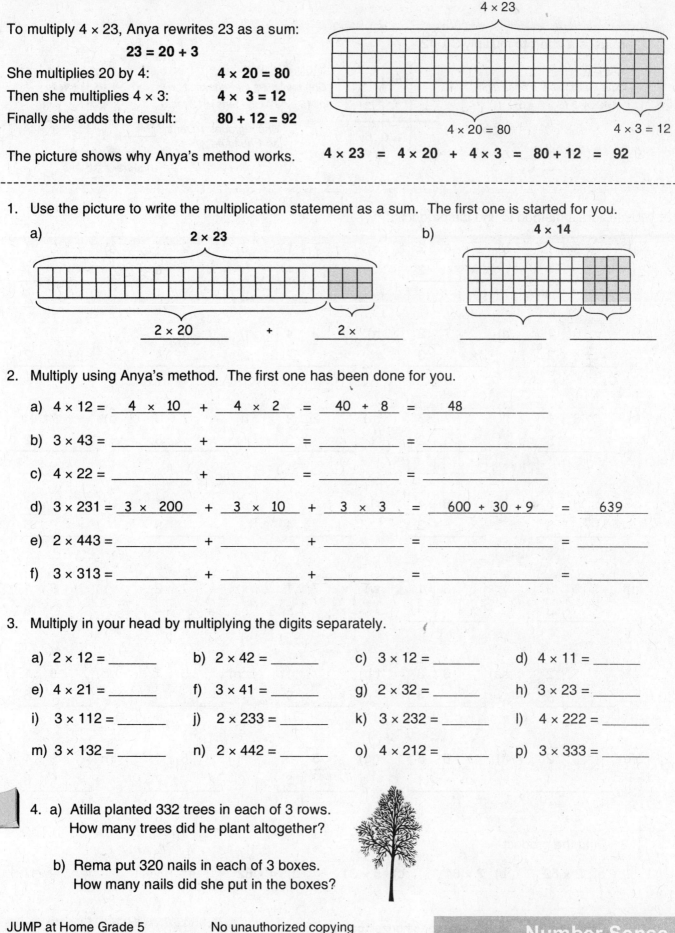

1. Use the picture to write the multiplication statement as a sum. The first one is started for you.

    a)   **2 × 23**

    2 × 20 _____ + 2 × _____

    b)   **4 × 14**

    _____   _____

2. Multiply using Anya's method. The first one has been done for you.

    a) 4 × 12 = __4 × 10__ + __4 × 2__ = __40 + 8__ = __48__

    b) 3 × 43 = _____ + _____ = _____ = _____

    c) 4 × 22 = _____ + _____ = _____ = _____

    d) 3 × 231 = __3 × 200__ + __3 × 10__ + __3 × 3__ = __600 + 30 + 9__ = __639__

    e) 2 × 443 = _____ + _____ + _____ = _____ = _____

    f) 3 × 313 = _____ + _____ + _____ = _____ = _____

3. Multiply in your head by multiplying the digits separately.

    a) 2 × 12 = _____   b) 2 × 42 = _____   c) 3 × 12 = _____   d) 4 × 11 = _____

    e) 4 × 21 = _____   f) 3 × 41 = _____   g) 2 × 32 = _____   h) 3 × 23 = _____

    i) 3 × 112 = _____   j) 2 × 233 = _____   k) 3 × 232 = _____   l) 4 × 222 = _____

    m) 3 × 132 = _____   n) 2 × 442 = _____   o) 4 × 212 = _____   p) 3 × 333 = _____

4. a) Atilla planted 332 trees in each of 3 rows.
        How many trees did he plant altogether?

    b) Rema put 320 nails in each of 3 boxes.
        How many nails did she put in the boxes?

Clara uses a chart to multiply 3 × 42.

Step 1:
She multiplies the ones digit
of 42 by 3 (3 × 2 = 6).

	4	2
×		3
		6

Step 2:
She multiplies the tens digit
of 42 by 3 (3 × 4 tens = 12 tens).

She regroups 10 tens
as 1 hundred.

	4	2
×		3
1	2	6

hundreds   tens

1. Use Clara's method to find the product.

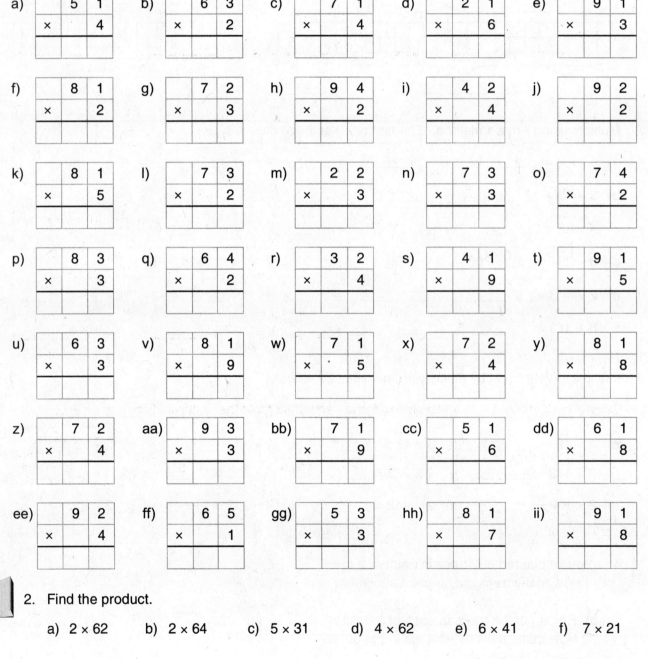

a)
	5	1
×		4

b)
	6	3
×		2

c)
	7	1
×		4

d)
	2	1
×		6

e)
	9	1
×		3

f)
	8	1
×		2

g)
	7	2
×		3

h)
	9	4
×		2

i)
	4	2
×		4

j)
	9	2
×		2

k)
	8	1
×		5

l)
	7	3
×		2

m)
	2	2
×		3

n)
	7	3
×		3

o)
	7	4
×		2

p)
	8	3
×		3

q)
	6	4
×		2

r)
	3	2
×		4

s)
	4	1
×		9

t)
	9	1
×		5

u)
	6	3
×		3

v)
	8	1
×		9

w)
	7	1
×		5

x)
	7	2
×		4

y)
	8	1
×		8

z)
	7	2
×		4

aa)
	9	3
×		3

bb)
	7	1
×		9

cc)
	5	1
×		6

dd)
	6	1
×		8

ee)
	9	2
×		4

ff)
	6	5
×		1

gg)
	5	3
×		3

hh)
	8	1
×		7

ii)
	9	1
×		8

2. Find the product.

a) 2 × 62   b) 2 × 64   c) 5 × 31   d) 4 × 62   e) 6 × 41   f) 7 × 21

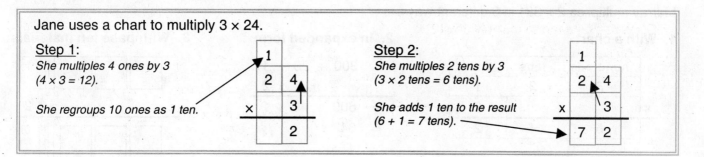

Jane uses a chart to multiply 3 × 24.

Step 1:
She multiples 4 ones by 3 (4 × 3 = 12).

She regroups 10 ones as 1 ten.

Step 2:
She multiples 2 tens by 3 (3 × 2 tens = 6 tens).

She adds 1 ten to the result (6 + 1 = 7 tens).

1. Using Jane's method, complete the first step of the multiplication. The first one has been done.

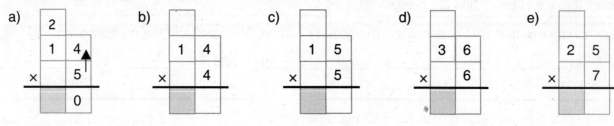

2. Using Jane's method, complete the second step of the multiplication.

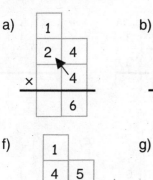 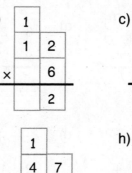 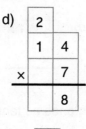 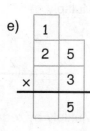

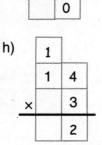 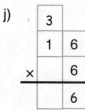

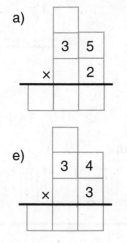 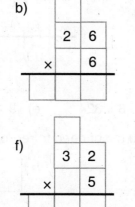 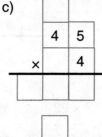 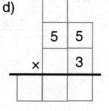

3. Using Jane's method, complete the first and second steps of the multiplication.

PARENT: Be sure to give your child extra practice at this skill.

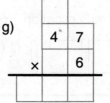 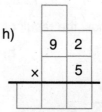 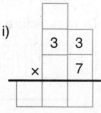

NS5-21: Multiplying – 3-Digit by 1-Digit

Murray multiplies 2 × 321 in 3 different ways.

1. With a chart:

	hundreds	tens	ones
	3	2	1
×			2
	6	4	2

2. In expanded form:

$$300 + 20 + 1$$
$$\times\ 2$$
$$= 600 + 40 + 2$$
$$= 642$$

3. With base ten materials:

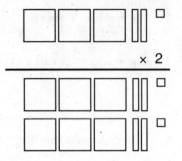

---

1. Rewrite the multiplication statement in expanded notation. Then perform the multiplication.

   a) 412   _____ + _____ + _____
       × 3   _____ × 3
                  = _____ + _____ + _____
                  = _____

   b) 323   _____ + _____ + _____
       × 2   _____ × 2
                  = _____ + _____ + _____
                  = _____

2. Multiply:

   a) | | 3 | 4 |
       | × | | 2 |
       | | | |

   b) | 3 | 1 | 2 |
       | × | | 3 |
       | | | |

   c) | 2 | 1 | 2 |
       | × | | 4 |
       | | | |

   d) | 3 | 2 | 3 |
       | × | | 3 |
       | | | |

   e) | 2 | 1 | 3 |
       | × | | 3 |
       | | | |

3. Multiply by regrouping ones as tens.

   a) | 1 | 1 | 4 |
       | × | | 4 |

   b) | 2 | 2 | 6 |
       | × | | 3 |

   c) | 2 | 2 | 4 |
       | × | | 4 |

   d) | 2 | 1 | 6 |
       | × | | 3 |

   e) | 1 | 1 | 4 |
       | × | | 6 |

4. Multiply by regrouping tens as hundreds. In the last question, you will also regroup ones as tens.

   a) | 2 | 5 | 2 |
       | × | | 3 |

   b) | 1 | 6 | 1 |
       | × | | 5 |

   c) | 2 | 5 | 3 |
       | × | | 3 |

   d) | 1 | 4 | 2 |
       | × | | 4 |

   e) | 2 | 7 | 4 |
       | × | | 3 |

5. Multiply.

   a) 4 × 142   b) 6 × 311   c) 7 × 223   d) 8 × 324   e) 9 × 1 432   f) 6 × 2 537

5. Draw a picture to show the result of the multiplication. You might need to regroup.

   a) _____ × 2

   b) _____ × 3

   c) _____ × 4

Erin wants to multiply 20 × 32. She knows how to find 10 × 32. She rewrites 20 x 32 as **double** 10 × 32.

$$20 \times 32 = 2 \times \mathbf{10 \times 32}$$
$$= 2 \times 320$$
$$= 640$$

The picture shows why this works: a 20 by 32 array contains the same number of squares as **two** 10 by 32 arrays.

----

1. Write the number as a product of 2 factors (where one of the factors is 10).

a) 30 = _____

b) 40 = _____

c) 70 = _____

2. Write 2 equivalent products of the array. The first one is done for you.

a)

$$20 \times 33 = 2 \times 10 \times 33$$

b)

$$20 \times 22 =$$ _____

c)

$$30 \times 17 =$$ _____

3. Find the product in 2 steps:

Step 1: *Multiply the second number by 10.*
Step 2: *Multiply the result by the tens digit of the first number.*

a) 20 × 34 = _2 × 340_

= _680_

b) 30 × 13 = _____

= _____

c) 40 × 22 = _____

= _____

d) 50 × 31 = _____

= _____

4. Find the product mentally.

a) 30 × 22 = _____

b) 20 × 40 = _____

c) 20 × 60 = _____

d) 40 × 27 = _____

e) 20 × 41 = _____

f) 30 × 92 = _____

g) 51 × 20 = _____

h) 30 × 64 = _____

i) 60 × 41 = _____

j) 61 × 50 = _____

k) 70 x 30 = _____

l) 80 x 20 = _____

5. Estimate the product.

HINT: Round each factor to the leading digit.

a) 27 × 39 ≈ 30 × 40 = _1200_

b) 43 × 51 ≈ _____

c) 22 × 47 ≈ _____

d) 62 x 41 ≈ _____

e) 72 × 49 ≈ _____

f) 38 x 17 ≈ _____

NS5-23: Multiplying 2-Digit Numbers by Multiples of Ten

Ed multiplies **20 × 37** by splitting the product into a sum of two smaller products:

$$20 × 37 = (20 × 7) + (20 × 30)$$
$$= 140 + 600$$
$$= 740$$

He keeps track of the steps of the multiplication in a chart:

Step 1:
Ed multiplies 2 × 7 = 14. He is really multiplying **20 × 7** so he first writes a zero in the ones place.

Step 2:
Next, since 2 × 7 = 14, Ed writes the 4 in the tens place and the 1 at the top of the hundreds column.

Step 3:
Ed then multiplies **20 × 30** (= 600). As a short cut, he multiplies 2 × 3 = 6 and then he adds the 1 from the top of the hundreds column: 6 + 1 = 7 (= 700).

1. Practise the first two steps of the multiplication.
   NOTE: In one of the questions, you will not need to regroup the hundreds.

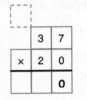

2. Multiply:

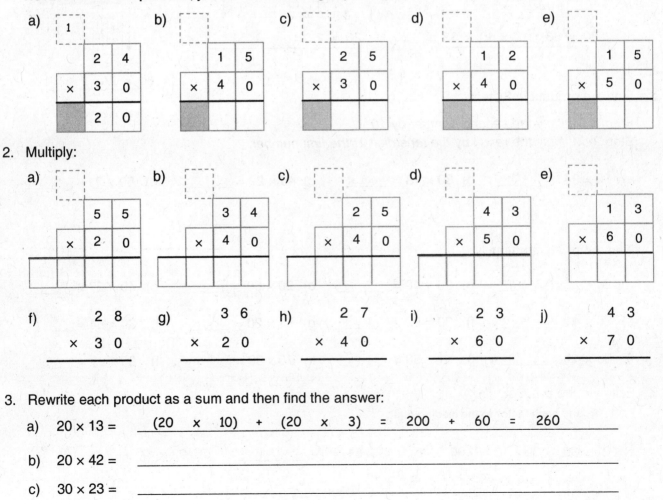

3. Rewrite each product as a sum and then find the answer:

   a) 20 × 13 = (20 × 10) + (20 × 3) = 200 + 60 = 260

   b) 20 × 42 = _____

   c) 30 × 23 = _____

No unauthorized copying **Number Sense 1**

Grace multiplies 26 × 28 by splitting the product into a sum
of two smaller products:

26 × 28 **= 6 × 28 + 20 × 28**

= 168 + 560

= 728

She keeps track of the steps of the multiplication using a chart.

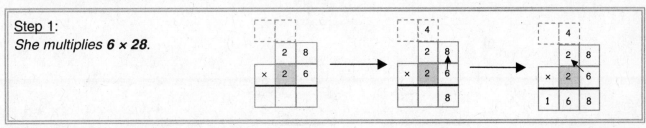

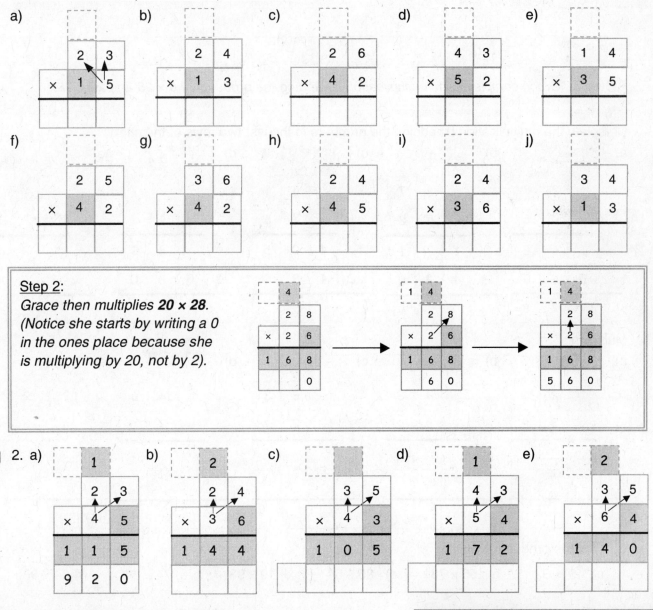

Step 1:
*She multiplies **6 × 28**.*

1.   Practice the first step of the multiplication:

a)   b)   c)   d)   e)

f)   g)   h)   i)   j)

Step 2:
*Grace then multiplies **20 × 28**.
(Notice she starts by writing a 0
in the ones place because she
is multiplying by 20, not by 2).*

2. a)   b)   c)   d)   e)

3. Practise the first 2 steps of the multiplication.

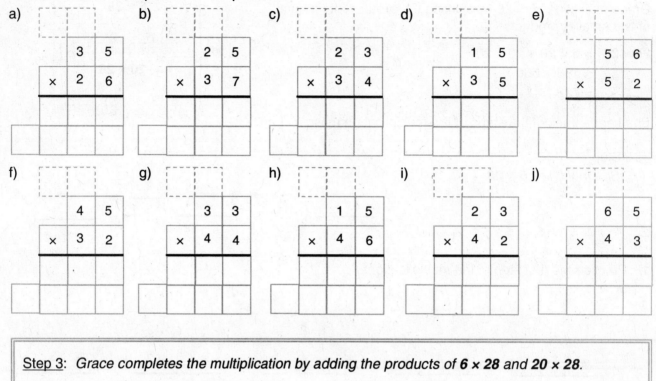

a)
```
    3  5
×   2  6
```

b)
```
    2  5
×   3  7
```

c)
```
    2  3
×   3  4
```

d)
```
    1  5
×   3  5
```

e)
```
    5  6
×   5  2
```

f)
```
    4  5
×   3  2
```

g)
```
    3  3
×   4  4
```

h)
```
    1  5
×   4  6
```

i)
```
    2  3
×   4  2
```

j)
```
    6  5
×   4  3
```

Step 3: *Grace completes the multiplication by adding the products of **6 × 28** and **20 × 28**.*

---

4. Complete the multiplication by adding the numbers in the last two rows of the chart.

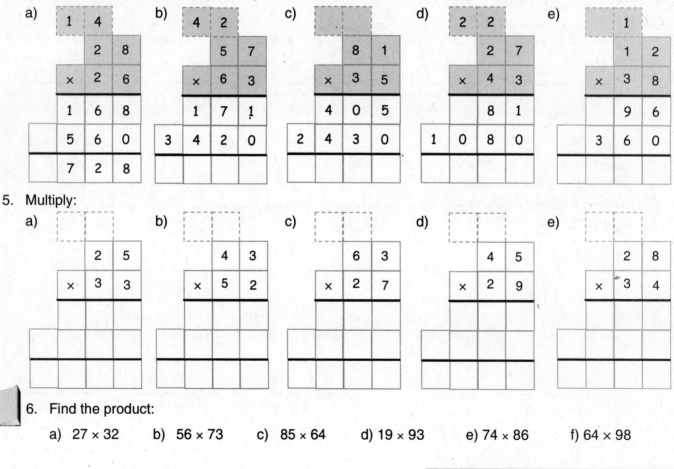

a)
```
   1  4
   2  8
×  2  6
   1  6  8
   5  6  0
   7  2  8
```

b)
```
   4  2
   5  7
×  6  3
   1  7  1
 3 4  2  0
```

c)
```
   8  1
×  3  5
   4  0  5
 2 4  3  0
```

d)
```
   2  2
   2  7
×  4  3
   8  1
 1 0  8  0
```

e)
```
      1
   1  2
×  3  8
   9  6
 3 6  0
```

5. Multiply:

a)
```
    2  5
×   3  3
```

b)
```
    4  3
×   5  2
```

c)
```
    6  3
×   2  7
```

d)
```
    4  5
×   2  9
```

e)
```
    2  8
×   3  4
```

6. Find the product:

a) 27 × 32   b) 56 × 73   c) 85 × 64   d) 19 × 93   e) 74 × 86   f) 64 × 98

NS5-25: Mental Math: Rearranging Products

1. Double each number mentally by doubling the ones digit and the tens digit separately.

	23	44	12	31	43	54	83	92	71
Double									

2. Double the ones and tens separately and add the result: $2 \times 36 = 2 \times 30 + 2 \times 6 = 60 + 12 = 72$.

	25	45	16	28	18	17	35	55	39
Double									

3. a) One flower costs 34¢. How much do two flowers cost? _____

   b) One lizard costs 48¢. How much do two lizards cost? _____

4. From the arrays you can see:
   3×2 is the same as 2×3.

   Is 4×5 the same as 5×4? Explain.

   3×2
   (3 rows of 2)

   2×3
   (2 rows of 3)

5. Rearrange the products so you can find the answer mentally.

   Example: $2 \times 8 \times 35$
   $= 2 \times 35 \times 8$
   $= 70 \times 8$
   $= 560$

   Example: $4 \times 18 \times 25$
   $= 4 \times 25 \times 18$
   $= 100 \times 18$
   $= 1800$

   a) $2 \times 4 \times 25$

   b) $2 \times 3 \times 45$

   c) $2 \times 6 \times 35$

   d) $2 \times 27 \times 50$

   e) $4 \times 75 \times 250$

   f) $2 \times 97 \times 500$

   g) $372 \times 4 \times 25$

   h) $2 \times 2 \times 15 \times 250$

   i) $25 \times 2 \times 50 \times 4$

6. Double the number in the box and halve the number in the circle.

   Example: 8 × ④ → 16 × ②

   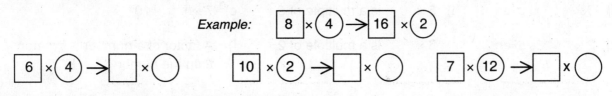

   Does the product change or stay the same? Explain

6. Use halving and doubling to find each product mentally.

   Example: 32×5
   $= 16 \times 10$
   $= 160$

   a) 42×5

   b) 64×5

   c) 86×5

1. Fill in the blanks.

a)

$3 \times \underline{2} + 3 \times \underline{1}$

$= 3 \times (\underline{2} + \underline{1})$

$= 3 \times \underline{3}$

b)

$3 \times \underline{} + 3 \times \underline{}$

$= 3 \times (\underline{} + \underline{})$

$= 3 \times \underline{}$

c)

$3 \times \underline{} + 3 \times \underline{}$

$= 3 \times (\underline{} + \underline{})$

$= 3 \times \underline{}$

d)

$3 \times \underline{} + 3 \times \underline{}$

$= 3 \times (\underline{} + \underline{})$

$= 3 \times \underline{}$

e) $3 \times 5 + 3 \times 4$

$= 3 \times (\underline{5} + \underline{4})$

$= 3 \times \underline{9}$

f) $3 \times 2 + 3 \times 6$

$= 3 \times (\underline{} + \underline{})$

$= 3 \times \underline{}$

g) $7 \times 4 + 7 \times 3$

$= 7 \times (\underline{} + \underline{})$

$= 7 \times \underline{}$

h) $9 \times 3 + 9 \times 2$

$= 9 \times (\underline{} + \underline{})$

$= 9 \times \underline{}$

2. Write each number in expanded form.

a) $32\,753 = \underline{\quad 3 \times 10\,000 + 2 \times 1000 + 7 \times 100 + 5 \times 10 + 3 \quad}$

b) $45\,326 = \underline{}$

c) $72\,023 = \underline{}$

3. Write as many statements as you can for the array using multiplication, addition, or both.

Example: $(2 \times 3) + (2 \times 3) + (2 \times 3) + (2 \times 3) = 24$

4. Is the given statement always, sometimes, or never true? Explain.

a) $3 \times \boxed{}$ is even

b) $5 \times \boxed{}$ is a multiple of 5

c) $7 \times \boxed{}$ is 0

d) $2 \times \boxed{}$ is even

e) $6 \times \boxed{}$ is a multiple of 2

f) A factor of a number is greater than the number

5. Explain why the product of two 2-digit numbers must be at least 100.

6. Using the digits 1, 2, 3, and 4, create:

a) the greatest product

$\boxed{} \times \boxed{}\boxed{}\boxed{}$

b) the least product

$\boxed{} \times \boxed{}\boxed{}\boxed{}$

NS5-27: Concepts in Multiplication

Answer the following questions in a notebook.

1. A bee has 6 legs. How many legs do 325 bees have?

2. How many hours are there in the month of January?

3. A 12-sided field has sides 87 metres long.

   What is the perimeter of the field?

4. Sapin's heart beats 98 times a minute.

   How many times would it beat in an hour?

5. A harp has 47 strings. How many strings do 12 harps have?

7. A hummingbird flaps its wings 15 times a second.

   How many times does it flap its wings in a minute?

6. Find the first four products. (Show your work on a separate piece of paper.) Use the pattern in the products to find the products in e) and f) without multiplying:

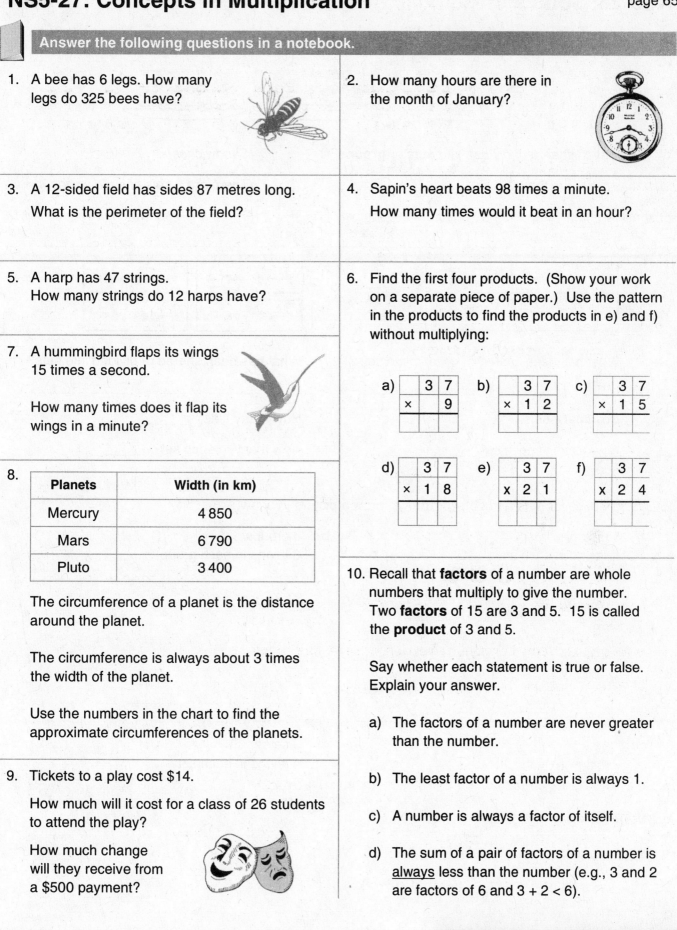

a)
	3	7
×		9

b)
	3	7
×	1	2

c)
	3	7
×	1	5

d)
	3	7
×	1	8

e)
	3	7
×	2	1

f)
	3	7
×	2	4

8.

Planets	Width (in km)
Mercury	4 850
Mars	6 790
Pluto	3 400

The circumference of a planet is the distance around the planet.

The circumference is always about 3 times the width of the planet.

Use the numbers in the chart to find the approximate circumferences of the planets.

9. Tickets to a play cost $14.

   How much will it cost for a class of 26 students to attend the play?

   How much change will they receive from a $500 payment?

10. Recall that **factors** of a number are whole numbers that multiply to give the number. Two **factors** of 15 are 3 and 5. 15 is called the **product** of 3 and 5.

   Say whether each statement is true or false. Explain your answer.

   a) The factors of a number are never greater than the number.

   b) The least factor of a number is always 1.

   c) A number is always a factor of itself.

   d) The sum of a pair of factors of a number is <u>always</u> less than the number (e.g., 3 and 2 are factors of 6 and 3 + 2 < 6).

Number Sense 1

Rita has 12 sandwiches. A tray holds 4 sandwiches:

There are 3 trays:

What has been shared or divided into **sets** or **groups**?   *(Sandwiches)*

How many sets are there?   *(There are 3 sets of sandwiches.)*

How many of the things being divided are in each set?   *(There are 4 sandwiches in each set.)*

---

1. a)

    What has been shared or divided into sets?
    _____

    How many sets? _____

    How many in each set? _____

    b)

    What has been shared or divided into sets?
    _____

    How many sets? _____

    How many in each set? _____

2. Using circles for **sets** and dots for **things**, draw a picture to show…

    a) 5 sets
        4 things in each set

    b) 6 groups
        3 things in each group

    c) 7 sets
        3 things in each set

    d) 3 sets
        4 things in each set

3.

		What has been shared or divided into sets?	How many sets?	How many in each set?
a)	24 toys 4 toys for each girl/boy 6 girls/boys	24 toys	6	4
b)	8 children 32 crackers 4 cookies for each child			
c)	18 flowers 3 bouquets 6 flowers in each bouquet			
d)	9 trees 45 oranges 5 oranges in each tree			
e)	8 apples in each pack 80 apples 10 packs			
f)	6 taxis 24 passengers 4 passengers in each taxi			
g)	35 cows 7 cows in each herd 5 herds			
h)	7 litters 42 puppies 6 puppies in each litter			

4. Draw a picture for Questions 3 a), b), and c) using **circles** for sets and **dots** for the things being divided.

Tory has 18 cookies. There are two ways she can share or <u>divide</u> her cookies equally:

I ☐ She can decide how many <u>sets</u> (or <u>groups</u>) of cookies she wants to make:

For example:
Tory wants to make 3 sets of cookies. She draws 3 circles:

She then puts one cookie at a time into the circles until she has placed 18 cookies.

II ☐ She can decide how many cookies she wants to put <u>in each set</u>:

For example:
Tory wants to put 6 cookies in each set. She counts out 6 cookies:

She counts out sets of 6 cookies until she has placed 18 cookies in sets.

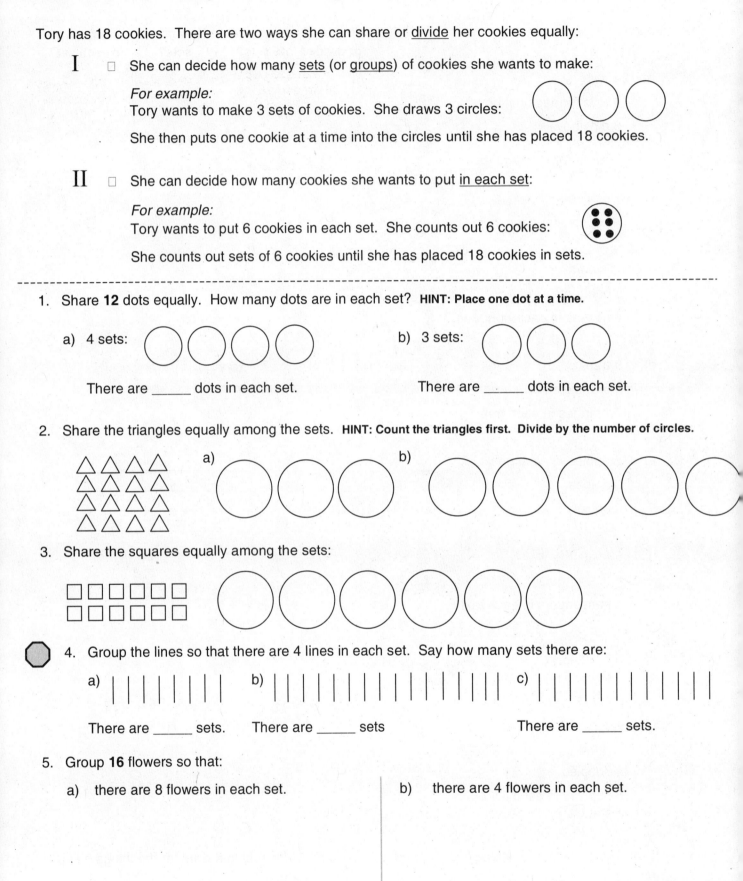

1. Share **12** dots equally. How many dots are in each set? **HINT: Place one dot at a time.**

a) 4 sets:

There are _____ dots in each set.

b) 3 sets:

There are _____ dots in each set.

2. Share the triangles equally among the sets. **HINT: Count the triangles first. Divide by the number of circles.**

a)

b)

3. Share the squares equally among the sets:

4. Group the lines so that there are 4 lines in each set. Say how many sets there are:

a) | | | | | | | |

There are _____ sets.

b) | | | | | | | | | | | | | | | | | |

There are _____ sets

c) | | | | | | | | | | | |

There are _____ sets.

5. Group **16** flowers so that:

a) there are 8 flowers in each set.

b) there are 4 flowers in each set.

6. In each question, fill in what you know. Write a question mark for what you don't know:

	What has been shared or divided into sets?	How many sets?	How many in each set?
a) Kathy has 30 stickers. She put 6 stickers in each box.	30 stickers	?	6
b) 24 children are in 6 vans.	24 children	6	?
c) Andy has 14 apples. He gives them to 7 friends.			
d) Manju has 24 comic books. She puts 3 in each bin.			
e) 35 children sit at 7 tables.			
f) 24 people are in 2 boats.			
g) 12 books are shared among 4 children.			
h) 10 flowers are in 2 rows.			
i) 8 hamsters are in 4 cages.			

7. Draw a picture using dots and circles to solve each question.

a) 10 dots; 5 sets

_____ dots in each set

b) 12 dots; 4 dots in each set

_____ sets

c) 15 dots; 5 dots in each set

_____ sets

d) 8 dots; 4 sets

_____ dots in each set

e) 3 friends share 12 tickets.

How many tickets does each friend get? _____

f) 10 students go canoeing in 5 boats.

How many kids are in each boat? _____

g) Pria has 14 stickers.
    She gives 7 to each friend.

How many friends receive stickers? _____

h) Each basket holds 5 plums.
    There are 15 plums altogether.

How many baskets are there? _____

i) 16 flowers are planted in 2 pots.

How many flowers are in each pot? _____

j) Keith has 15 stamps.
    He puts 3 on each page.

How many pages does he use? _____

Every **division** statement implies an **addition** statement.

For example, the statement "20 divided into sets of size 4 gives 5 sets" can be represented as:

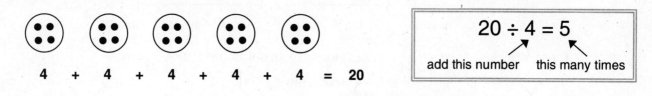

$$4 + 4 + 4 + 4 + 4 = 20$$

$$20 \div 4 = 5$$

add this number   this many times

Hence the division statement 20 ÷ 4 = 5 can be read as "add four five times."
The number 4 is called the **divisor** and the number 5 is called the **quotient** of the division statement.

----

1. Draw a picture and write an <u>addition</u> statement for each <u>division</u> statement.

   a)   12 ÷ 3 = 4   b)   8 ÷ 2 = 4   c)   20 ÷ 5 = 4

   _____3 + 3 + 3 + 3 = 12_____   _____   _____

2. Draw a picture and write a <u>division</u> statement for each <u>addition</u> statement.

   a)   6 + 6 + 6 + 6 = 24   b)   4 + 4 + 4 + 4 + 4 + 4 = 24

   _____   _____

   c)   7 + 7 + 7 = 21   d)   3 + 3 + 3 + 3 + 3 = 15

   _____   _____

   e)   4 + 4 + 4 + 4 = 16   f)   8 + 8 + 8 = 24

   _____   _____

You can solve the division problem **12 ÷ 4 = ?** by skip counting on the number line:

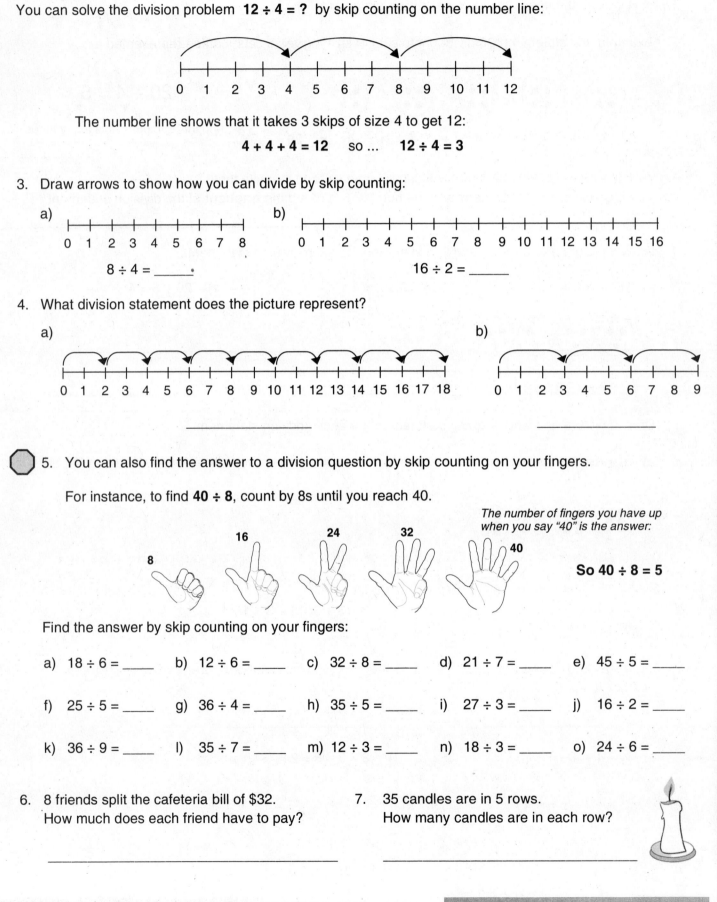

The number line shows that it takes 3 skips of size 4 to get 12:

4 + 4 + 4 = 12   so ...   **12 ÷ 4 = 3**

3. Draw arrows to show how you can divide by skip counting:

a)

8 ÷ 4 = _____ .

b)

16 ÷ 2 = _____

4. What division statement does the picture represent?

a)

_____

b)

_____

5. You can also find the answer to a division question by skip counting on your fingers.

For instance, to find **40 ÷ 8**, count by 8s until you reach 40.

The number of fingers you have up when you say "40" is the answer:

8   16   24   32   40

So 40 ÷ 8 = 5

Find the answer by skip counting on your fingers:

a) 18 ÷ 6 = _____   b) 12 ÷ 6 = _____   c) 32 ÷ 8 = _____   d) 21 ÷ 7 = _____   e) 45 ÷ 5 = _____

f) 25 ÷ 5 = _____   g) 36 ÷ 4 = _____   h) 35 ÷ 5 = _____   i) 27 ÷ 3 = _____   j) 16 ÷ 2 = _____

k) 36 ÷ 9 = _____   l) 35 ÷ 7 = _____   m) 12 ÷ 3 = _____   n) 18 ÷ 3 = _____   o) 24 ÷ 6 = _____

6. 8 friends split the cafeteria bill of $32. How much does each friend have to pay?

7. 35 candles are in 5 rows. How many candles are in each row?

_____   _____

Every division statement implies a multiplication statement. The statement:

"14 divided into sets of size 2 gives 7 sets" (or **14 ÷ 2 = 7**)

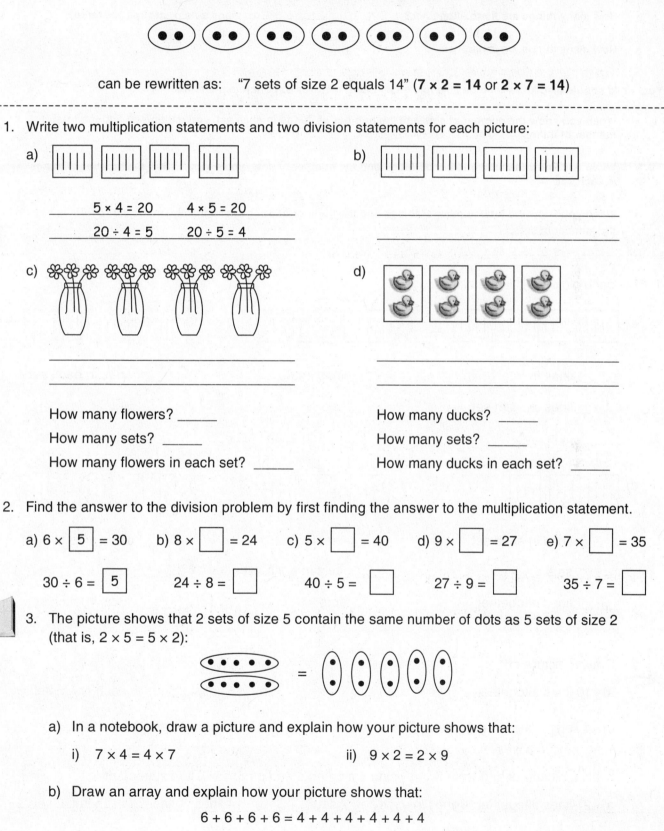

can be rewritten as: "7 sets of size 2 equals 14" (**7 × 2 = 14 or 2 × 7 = 14**)

----

1. Write two multiplication statements and two division statements for each picture:

   a)

   $5 × 4 = 20 \qquad 4 × 5 = 20$

   $20 ÷ 4 = 5 \qquad 20 ÷ 5 = 4$

   b)

   _____

   _____

   c)

   _____

   _____

   How many flowers? _____

   How many sets? _____

   How many flowers in each set? _____

   d)

   _____

   _____

   How many ducks? _____

   How many sets? _____

   How many ducks in each set? _____

2. Find the answer to the division problem by first finding the answer to the multiplication statement.

   a) $6 × \boxed{5} = 30$ b) $8 × \boxed{} = 24$ c) $5 × \boxed{} = 40$ d) $9 × \boxed{} = 27$ e) $7 × \boxed{} = 35$

   $30 ÷ 6 = \boxed{5}$ $24 ÷ 8 = \boxed{}$ $40 ÷ 5 = \boxed{}$ $27 ÷ 9 = \boxed{}$ $35 ÷ 7 = \boxed{}$

3. The picture shows that 2 sets of size 5 contain the same number of dots as 5 sets of size 2 (that is, $2 × 5 = 5 × 2$):

   a) In a notebook, draw a picture and explain how your picture shows that:

      i) $7 × 4 = 4 × 7$ ii) $9 × 2 = 2 × 9$

   b) Draw an array and explain how your picture shows that:

      $6 + 6 + 6 + 6 = 4 + 4 + 4 + 4 + 4 + 4$

NS5-32: Knowing When to Multiply or Divide

TEACHER:

To solve word problems involving multiplication or division, your child should ask:

- **How many things are there altogether?**
- **How many things are in each set?**
- **How many sets or groups are there?**

Your child should also know (and be able to explain using pictures or concrete materials):

- **When you know the number of sets and the number of things in each set, you multiply to find the total number of things.**
- **When you know the total number of things and the number of sets, you divide to find the number of things in each set.**
- **When you know the total number of things and the number of things in each set, you divide to find the number of sets.**

- -

1. For each picture, fill in the blanks:

a)

_____ lines in total

_____ lines in each set

_____ sets

b)

_____ lines in total

_____ sets

_____ lines in each set

c)

_____ lines in each set

_____ sets

_____ lines altogether

d)

_____ lines in each set

_____ sets

_____ lines altogether

e)

_____ lines

_____ lines in each set

_____ sets

f)

_____ lines in total

_____ sets

_____ lines in each set

2. Draw a picture of:

   a) 10 lines altogether; 2 lines in each set; 5 sets

   b) 15 lines; 3 lines in each set; 5 sets

   c) 4 sets; 7 lines in each set; 28 lines in total

   d) 18 lines; 3 sets; 6 lines in each set

3. Draw a picture of <u>and</u> write two division statements and a multiplication statement for:

   a) 21 lines altogether; 3 lines in each set; 7 sets

   b) 14 lines; 7 lines in each set; 2 sets

Number Sense 1

4. In each question, some information is missing (indicated by a question mark).

   Write a multiplication or division statement to find the missing information.

	Total number of things	Number of sets	Number of things in each set	Multiplication or division statement
a)	?	6	3	6 × 3 = 18
b)	20	4	?	20 ÷ 4 = 5
c)	15	?	5	
d)	10	2	?	
e)	?	4	6	
f)	21	7	?	

5. For each question, write a multiplication or a division statement to solve the problem:

a) 15 things in total
   5 things in each set

   _____

   How many sets?

   _____

b) 6 sets
   4 things in each set

   _____

   How many things in total?

   _____

c) 25 things in total
   5 sets

   _____

   How many things in each set?

   _____

d) 9 groups
   4 things in each group

   _____

   How many things in total?

   _____

e) 9 things in each set
   18 things in total

   _____

   How many sets?

   _____

f) 3 groups
   18 things altogether

   _____

   How many in each group?

   _____

g) 16 things in each set
   3 sets

   _____

   How many things in total?

   _____

h) 8 things in each set
   24 things in total

   _____

   How many sets?

   _____

i) 20 things in total
   5 sets

   _____

   How many things in each set?

   _____

NS5-32: Knowing When to Multiply or Divide (continued)

6. Fill in the chart. Use a question mark to show what you don't know.
   Then write a multiplication or division statement in the right hand column.

	Total Number of things	Number of sets	Number in each set	Multiplication or division statement
a) 8 chairs at each table 3 tables	?	3	8	$3 \times 8 = 24$ How many chairs? _____ 8
b) 9 marbles in each jar 5 jars				How many marbles? _____
c) 35 flowers 7 pots				How many flowers in each pot? _____
d) 32 people 4 boats				How many people in each boat? _____
e) 24 flowers 6 plants				How many flowers on each plant? _____
f) 36 candles 6 candles in each packet				How many packets? _____

7. The fact family for the multiplication statement $3 \times 5 = 15$ is: $5 \times 3 = 15$; $15 \div 3 = 5$ and $15 \div 5 = 3$.
   Write the fact family of equations for the multiplication statements:

   a) $4 \times 2 = 8$ b) $6 \times 3 = 18$ c) $7 \times 8 = 56$ d) $9 \times 4 = 36$

   _____   _____   _____   _____

   _____   _____   _____   _____

   _____   _____   _____   _____

Guy wants to share 9 apples with 3 friends.
He sets out 4 plates, one for himself and one for each of his friends.
He puts one apple at a time on a plate:

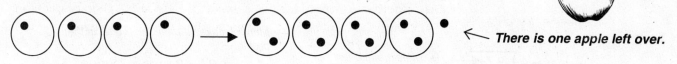

← *There is one apple left over.*

9 apples cannot be shared equally into 4 sets. Each person gets 2 apples, but one is left over.

$$9 \div 4 = 2 \text{ Remainder } 1 \quad OR \quad 9 \div 4 = 2 \text{ R } 1$$

---

1. Can you share 7 apples equally onto 2 plates? Show your work using dots and circles:

2. Share the dots as equally as possible among the circles.

   a) 8 dots in 3 circles

   b) 13 dots in 4 circles

   ____ dots in each circle; ____ dots remaining

   ____ dots in each circle; ____ dot remaining

3. Share the dots as equally as possible. Draw a picture and write a division statement.

   Example: 9 dots
   in 2 circles

   $9 \div 2 = 4 \text{ R}1$

   a) 14 dots
       in 4 circles

   b) 18 dots
       in 6 circles

   c) 17 dots
       in 4 circles

   d) 22 dots
       in 3 circles

4. Five children want to share 22 sea shells.
   How many shells will each child receive?
   How many will be left over?

5. Find two different ways to share 29 pens into equal groups
   so that one is left over.

6. Four friends have more than 7 stickers and less than 13 stickers.
   They share the stickers evenly. How many stickers do they have?
   (Is there more than one answer?)

Number Sense 1

NS5-34: Long Division — 2-Digit by 1-Digit

Manuel is preparing snacks for 4 classes.
He needs to divide 97 oranges into 4 groups.
He will use long division and a model to solve the problem:

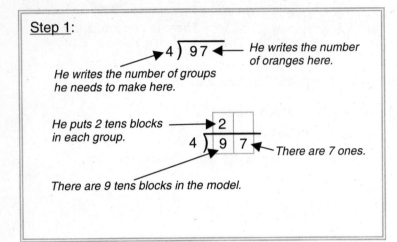

Step 1:

4) 97 — He writes the number of oranges here.

He writes the number of groups he needs to make here.

He puts 2 tens blocks in each group. → 2

4) 9 7 — There are 7 ones.

There are 9 tens blocks in the model.

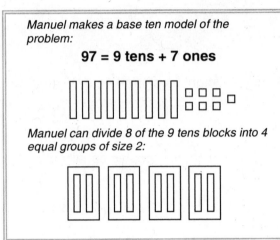

Manuel makes a base ten model of the problem:

97 = 9 tens + 7 ones

Manuel can divide 8 of the 9 tens blocks into 4 equal groups of size 2:

1. Manuel has written a division statement to solve a problem.
   How many groups does he want to make?
   How many tens and how many ones would he need to model the problem?

   a) 3) 76

   groups _____

   tens blocks _____

   ones _____

   b) 4) 95

   groups _____

   tens blocks _____

   ones _____

   c) 4) 92

   groups _____

   tens blocks _____

   ones _____

   d) 5) 86

   groups _____

   tens blocks _____

   ones _____

2. How many tens blocks can be put in each group?

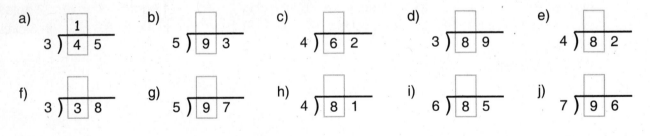

   a) 1
      3) 4 5

   b) 5) 9 3

   c) 4) 6 2

   d) 3) 8 9

   e) 4) 8 2

   f) 3) 3 8

   g) 5) 9 7

   h) 4) 8 1

   i) 6) 8 5

   j) 7) 9 6

3. For each division statement, how many groups have been made?
   How many tens are in each group?

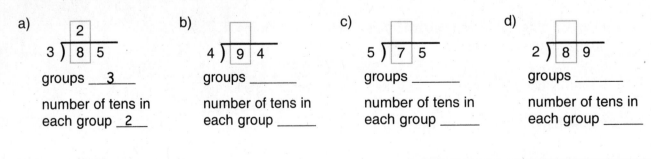

   a) 2
      3) 8 5

   groups ___3___

   number of tens in
   each group __2__

   b) 4) 9 4

   groups _____

   number of tens in
   each group _____

   c) 5) 7 5

   groups _____

   number of tens in
   each group _____

   d) 2) 8 9

   groups _____

   number of tens in
   each group _____

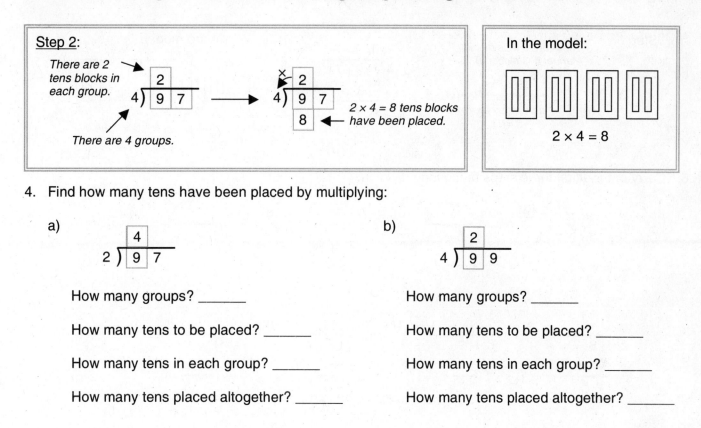

Step 2:

There are 2 tens blocks in each group.

$2 \times 4 = 8$ tens blocks have been placed.

There are 4 groups.

In the model:

$2 \times 4 = 8$

4. Find how many tens have been placed by multiplying:

a)

$$2 \overline{)\ 9\ 7}$$ with 4 above

How many groups? _____

How many tens to be placed? _____

How many tens in each group? _____

How many tens placed altogether? _____

b)

$$4 \overline{)\ 9\ 9}$$ with 2 above

How many groups? _____

How many tens to be placed? _____

How many tens in each group? _____

How many tens placed altogether? _____

5. Use skip counting to find out how many tens can be placed in each group.
    Then use multiplication to find out how many tens have been placed:

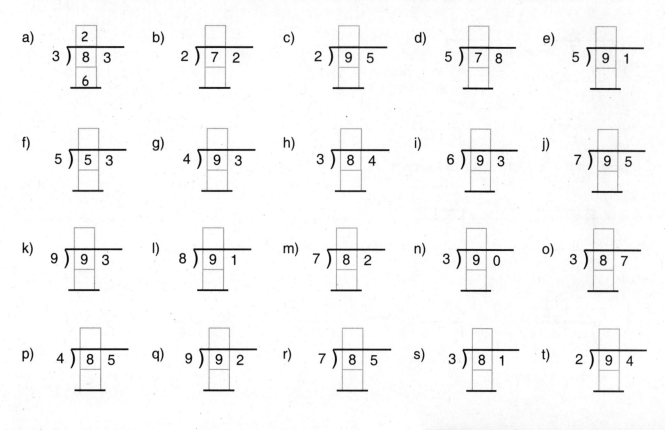

a) $3 \overline{)\ 8\ 3}$ with 2 above, 6 below

b) $2 \overline{)\ 7\ 2}$

c) $2 \overline{)\ 9\ 5}$

d) $5 \overline{)\ 7\ 8}$

e) $5 \overline{)\ 9\ 1}$

f) $5 \overline{)\ 5\ 3}$

g) $4 \overline{)\ 9\ 3}$

h) $3 \overline{)\ 8\ 4}$

i) $6 \overline{)\ 9\ 3}$

j) $7 \overline{)\ 9\ 5}$

k) $9 \overline{)\ 9\ 3}$

l) $8 \overline{)\ 9\ 1}$

m) $7 \overline{)\ 8\ 2}$

n) $3 \overline{)\ 9\ 0}$

o) $3 \overline{)\ 8\ 7}$

p) $4 \overline{)\ 8\ 5}$

q) $9 \overline{)\ 9\ 2}$

r) $7 \overline{)\ 8\ 5}$

s) $3 \overline{)\ 8\ 1}$

t) $2 \overline{)\ 9\ 4}$

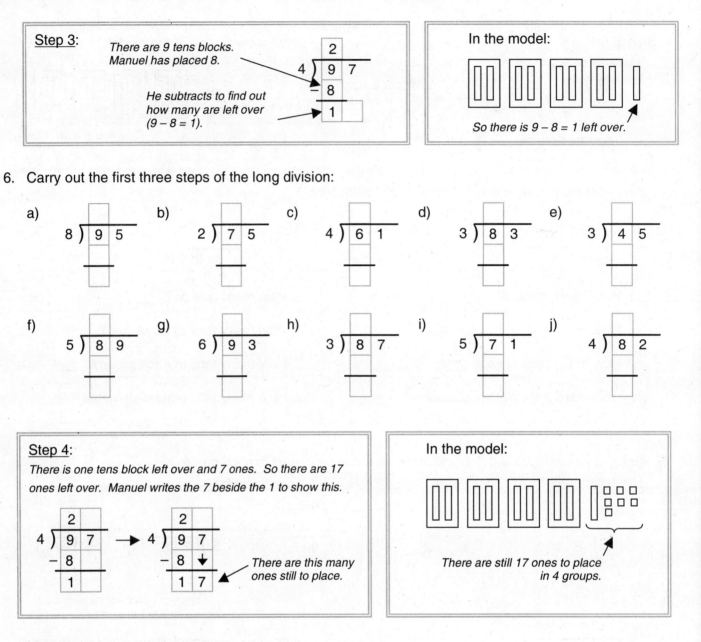

Step 3: There are 9 tens blocks. Manuel has placed 8.

He subtracts to find out how many are left over (9 − 8 = 1).

In the model:

So there is 9 − 8 = 1 left over.

6. Carry out the first three steps of the long division:

a) 8) 9 5

b) 2) 7 5

c) 4) 6 1

d) 3) 8 3

e) 3) 4 5

f) 5) 8 9

g) 6) 9 3

h) 3) 8 7

i) 5) 7 1

j) 4) 8 2

Step 4:
There is one tens block left over and 7 ones. So there are 17 ones left over. Manuel writes the 7 beside the 1 to show this.

$$4 \overline{)97} \ -8 \ \overline{1} \quad \rightarrow \quad 4\overline{)97} \ -8 \ \overline{17}$$

There are this many ones still to place.

In the model:

There are still 17 ones to place in 4 groups.

7. Carry out the first four steps of the division:

a) 5) 7 5

b) 3) 5 7

c) 4) 9 3

d) 2) 7 3

e) 5) 9 6

f) 9) 9 3

g) 4) 7 6

h) 8) 9 8

i) 7) 9 1

j) 8) 9 6

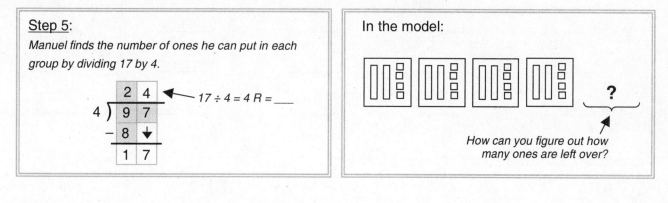

Step 5:

Manuel finds the number of ones he can put in each group by dividing 17 by 4.

17 ÷ 4 = 4 R = ___

In the model:

How can you figure out how many ones are left over?

8. Carry out the **first** five steps of the division:

a) 4) 9 6

b) 5) 8 5

c) 2) 7 5

d) 3) 5 1

e) 5) 7 2

f) 7) 8 5

g) 2) 9 5

h) 8) 9 6

i) 3) 9 2

j) 2) 9 3

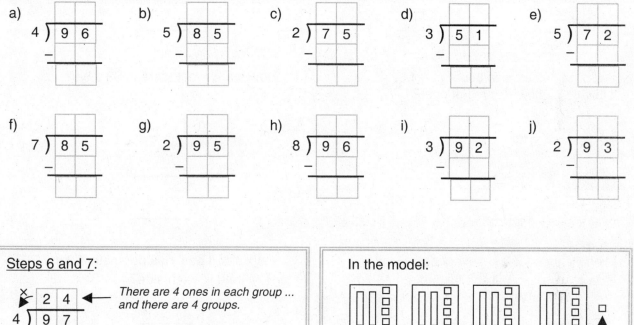

Steps 6 and 7:

There are 4 ones in each group ... and there are 4 groups.

So there are 16 ones altogether in the groups (4 × 4 = 16).

There were 17 ones so there is 1 one left over (17 − 16 = 1).

In the model:

*There are 16 ones in the groups so there is 1 one left: **17 − 16 = 1**.*

The division statement and the model both show that he can give each class 24 oranges with one left over.

9. Carry out all seven steps of the division:

a) 5) 7 4

b) 3) 7 7

c) 2) 6 7

d) 4) 7 0

e) 4) 9 0

f)   )8 1

g)   4)8 4

h)   5)9 6

i)   6)8 9

j)   9)9 7

k)   4)9 3

l)   8)9 7

m)   6)8 6

n)   7)9 5

o)   2)8 0

10. Avi put 98 flowers in bouquets of 8. How many flowers are left over?

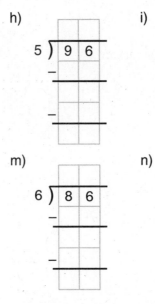

11. How many weeks are in 93 days?

12. Michelle jogs for 3 km every day. How many days will she take to run 45 km?

13. A six sided pool has perimeter 72 m. How long is each side?

14. Guerdy packs 85 books into boxes of 6, and Tyree packs 67 books into boxes of 4. Who uses more boxes?

NS5-35: Long Division — 3- and 4-Digit by 1-Digit

1. Find 335 ÷ 2 by drawing a base ten model and by long division:

   Step 1:   *Draw a base ten model of 335.*

   Draw your model here.

   Step 2:   *Divide the hundreds squares into 2 equal groups.*

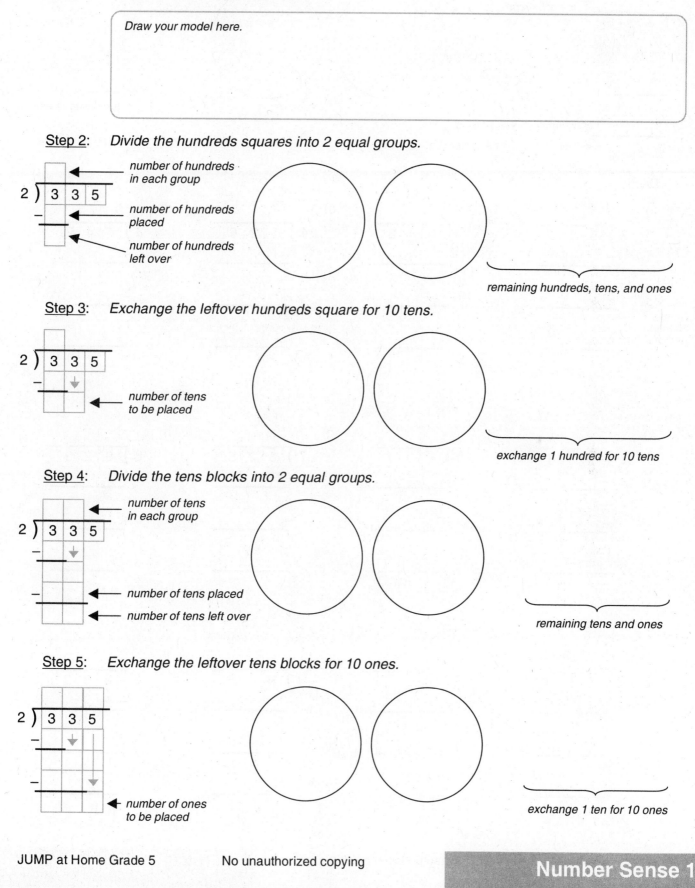

   number of hundreds in each group

   number of hundreds placed

   number of hundreds left over

   remaining hundreds, tens, and ones

   Step 3:   *Exchange the leftover hundreds square for 10 tens.*

   number of tens to be placed

   exchange 1 hundred for 10 tens

   Step 4:   *Divide the tens blocks into 2 equal groups.*

   number of tens in each group

   number of tens placed

   number of tens left over

   remaining tens and ones

   Step 5:   *Exchange the leftover tens blocks for 10 ones.*

   number of ones to be placed

   exchange 1 ten for 10 ones

<u>Steps 6 and 7</u>: *Divide the ones into 2 equal groups.*

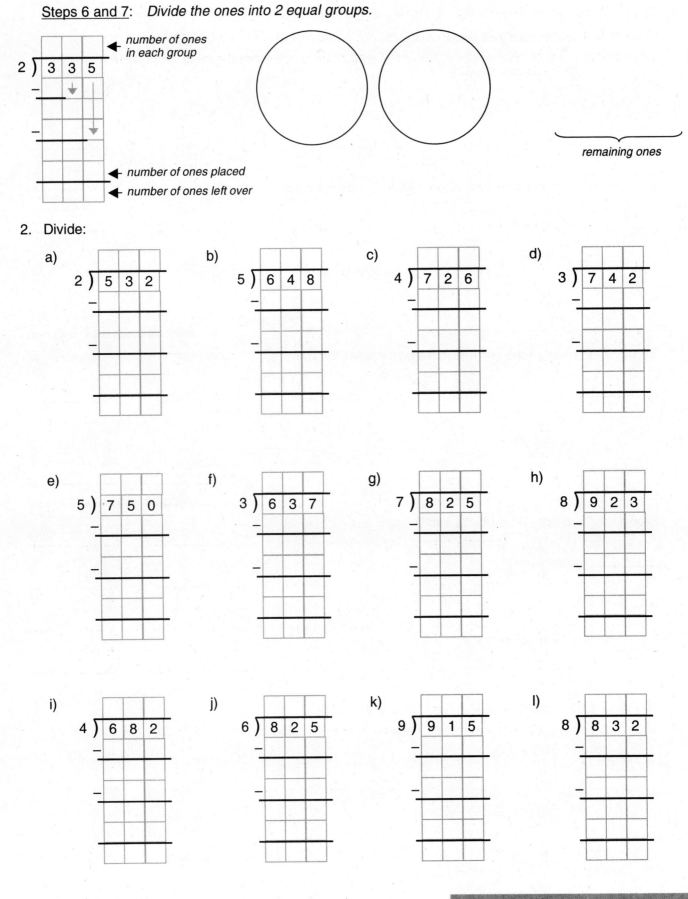

2. Divide:

a)   2) 5 3 2

b)   5) 6 4 8

c)   4) 7 2 6

d)   3) 7 4 2

e)   5) 7 5 0

f)   3) 6 3 7

g)   7) 8 2 5

h)   8) 9 2 3

i)   4) 6 8 2

j)   6) 8 2 5

k)   9) 9 1 5

l)   8) 8 3 2

3. In each question, there are fewer hundreds than the number of groups.

Write a '0' in the hundreds position to show that no hundreds can be placed in equal groups.

Then perform the division as if the hundreds had automatically been exchanged for tens.

Divide. The first one has been done for you:

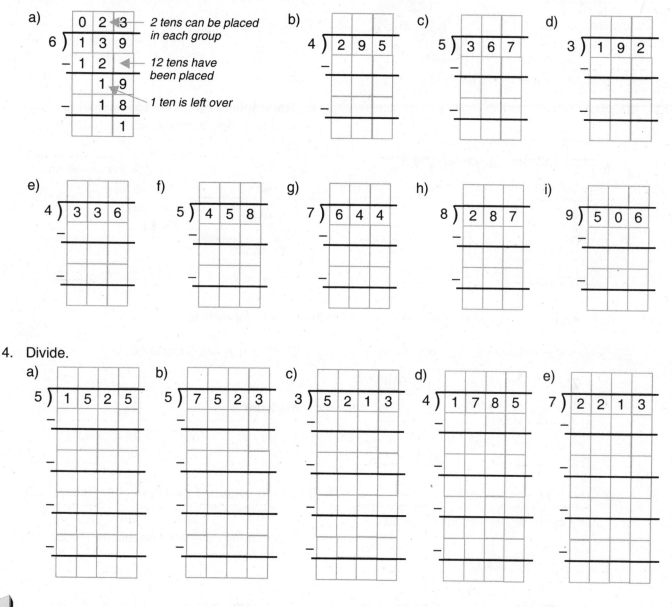

a)

```
      0 2 3  ← 2 tens can be placed
6 ) 1 3 9     in each group
  - 1 2    ← 12 tens have
      1 9      been placed
  -   1 8   ← 1 ten is left over
        1
```

b) 4) 2 9 5

c) 5) 3 6 7

d) 3) 1 9 2

e) 4) 3 3 6

f) 5) 4 5 8

g) 7) 6 4 4

h) 8) 2 8 7

i) 9) 5 0 6

4. Divide.

a) 5) 1 5 2 5

b) 5) 7 5 2 3

c) 3) 5 2 1 3

d) 4) 1 7 8 5

e) 7) 2 2 1 3

5. Ken swims 4 laps of a pool. Altogether he swims 144 metres. How long is the pool?

6. The perimeter of a hexagonal park is 852 km. How long is each side of the park?

7. Seven friends collect 2 744 books for charity. Each friend collects the same number of books. How many books did each friend collect?

Answer the following questions in a notebook.

1. A class paid $20 for a cake and $4 per child for a slice of pizza.

    They paid $140.

    How many children are in the class?

    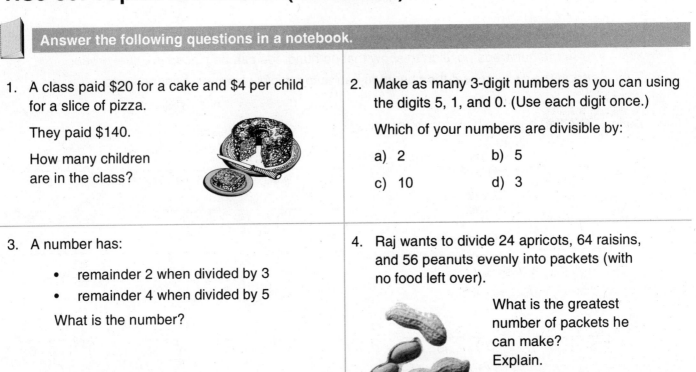

2. Make as many 3-digit numbers as you can using the digits 5, 1, and 0. (Use each digit once.)

    Which of your numbers are divisible by:

    a) 2   b) 5

    c) 10   d) 3

3. A number has:

    - remainder 2 when divided by 3
    - remainder 4 when divided by 5

    What is the number?

4. Raj wants to divide 24 apricots, 64 raisins, and 56 peanuts evenly into packets (with no food left over).

    What is the greatest number of packets he can make? Explain.

In the questions below, you will have to interpret what the remainder means.

   Example: Cindy wants to put 64 cookies onto trays. Each tray holds 5 cookies.

   How many trays will she need?

   ### 64 ÷ 5 = 12 remainder 4

   She will need 13 trays (because she needs a tray for the four leftover cookies).

5. A car can hold 5 passengers.

    How many cars will 29 passengers need?

    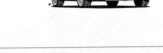

6. Manu colours 4 pictures in her picture book every day.

    How many days will she take to colour 50 pictures?

7. Jay shares 76 plums as evenly as possible among 9 friends.

    How many plums does each friend get?

8. Siru wants to place her stamps in an album.

    Each page holds 9 stamps.

    How many pages will she need for 95 stamps?

Answer the following questions in a notebook.

1. A bus carries 36 students.

   How many students can 25 buses carry?

2. A racer snake lays at least 3 eggs and no more than 40 eggs.

   What is the least number of eggs 6 snakes would lay?

   What is the greatest number?

3. If 2 pencils cost 17¢, how much will 8 pencils cost? Show your work.

4. How much do 7 books cost at $19 per book?

5. A tiger beetle is the fastest land insect It can scuttle 9 km in an hour.

   How many metres could it crawl in half an hour?

6. Create a division problem to go with the expression below.

   $$72 \div 8$$

7. What is the least number of whole apples that can be shared equally among 2, 3, or 4 people?

8. a) Alice is between 20 and 40 years old. Last year, her age was a multiple of 4. This year, her age is a multiple of 5. How old is Alice?

   b) George is between 30 and 50 years old. Last year, his age was a multiple of 6. This year it is a multiple of 7. How old is George?

9. Nandita ran 24 laps of her school track. The track is 75 metres long.

   a) How far has she run?

   b) How much farther must she run if she wants to run 2000 metres?

   c) About how many extra laps must she run?

10. If 3 CDs cost $23, how would you calculate the cost of 12 CDs?

11. What digit could be in the box? Explain.

   □ **569 ÷ 6** is about 400.

12. Three letter carriers delivered a different number of letters in 1 week:

   ♣ Carl: 2 624 letters

   ♣ Sally: 1 759 letters

   ♣ Selma: 3 284 letters

   Did any one letter carrier deliver more than half of all the letters?

1. Draw an arrow to the 0 or 10 to show whether the circled number is closer to **0 or 10**:

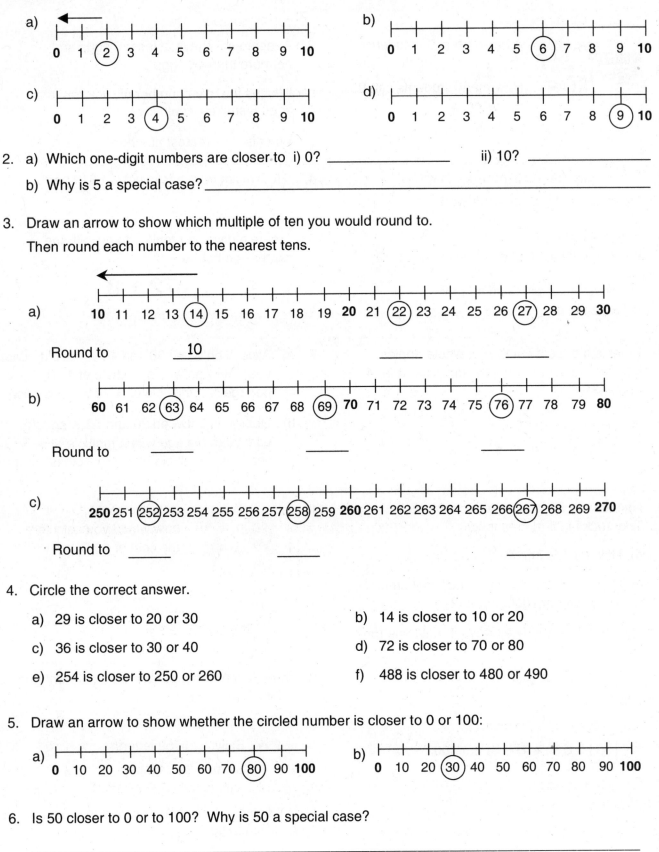

a)

0 1 ② 3 4 5 6 7 8 9 **10**

b)

0 1 2 3 4 5 ⑥ 7 8 9 **10**

c)

0 1 2 3 ④ 5 6 7 8 9 **10**

d)

0 1 2 3 4 5 6 7 8 ⑨ **10**

2. a) Which one-digit numbers are closer to i) 0? _____ ii) 10? _____

   b) Why is 5 a special case? _____

3. Draw an arrow to show which multiple of ten you would round to.

   Then round each number to the nearest tens.

   a)

   10 11 12 13 ⑭ 15 16 17 18 19 **20** 21 ㉒ 23 24 25 26 ㉗ 28 29 **30**

   Round to ___10___   _____   _____

   b)

   60 61 62 ㉖③ 64 65 66 67 68 ㉗⑨ **70** 71 72 73 74 75 ㉗⑥ 77 78 79 **80**

   Round to _____   _____   _____

   c)

   250 251 ㉒⑤② 253 254 255 256 257 ㉒⑤⑧ 259 **260** 261 262 263 264 265 266㉖⑦ 268 269 **270**

   Round to _____   _____   _____

4. Circle the correct answer.

   a) 29 is closer to 20 or 30   b) 14 is closer to 10 or 20

   c) 36 is closer to 30 or 40   d) 72 is closer to 70 or 80

   e) 254 is closer to 250 or 260   f) 488 is closer to 480 or 490

5. Draw an arrow to show whether the circled number is closer to 0 or 100:

   a)

   0 10 20 30 40 50 60 70 ㊇⓪ 90 **100**

   b)

   0 10 20 ㉚⓪ 40 50 60 70 80 90 **100**

6. Is 50 closer to 0 or to 100? Why is 50 a special case?

   _____

7. Circle the correct answer:

    a) 80 is closer to: 0 or 100

    b) 20 is closer to: 0 or 100

    c) 40 is closer to: 0 or 100

    d) 60 is closer to: 0 or 100

8. Show the approximate position of each number on the line. What multiple of 100 would you round to?

    a) 627   b) 683   c) 795   d) 706

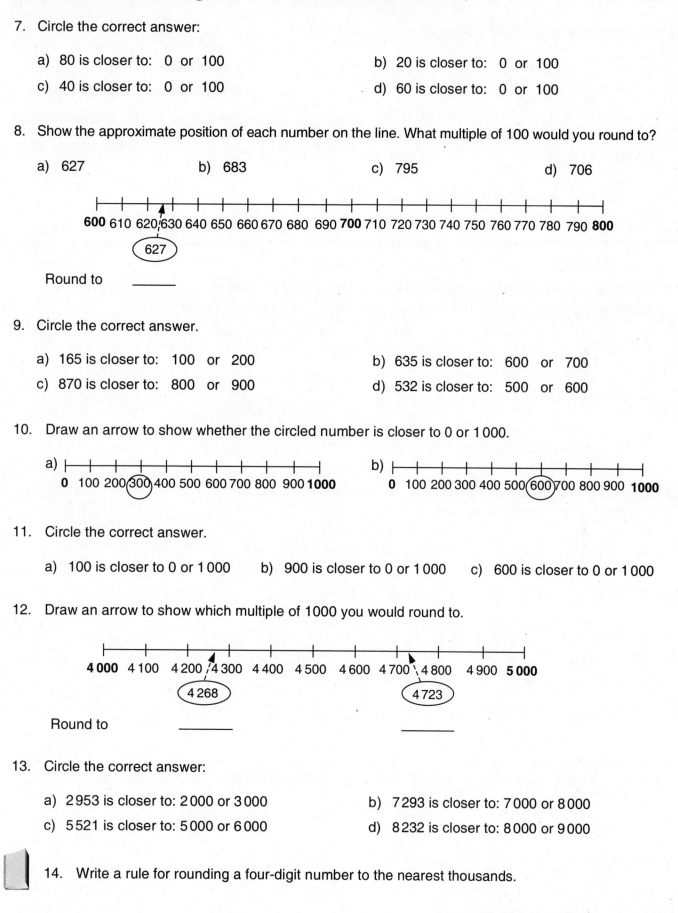

    Round to   _____

9. Circle the correct answer.

    a) 165 is closer to: 100 or 200

    b) 635 is closer to: 600 or 700

    c) 870 is closer to: 800 or 900

    d) 532 is closer to: 500 or 600

10. Draw an arrow to show whether the circled number is closer to 0 or 1 000.

    a)   b)

11. Circle the correct answer.

    a) 100 is closer to 0 or 1 000   b) 900 is closer to 0 or 1 000   c) 600 is closer to 0 or 1 000

12. Draw an arrow to show which multiple of 1000 you would round to.

    Round to   _____   _____

13. Circle the correct answer:

    a) 2 953 is closer to: 2 000 or 3 000

    b) 7 293 is closer to: 7 000 or 8 000

    c) 5 521 is closer to: 5 000 or 6 000

    d) 8 232 is closer to: 8 000 or 9 000

14. Write a rule for rounding a four-digit number to the nearest thousands.

NS5-39: Rounding

1. Round to the nearest **tens** place:

    a) 22 [   ]   b) 26 [   ]

    c) 73 [   ]   d) 58 [   ]

    e) 94 [   ]   f) 83 [   ]

    g) 15 [   ]   h) 49 [   ]

    i) 27 [   ]   j) 37 [   ]   k) 91 [   ]

    > **REMEMBER:**
    > If the number in the ones digit is:
    >   0, 1, 2, 3 or 4 – you round <u>down</u>
    >   5, 6, 7, 8 or 9 – you round <u>up</u>

2. Round to the nearest **tens** place. Underline the tens digit first. Then put your pencil on the digit to the right (the ones digit). This digit tells you whether to round up or down:

    a) 14<u>5</u> [150]   b) 183 [   ]   c) 361 [   ]

    d) 342 [   ]   e) 554 [   ]   f) 667 [   ]

    g) 656 [   ]   h) 847 [   ]   i) 938 [   ]

3. Round to the nearest **hundreds** place. Underline the hundreds digit first. Then put your pencil on the digit to the right (the tens digit):

    a) <u>7</u>30 [700]   b) 490 [   ]   c) 540 [   ]

    d) 270 [   ]   e) 167 [   ]   f) 317 [   ]

    g) 160 [   ]   h) 873 [   ]   i) 791 [   ]

    j) 6 <u>2</u>37 [6 200]   k) 1 286 [   ]   l) 8 218 [   ]

    m) 4 905 [   ]   n) 6 321 [   ]   o) 9 583 [   ]

4. Round to the nearest thousands place. Underline the thousands digit first. Then put your pencil on the digit to the right (the hundreds digit).

    a) <u>7</u> 872 [8 000]   b) 8 952 [   ]   c) 5 231 [   ]

    d) 3 092 [   ]   e) 3 871 [   ]   f) 1680 [   ]

1. Underline the digit you wish to round to. Then say whether you would round up or down.

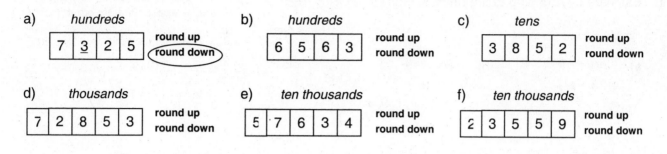

a) hundreds
| 7 | 3 | 2 | 5 |

round up
(round down)

b) hundreds
| 6 | 5 | 6 | 3 |

round up
round down

c) tens
| 3 | 8 | 5 | 2 |

round up
round down

d) thousands
| 7 | 2 | 8 | 5 | 3 |

round up
round down

e) ten thousands
| 5 | 7 | 6 | 3 | 4 |

round up
round down

f) ten thousands
| 2 | 3 | 5 | 5 | 9 |

round up
round down

2. Complete the steps of rounding from Question 1. Then follow these steps:

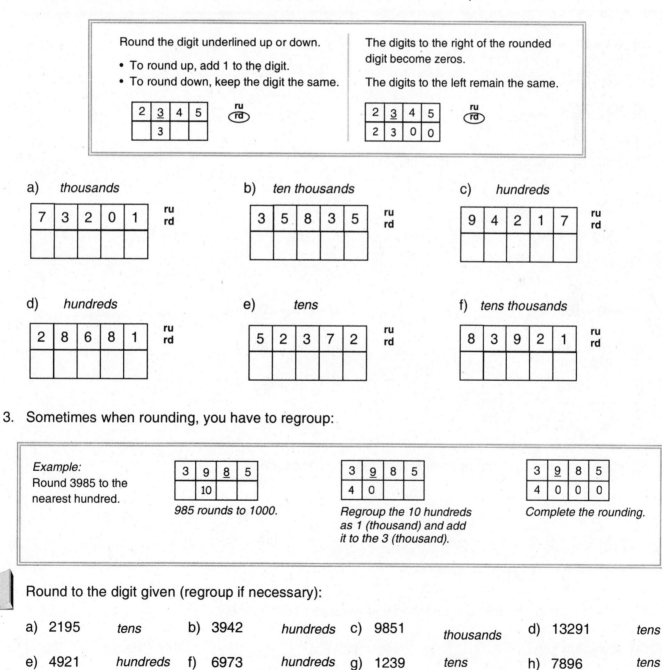

Round the digit underlined up or down.

- To round up, add 1 to the digit.
- To round down, keep the digit the same.

| 2 | 3 | 4 | 5 |
| 3 | | | |

ru (rd)

The digits to the right of the rounded digit become zeros.

The digits to the left remain the same.

| 2 | 3 | 4 | 5 |
| 2 | 3 | 0 | 0 |

ru (rd)

a) thousands
| 7 | 3 | 2 | 0 | 1 |
| | | | | |

ru
rd

b) ten thousands
| 3 | 5 | 8 | 3 | 5 |
| | | | | |

ru
rd

c) hundreds
| 9 | 4 | 2 | 1 | 7 |
| | | | | |

ru
rd

d) hundreds
| 2 | 8 | 6 | 8 | 1 |
| | | | | |

ru
rd

e) tens
| 5 | 2 | 3 | 7 | 2 |
| | | | | |

ru
rd

f) tens thousands
| 8 | 3 | 9 | 2 | 1 |
| | | | | |

ru
rd

3. Sometimes when rounding, you have to regroup:

Example:
Round 3985 to the nearest hundred.

| 3 | 9 | 8 | 5 |
| | 10 | | |

985 rounds to 1000.

| 3 | 9 | 8 | 5 |
| 4 | 0 | | |

Regroup the 10 hundreds as 1 (thousand) and add it to the 3 (thousand).

| 3 | 9 | 8 | 5 |
| 4 | 0 | 0 | 0 |

Complete the rounding.

Round to the digit given (regroup if necessary):

a) 2195   tens   b) 3942   hundreds   c) 9851   thousands   d) 13291   tens

e) 4921   hundreds   f) 6973   hundreds   g) 1239   tens   h) 7896   tens

NS5-41: Estimating Sums and Differences

1. Estimate by rounding to the nearest tens.

> ≈ ← Mathematicians use this symbol to mean **"approximately equal to."**

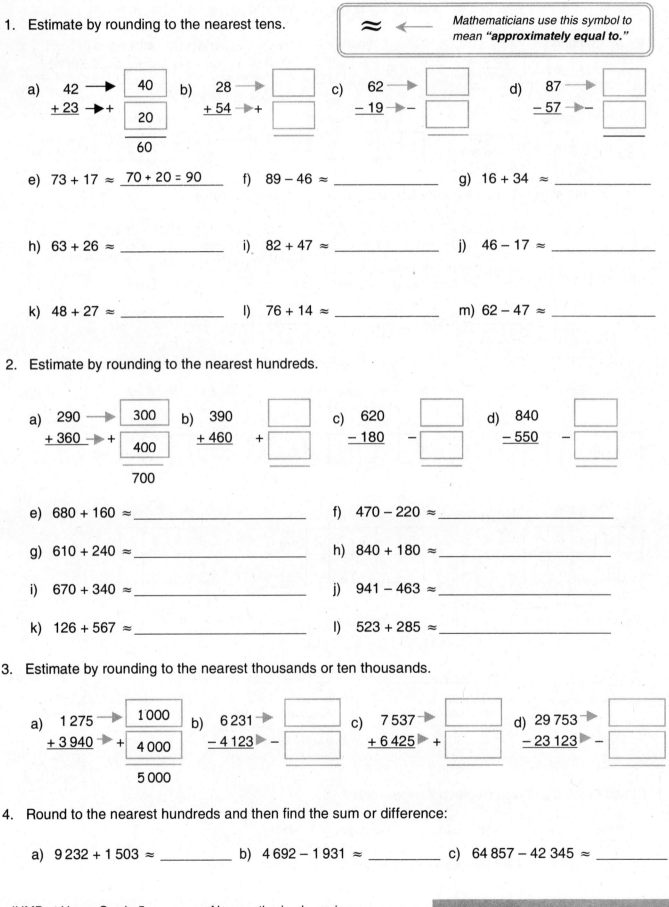

a) 42 → 40
   + 23 → + 20
   ────────
        60

b) 28 → ☐
   + 54 → + ☐

c) 62 → ☐
   − 19 → − ☐

d) 87 → ☐
   − 57 → − ☐

e) 73 + 17 ≈ _70 + 20 = 90_   f) 89 − 46 ≈ _____   g) 16 + 34 ≈ _____

h) 63 + 26 ≈ _____   i) 82 + 47 ≈ _____   j) 46 − 17 ≈ _____

k) 48 + 27 ≈ _____   l) 76 + 14 ≈ _____   m) 62 − 47 ≈ _____

2. Estimate by rounding to the nearest hundreds.

a) 290 → 300
   + 360 → + 400
   ──────────
        700

b) 390 → ☐
   + 460 → + ☐

c) 620 → ☐
   − 180 → − ☐

d) 840 → ☐
   − 550 → − ☐

e) 680 + 160 ≈ _____   f) 470 − 220 ≈ _____

g) 610 + 240 ≈ _____   h) 840 + 180 ≈ _____

i) 670 + 340 ≈ _____   j) 941 − 463 ≈ _____

k) 126 + 567 ≈ _____   l) 523 + 285 ≈ _____

3. Estimate by rounding to the nearest thousands or ten thousands.

a) 1 275 → 1 000
   + 3 940 → + 4 000
   ────────────
        5 000

b) 6 231 → ☐
   − 4 123 → − ☐

c) 7 537 → ☐
   + 6 425 → + ☐

d) 29 753 → ☐
   − 23 123 → − ☐

4. Round to the nearest hundreds and then find the sum or difference:

a) 9 232 + 1 503 ≈ _____   b) 4 692 − 1 931 ≈ _____   c) 64 857 − 42 345 ≈ _____

Number Sense 1

NS5-42: Estimation

Answer the following questions in a notebook.

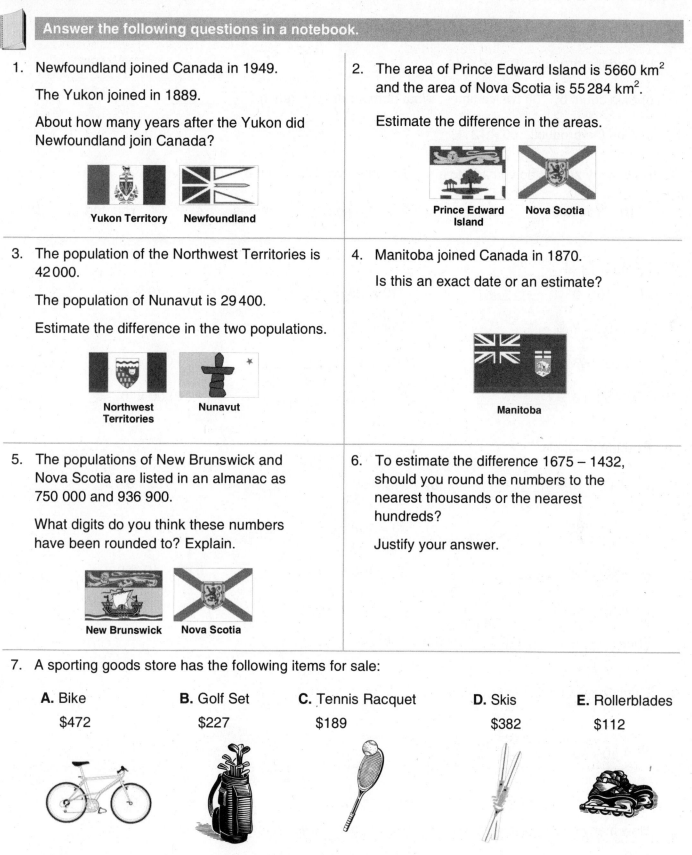

1. Newfoundland joined Canada in 1949.

   The Yukon joined in 1889.

   About how many years after the Yukon did Newfoundland join Canada?

   Yukon Territory   **Newfoundland**

2. The area of Prince Edward Island is 5660 km^2 and the area of Nova Scotia is 55 284 km^2.

   Estimate the difference in the areas.

   Prince Edward Island   **Nova Scotia**

3. The population of the Northwest Territories is 42 000.

   The population of Nunavut is 29 400.

   Estimate the difference in the two populations.

   Northwest Territories   **Nunavut**

4. Manitoba joined Canada in 1870.

   Is this an exact date or an estimate?

   Manitoba

5. The populations of New Brunswick and Nova Scotia are listed in an almanac as 750 000 and 936 900.

   What digits do you think these numbers have been rounded to? Explain.

   New Brunswick   **Nova Scotia**

6. To estimate the difference 1675 – 1432, should you round the numbers to the nearest thousands or the nearest hundreds?

   Justify your answer.

7. A sporting goods store has the following items for sale:

   A. Bike   **B.** Golf Set   **C.** Tennis Racquet   **D.** Skis   **E.** Rollerblades
   $472 $227 $189 $382 $112

   a) What could you buy if you had $800 to spend? Estimate to find out. Then add the actual prices.

   b) List a different set of items you could buy.

NS5-43: Multiplying by 10, 100, 1 000, and 10 000

1. a) Skip count by 10 <u>twelve</u> times. What number did you reach? _____

   b) Find the product: 10 × 12 = _____

   c) Skip count by 100 twelve times. What number did you reach? _____

   d) Find the product: 100 × 12 = _____

2. How many zeroes do you add to a number when you multiply the number by:

   a) 10: You add _____ zero.   b) 100: You add _____ zeroes.   c) 1000: You add _____ zeroes.

3. Continue the pattern.

   a)   10 × 8 = _____   b)   10 x 25 = _____   c)   10 x 62 = _____

        100 × 8 = _____   100 × 25 = _____   100 × 62 = _____

        1 000 × 8 = _____   1 000 × 25 = _____   1 000 × 62 = _____

        10 000 × 8 = _____   10 000 × 25 = _____   10 000 × 62 = _____

4. Find the products.

   a)   17 × 10 = _____   b)   10 × 50 = _____   c)   10 × 97 = _____

   d)   69 × 100 = _____   e)   20 × 100 = _____   f)   19 × 100 = _____

   g)   100 × 89 = _____   h)   37 × 100 = _____   i) 46 × 10 000 = _____

5. Round each number to the leading digit.
   Then find the product of the rounded numbers:

   leading digit

   a) 11 × 79   b) 12 × 22   c) 13 × 79   d) 11 × 64   e) 59 × 110   f) 91 × 120

10 × 80
= 800

   =   =   =   =   =

6. How many digits will the answer have? Write your answer in the box provided.

   a) (2 + 5) × 100: [ ] digits   b) (7 + 5) × 100: [ ] digits   c) (5 + 69) × 1000: [ ] digits

NS5-44: Counting Coins

1. Count by the first number given, then by the second number after the vertical line.

   a) __5__ , ____ , ____ , ____ , ____ | ____ , ____ , ____
      Count by 5s | *Continue counting by 1s*

   b) __5__ , ____ , ____ , ____ | ____ , ____ , ____
      Count by 5s | *Continue counting by 1s*

2. Complete each pattern.

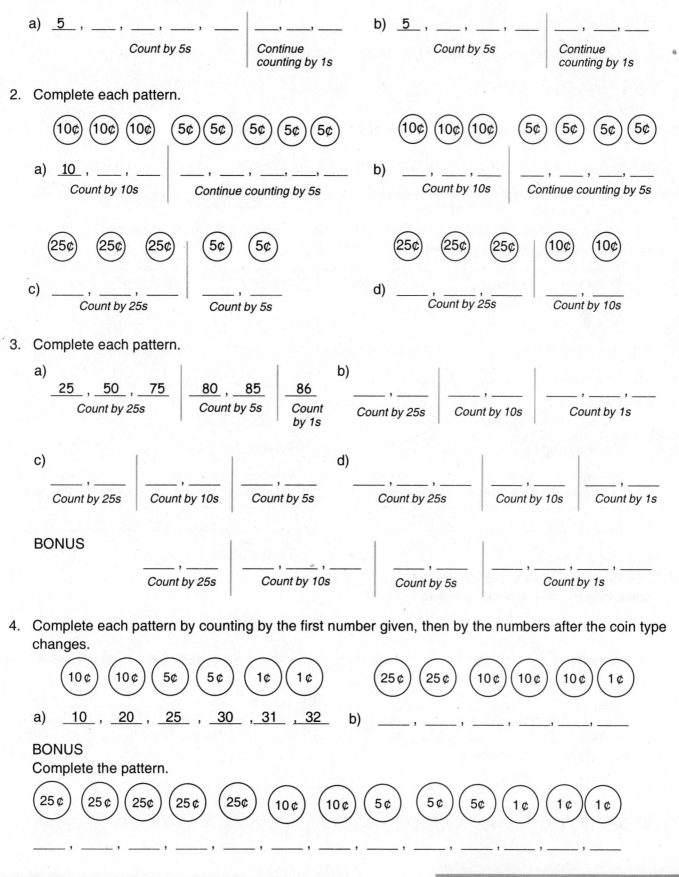

   a) __10__ , ____ , ____ | ____ , ____ , ____ , ____ , ____
      Count by 10s | *Continue counting by 5s*

   b) ____ , ____ , ____ | ____ , ____ , ____ , ____
      Count by 10s | *Continue counting by 5s*

   c) ____ , ____ , ____ | ____ , ____
      Count by 25s | *Count by 5s*

   d) ____ , ____ , ____ | ____ , ____
      Count by 25s | *Count by 10s*

3. Complete each pattern.

   a) __25__ , __50__ , __75__ | __80__ , __85__ | __86__
      Count by 25s | *Count by 5s* | *Count by 1s*

   b) ____ , ____ | ____ , ____ | ____ , ____ , ____
      Count by 25s | *Count by 10s* | *Count by 1s*

   c) ____ , ____ | ____ , ____ | ____ , ____
      Count by 25s | *Count by 10s* | *Count by 5s*

   d) ____ , ____ , ____ | ____ , ____ | ____ , ____
      Count by 25s | *Count by 10s* | *Count by 1s*

   BONUS

   ____ , ____ | ____ , ____ , ____ | ____ , ____ | ____ , ____ , ____ , ____
   Count by 25s | *Count by 10s* | *Count by 5s* | *Count by 1s*

4. Complete each pattern by counting by the first number given, then by the numbers after the coin type changes.

   a) __10__ , __20__ , __25__ , __30__ , __31__ , __32__

   b) ____ , ____ , ____ , ____ , ____ , ____

   BONUS
   Complete the pattern.

   ____ , ____ , ____ , ____ , ____ , ____ , ____ , ____ , ____ , ____ , ____ , ____ , ____

5. Complete the pattern by counting each number given:

a)

<u>10</u> , <u>20</u> , <u>30</u> | <u>35</u> , <u>40</u> | <u>41</u>

Count by 10s | *Count by 5s* | *Count by 1s*

b)

____ , ____ | ____ , ____ | ____ , ____ , ____

Count by 25s | *Count by 5s* | *Count by 1s*

c)

____ , ____ | ____ , ____ | ____ , ____

Count by 25s | *Count by 10s* | *Count by 1s*

d)

____ , ____ , ____ | ____ , ____ | ____ , ____

Count by 25s | *Count by 10s* | *Count by 5s*

BONUS

e)   ____ , ____ | ____ , ____ , ____ | ____ , ____ | ____ , ____ , ____ , ____

Count by 25s | *Count by 10s* | *Count by 5s* | *Count by 1s*

6. Write the total amount of money in cents for the number of coins given in the charts below.
   HINT: Count by the greatest amount first.

a)

Nickels	Pennies
6	7

Total amount = _____

b)

Quarters	Dimes
3	2

Total amount = _____

c)

Quarters	Nickels
5	5

Total amount = _____

d)

Quarters	Nickels	Pennies
4	2	4

Total amount = _____

e)

Quarters	Dimes	Nickels
6	3	7

Total amount = _____

f)

Quarters	Dimes	Nickels	Pennies
2	3	1	5

Total amount = _____

g)

Quarters	Dimes	Nickels	Pennies
5	2	2	2

Total amount = _____

7. Count the given coins and write the total amount:
   HINT: Count by the greatest amount first.

a)   Total amount = _____

25¢ 1¢ 1¢ 5¢ 5¢ 10¢ 1¢

b)   Total amount = _____

10¢ 1¢ 10¢ 25¢ 25¢ 1¢ 25¢

c)   Total amount = _____

10¢ 1¢ 25¢ 5¢ 10¢ 25¢ 10¢

d)   Total amount = _____

5¢ 10¢ 25¢ 5¢ 1¢ 5¢ 25¢

BONUS
e)   Total amount = _____

5¢ 1¢ 5¢ 1¢ 1¢ 5¢ 25¢ 5¢ 1¢ 10¢ 10¢ 25¢ 25¢

NS5-45: Counting by Different Denominations

1. Draw the additional coins needed to make each total:

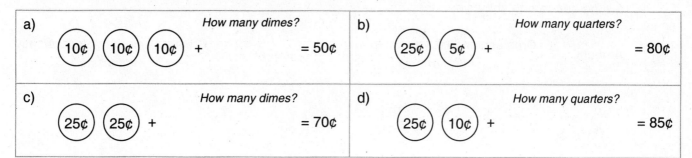

a) *How many dimes?* 10¢ 10¢ 10¢ + = 50¢	b) *How many quarters?* 25¢ 5¢ + = 80¢
c) *How many dimes?* 25¢ 25¢ + = 70¢	d) *How many quarters?* 25¢ 10¢ + = 85¢

2. Draw the <u>additional</u> coins needed to make each total.
   You can only draw **two** coins for each question:

a) 26¢ 10¢ 10¢	b) 50¢ 25¢ 10¢
c) 50¢ 25¢ 10¢	d) 85¢ 25¢ 25¢
e) 31¢ 10¢ 1¢	f) 65¢ 25¢ 25¢
g) 105¢ 25¢ 25¢ 25¢	h) 95¢ 25¢ 25¢ 25¢
i) $5 $2	j) $7 $2 $2
k) $3 $1	l) $10 $2 $2 $2 $1
m) 131¢ $1 5¢	n) 340¢ $2 $1 25¢

3. Draw a picture to show the fewest extra coins the child will need to pay for the item:

   a) Ron has 25¢. He wants to buy an eraser for 55¢.

   b) Alan has 3 quarters, a dime, and a nickel. He wants to buy a notebook for 97¢.

   c) Jane has 2 toonies and 2 loonies. She wants to buy a plant for ten dollars.

   d) Raiz has 3 toonies and a loonie. He wants to buy a book for nine dollars and forty-five cents.

4. Show how to make 80¢ using only:

   a) dimes and quarters   b) nickels and quarters

5. Make up a problem like one of the problems in Question 3 and exchange it with a parent to solve.

1. What is the greatest amount you could pay in quarters without exceeding the amount?
   Draw the quarters to show your answer:

Amount	Greatest amount you could pay in quarters	Amount	Greatest amount you could pay in quarters
a) 45¢		b) 52¢	
c) 79¢		d) 83¢	
e) 63¢		f) 64¢	
g) 49¢		h) 31¢	
i) 82¢		j) 96¢	

2. Find the greatest amount you could pay in quarters.
   Represent the amount remaining using the least number of coins:

Amount	Amount paid in quarters	Amount remaining	Amount remaining in coins
a) 82¢	75¢	82¢ - 75¢ = 7¢	5¢ 1¢ 1¢
b) 57¢			
c) 85¢			
d) 95¢			

3. Trade coins to make each amount with the least number of coins.
   Draw a picture in a notebook to show your final answer:

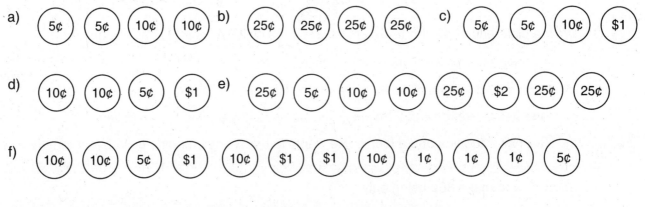

4. Show how you could trade the amounts for the least number of coins:

   a) 6 quarters
   b) 6 dimes and 2 nickels
   c) 8 loonies
   d) 9 loonies and 5 dimes
   e) 10 loonies, 6 dimes, 2 nickels, and 5 pennies

NS5-47: Dollar and Cent Notation

1. Write the given amount in dollars, dimes, and pennies, then in dollar notation.

Dollars	Dimes	Pennies	Amount in $
1	7	3	$ 1.73

a) 173¢   b) 465¢

Dollars	Dimes	Pennies	Amount in $

c) 62¢   d) 2¢

2. Change the amount to cent notation, then dollar notation.

a) 7 pennies = ___7¢___ = ___$ .07___   b) 4 nickels = _____ = _____   c) 6 dimes = _____ = _____

d) 4 pennies = _____ = _____   e) 13 pennies = _____ = _____   f) 1 quarter = _____ = _____

g) 5 nickels = _____ = _____   h) 3 quarters = _____ = _____   i) 8 dimes = _____ = _____

j) 6 toonies = _____ = _____   k) 4 loonies = _____ = _____   l) 7 loonies = _____ = _____

3. Count the dollar amount and the cent amount. Write the total amount in dollar (decimal) notation.

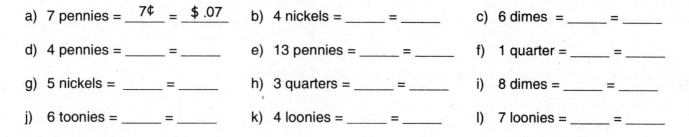

Dollar Amount	Cent Amount	Total
a) $2 $2 $1 = _____	25¢ 25¢ 5¢ = _____	_____
b) [10] [5] = _____	25¢ 10¢ 1¢ = _____	_____
c) [10] [10] = _____	25¢ 25¢ 1¢ = _____	_____

4. Count the given coins. Write the total amount in cents and in dollars (decimals).

Coins	Cent Notation	Dollar Notation
a) 25¢ 25¢ 25¢ 25¢ 5¢	105¢	$1.05
b) 25¢ 25¢ 25¢ 10¢ 10¢ 10¢ 5¢	_____	_____

5. Write each number of cents in dollar notation.

a) 325¢ = _____   b) 20¢ = _____   c) 6¢ = _____   d) 283¢ = _____   e) 205¢ = _____

Number Sense 1

NS5-47: Dollar and Cent Notation *(continued)*

6. Write each amount of money in cents notation.

   a) $2.99 = _____   b) $3.43 = _____   c) $1.41 = _____   d) $0.08 = _____

7. Circle the greater amount of money in each pair:

   a)   193¢   or $1.96   b) $1.01   or   103¢   c)   840¢   or $8.04

8. Circle the larger amount of money in each pair:

   a) seven dollars and sixty-five cents   or   seven dollars and seventy cents

   b) nine dollars and eighty-three cents   or   978¢

   c) fifteen dollars and eighty cents   or $15.08

9. Tally the amount of each type of denomination and then find the total.

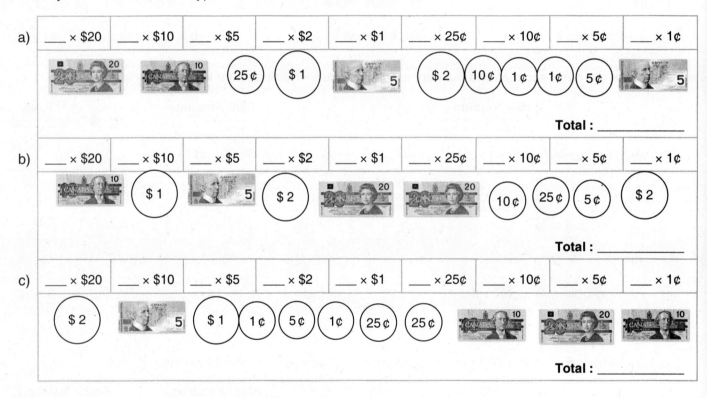

10. Which is a greater amount of money: 256¢ or $2.62? Explain how you know.

11. Alan bought a pack of markers for $3.50. He paid for it with 4 coins. Which coins did he use?

12. Tanya's weekly allowance is $5.25. Her mom gave her 6 coins. Which coins did she use? Can you find more than one answer?

13. Write words for the following amounts:

    a) $3.57   b) $12.23   c) $604.80   d) $327.25   e) $26.93   f) $766.03

1. Find the number of coins you need to make the amount in the right hand column of the chart.

   HINT: Count up by quarters until you are as close to the amount as possible. Then count on by dimes, and so on.

	Number of Quarters	Subtotal	Number of Dimes	Subtotal	Number of Nickels	Subtotal	Number of Pennies	Total Amount
a)	3	75¢	0	75¢	1	80¢	3	83¢
b)								52¢
c)								97¢
d)								23¢
e)								42¢
f)								94¢

2. Write the greatest amount you could pay in $20 bills without exceeding the amount.

   a) **$45** = _____ b) **$32** = _____ c) **$27** = _____ d) **$48** = _____ e) **$37** = _____

3. Write the number of each type of bill (or coin) that you would need to get the amounts in **bold**:

		#	Type	#	Type	#	Type	#	Type	#	Type	#	Type
a)	**$21.00**	0	$50.00	1	$20.00	0	$10.00	0	$5.00	0	$2.00	1	$1.00
b)	**$30.00**		$50.00		$20.00		$10.00		$5.00		$2.00		$1.00
c)	**$54.00**		$50.00		$20.00		$10.00		$5.00		$2.00		$1.00
d)	**$85.00**		$50.00		$20.00		$10.00		$5.00		$2.00		$1.00
e)	**$64.00**		$50.00		$20.00		$10.00		$5.00		$2.00		$1.00

4. Draw the least number of coins you need to make the following amounts.

   a) 72¢   b) 93¢   c) 82¢   d) 52¢

5. Draw the least number of coins and bills you need to make the following amounts.

   a) $55.00   b) $67.00   c) $64.00   d) $123.00

   e) $62.35   f) $42.12   g) $57.61   h) $78.18

   i) $73.08   j) $157.50   k) $92.82   l) $85.23

NS5-49: Making Change Using Mental Math

1. Calculate the change owing for each purchase.

   a) Price of a pencil = 44¢
      Amount paid = 50¢

      Change = _____

   b) Price of an eraser = 41¢
      Amount paid = 50¢

      Change = _____

   c) Price of a sharpener = 84¢
      Amount paid = 90¢

      Change = _____

   d) Price of a ruler = 53¢
      Amount paid = 60¢

      Change = _____

   e) Price of a marker = 76¢
      Amount paid = 80¢

      Change = _____

   f) Price of a notebook = 65¢
      Amount paid = 70¢

      Change = _____

   g) Price of a folder = 68¢
      Amount paid = 70¢

      Change = _____

   h) Price of a juice box = 49¢
      Amount paid = 50¢

      Change = _____

   i) Price of a freezie = 28¢
      Amount paid = 30¢

      Change = _____

2. Count up by 10s to find the change owing from a dollar (100¢):

Price Paid	Change	Price Paid	Change	Price Paid	Change
a) 90¢		b) 40¢		c) 20¢	
d) 70¢		e) 10¢		f) 60¢	
g) 50¢		h) 30¢		i) 80¢	

3. Find the change owing for each purchase:

   a) Price of a binder = 80¢
      Amount paid = $1.00

      Change = _____

   b) Price of an eraser = 70¢
      Amount paid = $1.00

      Change = _____

   c) Price of an apple = 20¢
      Amount paid = $1.00

      Change = _____

   d) Price of a marker = 60¢
      Amount paid = $1.00

      Change = _____

   e) Price of a patty = 50¢
      Amount paid = $1.00

      Change = _____

   f) Price of a pencil = 30¢
      Amount paid = $1.00

      Change = _____

   g) Price of a sharpener = 10¢
      Amount paid = $1.00

      Change = _____

   h) Price of juice = 40¢
      Amount paid = $1.00

      Change = _____

   i) Price of a popsicle = 60¢
      Amount paid = $1.00

      Change = _____

4. Find the smallest two-digit number ending in zero (i.e., 10, 20, 30, ...) <u>greater</u> than the number given.

   a) 74 __80__   b) 56 _____   c) 43 _____   d) 28 _____   e) 57 _____   f) 4 _____

     Number Sense 1

NS5-49: Making Change Using Mental Math *(continued)*

5. Make change for the number written below. Follow steps that are shown for 16¢:

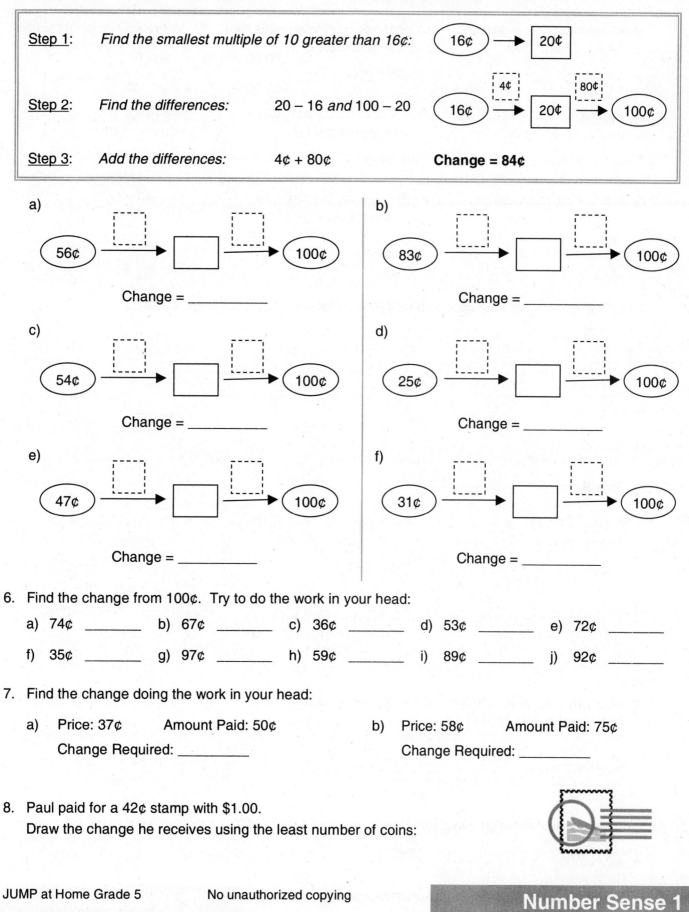

Step 1: *Find the smallest multiple of 10 greater than 16¢:* 16¢ ⟶ 20¢

Step 2: *Find the differences:* 20 − 16 *and* 100 − 20

Step 3: *Add the differences:* 4¢ + 80¢ **Change = 84¢**

a) 56¢ ⟶ ⬜ ⟶ 100¢

Change = _____

b) 83¢ ⟶ ⬜ ⟶ 100¢

Change = _____

c) 54¢ ⟶ ⬜ ⟶ 100¢

Change = _____

d) 25¢ ⟶ ⬜ ⟶ 100¢

Change = _____

e) 47¢ ⟶ ⬜ ⟶ 100¢

Change = _____

f) 31¢ ⟶ ⬜ ⟶ 100¢

Change = _____

6. Find the change from 100¢. Try to do the work in your head:

a) 74¢ _____ b) 67¢ _____ c) 36¢ _____ d) 53¢ _____ e) 72¢ _____

f) 35¢ _____ g) 97¢ _____ h) 59¢ _____ i) 89¢ _____ j) 92¢ _____

7. Find the change doing the work in your head:

a) Price: 37¢ Amount Paid: 50¢

Change Required: _____

b) Price: 58¢ Amount Paid: 75¢

Change Required: _____

8. Paul paid for a 42¢ stamp with $1.00.

Draw the change he receives using the least number of coins:

Number Sense 1

9. Find the change:

Amount Paid	Price	Change	Amount Paid	Price	Change
a) $30.00	$22.00		b) $70.00	$64.00	
c) $40.00	$34.00		d) $90.00	$87.00	
e) $50.00	$46.00		f) $20.00	$13.00	

10. Follow the steps shown below for finding the change from $50.00 on a payment of $22.00:

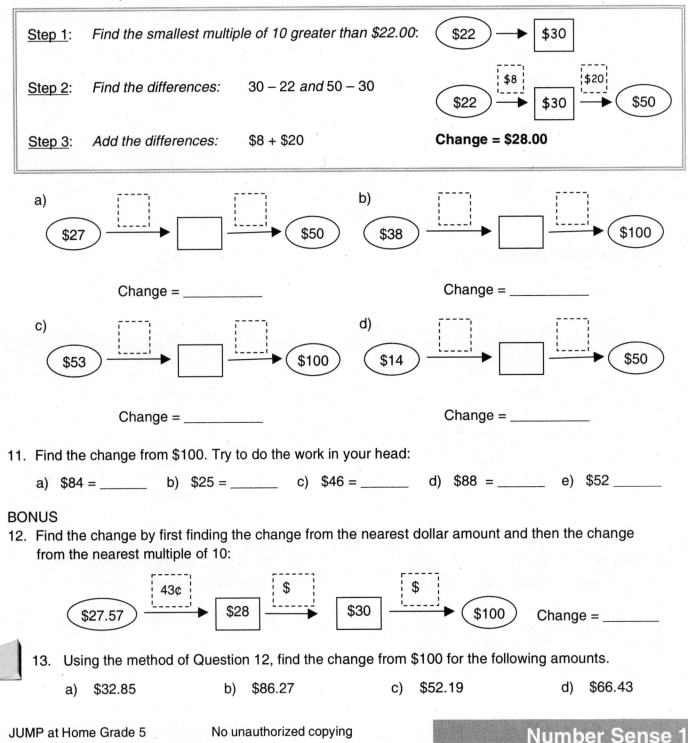

Step 1:   Find the smallest multiple of 10 greater than $22.00:

Step 2:   Find the differences: 30 – 22 and 50 – 30

Step 3:   Add the differences: $8 + $20   **Change = $28.00**

a)

Change = _____

b)

Change = _____

c)

Change = _____

d)

Change = _____

11. Find the change from $100. Try to do the work in your head:

a) $84 = _____   b) $25 = _____   c) $46 = _____   d) $88 = _____   e) $52 _____

BONUS

12. Find the change by first finding the change from the nearest dollar amount and then the change from the nearest multiple of 10:

Change = _____

13. Using the method of Question 12, find the change from $100 for the following amounts.

a) $32.85   b) $86.27   c) $52.19   d) $66.43

1. Sara spent $14.42 on a plant and $3.53 on a vase.
    To find out how much she spent, she added the amounts using the following steps:

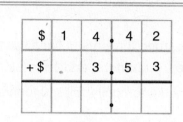

$	1	4 .	4	2
+ $	.	3 .	5	3
		.		

Step 1:
She lined up the numerals: she put dollars above dollars, dimes above dimes and pennies above pennies.

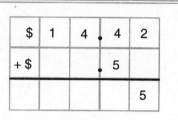

$	1	4 .	4	2
+ $		.	5	
				5

Step 2:
She added the numerals, starting with the ones digits (the pennies).

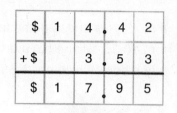

$	1	4 .	4	2
+ $		3 .	5	3
$	1	7 .	9	5

Step 3:
She added a decimal to show the amount in dollars.

Add:

a) $5.45 + $3.23

$	5 .	4	5
+ $	3 .	2	3
	.		

b) $26.15 + $32.23

$	.		
+ $	.		
	.		

c) $19.57 + $30.32

$	.		
+ $	.		
	.		

2. In order to add the amounts below, you will have to regroup:

a)

$	1	6 .	6	0
+ $	2	3 .	7	5
		.		

b)

$	2	7 .	4	5
+ $	4	5 .	1	2
		.		

c)

$	8	7 .	4	3
+ $		6 .	5	2
$		.		

d)

$	3	4 .	6	0
+ $	2	6 .	0	0
		.		

e)

$	3	8 .	4	0
+ $	4	4 .	2	5
		.		

f)

$	1	6 .	5	2
+ $	4	8 .	2	5
$		.		

3. Jasmine bought a pack of socks for $7.25 and a cap for $23.53.
    How much money does she need to pay the bill?

4. A library spent $270.25 on novels and $389.82 on non-fiction books.
    How much did the library spend in total?

5. Eli bought three CDs that cost $12.30 each.
    How much did he pay in total?

NS5-50: Adding Money (continued)

6. Sakku has $25.

   If he buys a chess game for $9.50 and a book for $10.35, will he have enough money left to buy a book which costs $5.10?

7. Find the amounts each child earned shovelling snow:

   a) Karen earned 3 twenty dollar bills, 1 toonie, 2 loonies, 2 quarters, and 1 nickel.

   b) Jill earned 4 ten dollar bills, 6 toonies, and 3 quarters.

   c) Sandor earned 2 twenty and 3 ten dollar bills, 2 loonies, and 5 quarters.

   d) Tory earned 5 ten dollar bills, 6 toonies, 2 loonies, and 6 dimes.

8. a) If you bought a watch and a soccer ball, how much would you pay?

   b) Which costs more: a watch and a cap or a pair of pants and a soccer ball?

   c) Could you buy a soccer ball, a pair of tennis rackets, and a pair of pants for $100?

   d) What is the total cost of the three most expensive things in the picture?

   e) Make up your own problem using the items.

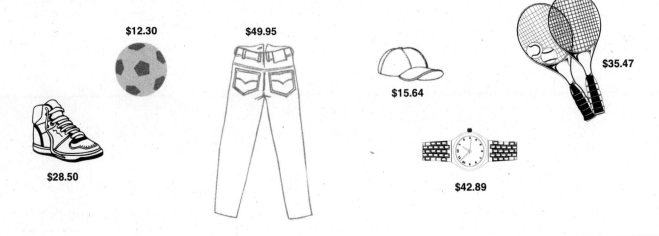

$12.30
$49.95
$15.64
$35.47
$28.50
$42.89

9. Try to find the answer mentally.

   a) How much do 4 loaves of bread cost at $2.30 each?

   b) How many apples, costing 40¢, could you buy with $3.00?

   c) Permanent markers cost $3.10.

   How many could you buy if you had $25.00?

   d) Is $10.00 enough to pay for a book costing $4.75 and a pen costing $5.34?

   e) Which costs more, 4 apples at 32¢ an apple, or 3 oranges at 45¢ an orange?

 Number Sense 1

1. Find the remaining amount by subtracting:

a)
	4 . 6	2
− $	2 . 3	0

b)
$	8 . 6	5
− $	4 . 2	3

c)
$	7 . 8	9
− $	3 . 6	8

d)
$	9 . 8	2
− $	7 . 8	1

e)
$	6 . 8	2
− $	5 . 2	1

2. Subtract the given money amounts by regrouping once or twice:

Example:

Step 1:
	6 10	
$	⁷̶ . ⁰̶	0
− $	2 . 4	3

Step 2:
	6 9̶10̶	
$	7 . 0	0
− $	2 . 4	3
$	4 . 5	7

a)
$	4 . 0	0
− $	2 . 2	9

b)
$	9 . 0	0
− $	6 . 2	4

c)
$	7 . 0	0
− $	5 . 7	2

d)
$	4 6 . 0	0
− $	2 3 . 4	5

e)
$	5 8 . 4	5
− $	2 7 . 7	8

f)
$	6 7 . 2	3
− $	3 4 . 6	4

3. Andrew spent $3.67 on his breakfast.

   He paid for it with a five dollar bill.

   Calculate his change.

4. Mera has $12.16 and Wendy has $13.47.

   How much more money does Wendy have than Mera?

5. Rita has $20.00. She wants to buy vegetables for $7.70, juice for $3.45, and dairy products for $9.75.

   Does she have enough money to buy all these items?

   If not, by how much is she short?

6. Mark has $30.00.

   He wants to buy a pair of shoes for $18.35 and pants for $14.53.

   How much more money does he need?

LSS-1: Organized Lists

Many problems in mathematics and science have more than one solution.

If a problem involves two quantities, list the values of one quantity in increasing order. Then you won't miss any solutions.

For instance, to find all the ways you can make 35¢ with dimes and nickels, start by assuming you have no dimes, then 1 dime, and so on up to 3 dimes (4 would be too many).

In each case, count on by 5s to 35 to find out how many nickels you need to make 35¢.

Step 1:

dimes	nickels
0	
1	
2	
3	

Step 2:

dimes	nickels
0	7
1	5
2	3
3	1

----

1. Fill in the amount of pennies, nickels, or dimes you need to:

a) make 17¢.

nickels	pennies
0	
1	
2	
3	

b) make 45¢.

dimes	nickels
0	
1	
2	
3	
4	

c) make 23¢.

nickels	pennies
0	
1	
2	
3	
4	

d) make 32¢.

dimes	pennies
0	
1	
2	
3	

e) make 65¢.

quarters	nickels
0	
1	
2	

f) make 85¢.

quarters	nickels
0	
1	
2	
3	

2.

quarters	nickels
0	
1	
2	

Ben wants to find all the ways he can make 60¢ using quarters and nickels. He lists the number of quarters in increasing order. Why did he stop at 2 quarters?

_____

_____

3. Make a chart to show all the ways you can make the given amount.

a) Make 27¢ using nickels and pennies.

b) Make 70¢ using quarters and nickels.

c) Make 65¢ using dimes and nickels.

d) Make $13 using loonies and toonies.

Logic and Systematic Search

Alana wants to find all pairs of numbers that multiply to give 15.

There are no numbers that will multiply by 2 or 4 to give 15, so Alana leaves those rows in her chart blank.

The numbers in the last row of the chart are the same as those in the 3rd row so Alana knows she has found all possible pairs of numbers that multiply to give 15: $1 \times 15 = 15$ and $3 \times 5 = 15$.

1st Number	2nd Number
1	15
2	---
3	5
4	---
5	3

----

4. Find all pairs of numbers that multiply to give the number provided.

a) **6**

First Number	Second Number

b) **8**

First Number	Second Number

5.

quarters	dimes
0	
1	
2	

Alicia wants to find all the ways she can make 70¢ using quarters and dimes.

One of the entries on her chart won't work. Which one is it?

6. Find all the ways to make the amounts using quarters and dimes. (Some entries on your chart may not work.)

a) 80¢

quarters	dimes
0	
1	
2	
3	

b) 105¢

quarters	dimes

7.

Width	1	2	3	4
Length				

Find all rectangles with side lengths that are whole numbers that have area 16 square units.

8. Make a chart to find all the pairs of numbers that multiply to give:

a) 12 b) 14 c) 20 d) 24

9. Find all the rectangles with side lengths that are whole numbers and with a perimeter of 14 units.

10. Find all the rectangles with side lengths that are whole numbers and with an area of 10 square units

Logic and Systematic Search

1. In the sequences below, the step or gap between the numbers increases or decreases.
    Can you see a pattern in the way the gap changes? Use the pattern to extend the sequence.

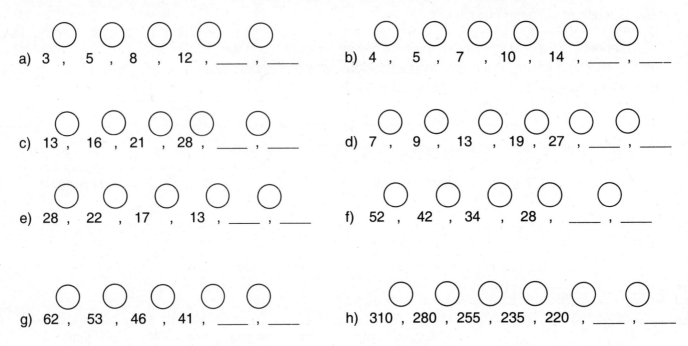

a) 3 , 5 , 8 , 12 , ____ , ____

b) 4 , 5 , 7 , 10 , 14 , ____ , ____

c) 13 , 16 , 21 , 28 , ____ , ____

d) 7 , 9 , 13 , 19 , 27 , ____ , ____

e) 28 , 22 , 17 , 13 , ____ , ____

f) 52 , 42 , 34 , 28 , ____ , ____

g) 62 , 53 , 46 , 41 , ____ , ____

h) 310 , 280 , 255 , 235 , 220 , ____ , ____

2. Complete the T-table for Figure 3 and Figure 4. Then use the pattern in the gap to predict the number
    of squares needed for Figures 5 and 6.

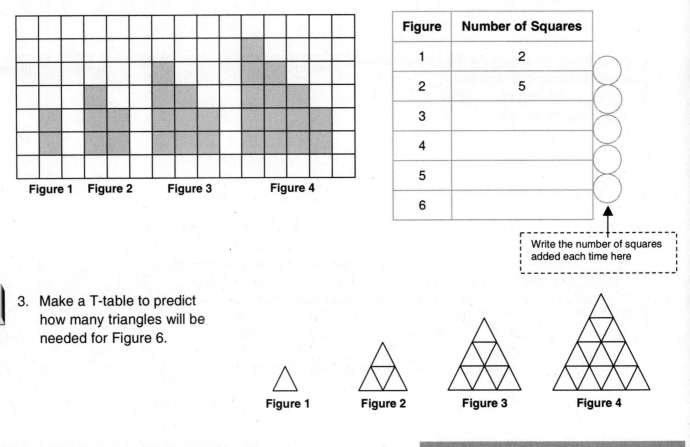

Figure	Number of Squares
1	2
2	5
3	
4	
5	
6	

Write the number of squares added each time here

Figure 1   Figure 2   Figure 3   Figure 4

3. Make a T-table to predict
    how many triangles will be
    needed for Figure 6.

Figure 1   Figure 2   Figure 3   Figure 4

(continued)

4. In each sequence below, the gap changes in a regular way. Write a rule for each pattern.

a) 2 , 5 , 10 , 17 , 26

     (+3) (+5) (+7) (+9)

    Rule: Start at 2. Add 3, 5, 7 … (The gap increases by 2.)

b) 7 , 11 , 9 , 13 , 11

     (+4) (-2) (+4) (-2)

    Rule : Start at 7. Add 4, then subtract 2. Repeat.

c) 1 , 2 , 4 , 7 , 11

    Rule: _____

d) 6 , 8 , 5 , 7 , 4

    Rule: _____

e) 24 , 23 , 20 , 15 , 8

    Rule: _____

f) 17 , 20 , 25 , 32 , 41

    Rule: _____

5. Write a rule for each pattern. Then give the value of the 5th term.

    a) 0 , 3 , 8 , 15   b) 1 , 3 , 9 , 27

6. Write a rule for the number of shaded squares or triangles in each figure.
    Use your rule to predict the number of shaded parts in the 5th figure.
    HINT: To count the number of triangles in the last figure in b), try skip counting by 3s.

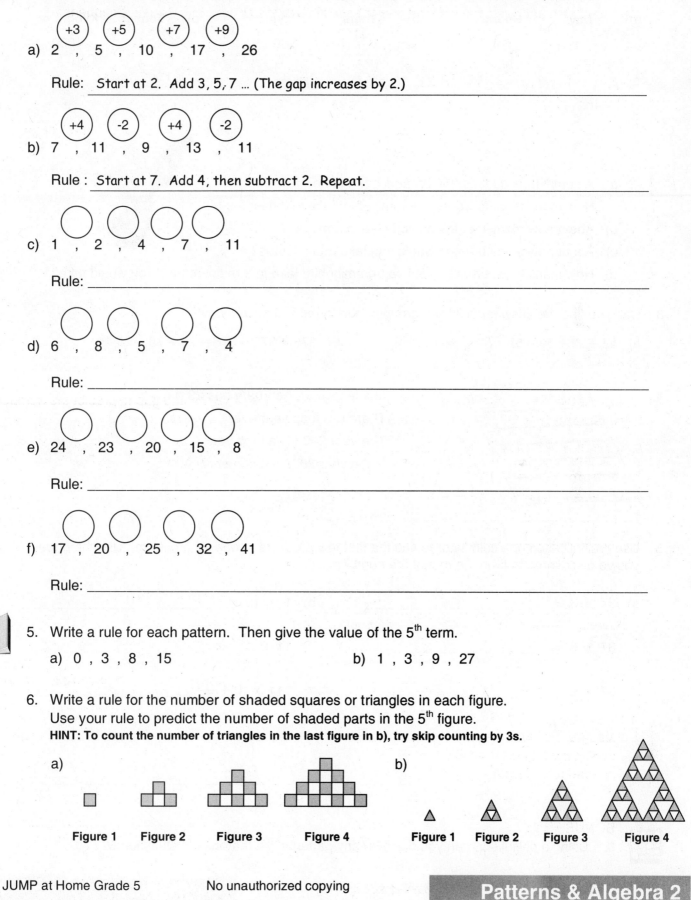

a)

Figure 1   Figure 2   Figure 3   Figure 4

b)

Figure 1   Figure 2   Figure 3   Figure 4

Patterns & Algebra 2

PA5-21: Patterns with Larger Numbers

1. Use addition or multiplication to complete the following charts.

a)
Days	Hours
1	24
2	
3	
4	
5	

b)
Years	Days
1	365
2	
3	

c)
Tonnes	Kilograms
1	1000
2	
3	
4	

2. a) A hummingbird takes 250 breaths per minute.
   How many breaths would a hummingbird take in 3 minutes?
   b) About how many breaths do you take in a minute?
   c) About how many breaths would you take in 3 minutes?
   d) How many more breaths would a hummingbird take in 3 minutes than you would take?

3. Can you find the answer quickly by grouping the terms in a clever way?

a) 52 − 52 + 52 − 52 + 52 − 52 + 52

b) 375 + 375 + 375 − 75 − 75 − 75

4. In a leap year, February has 29 days.
There is a leap year every 4 years.
The year 2008 is a leap year.
Is the year 2032 a leap year?

5. Use multiplication or a calculator to find the first few products. Look for a pattern. Use the pattern you've discovered to fill in the rest of the numbers.

a) 37 x 3 = _____

   37 x 6 = _____

   37 x 9 = _____

   _____ = _____

   _____ = _____

b) 1 x 1 = _____

   11 x 11 = _____

   111 x 111 = _____

   _____ = _____

   _____ = _____

BONUS
6. Using a calculator, can you discover any patterns like the ones in Question 5?

PA5-22: Introduction to Algebra

1. Some apples are inside a box and some are outside. The total number of apples is shown.
   Draw the missing apples in the box provided.

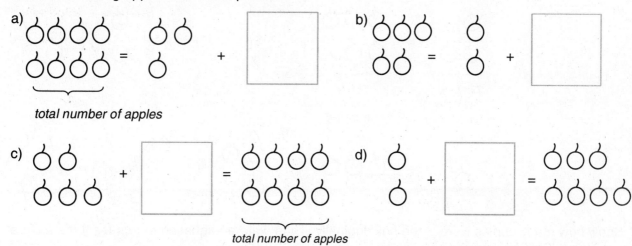

2. Draw the missing apples in the box given. Then write an equation (with numbers) to represent the picture.

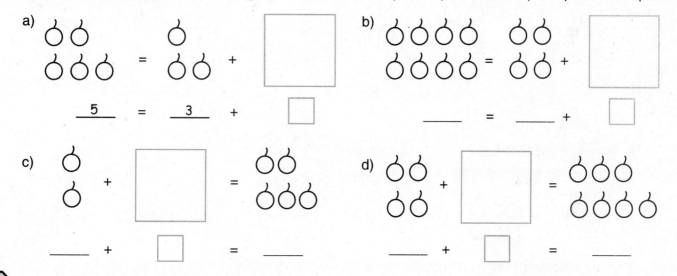

3. Write an equation for each situation. (Use a box to stand for the unknown quantity.)

   a) There are 9 apples altogether.
      5 are outside of a box.
      How many are inside?

      $$9 = 5 + \boxed{}$$

   b) There are 7 apples altogether.
      3 are outside of a box.
      How many are inside?

   c) There are 8 pears altogether.
      3 are inside a bag.
      How many are outside?

   d) 10 students are in a library.
      2 are inside the computer room.
      How many are outside?

   e) 7 children are in a gym.
      2 are in the pool.
      How many are out of the pool?

   f) Rena has 13 stamps.
      5 are Canadian.
      How many are from other countries?

   g) 15 children are in a camp.
      9 are girls.
      How many are boys?

   h) 9 dogs are in a pet store.
      5 are puppies.
      How many are adults?

Patterns & Algebra 2

1. Tim took some apples from a box. Show how many apples were in the box originally.

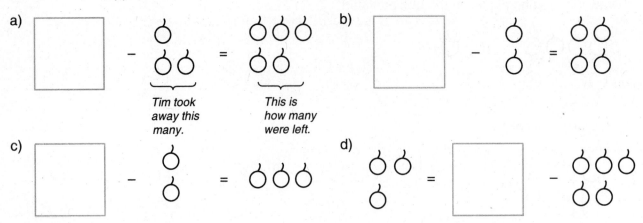

2. Show how many apples were in the box originally. Then write an equation to represent the picture.

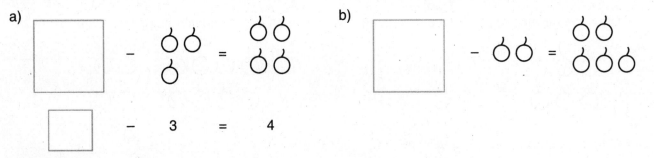

a)
    − 3 = 4

3. In the equations below, 2 × ☐ is a short form for two identical boxes.
    Show how many apples are in each box.

    a) 2 × 3 =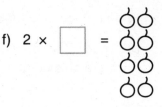

    b) 2 × ☐ =

    c) 3 × ☐ =

    d) 3 × ☐ =

    e) 4 × ☐ =

    f) 2 × ☐ =

4. Write an equation for each situation.

    a) Tom took 3 apples from a box. 2 apples were left.

       How many apples were in the box?

    b) Sarah took 3 eggs from a carton. 5 eggs were left.

       How many eggs were in the carton?

    c) Ed has 15 apples in 3 boxes.

       Each box contains the same number of apples.

       How many apples are in each box?

5. Write a problem to match each equation.

    a) ☐ + 2 = 5

    b) ☐ − 4 = 6

    c) 3 × ☐ = 12

A **variable** is a letter or symbol (such as **x**, **n**, or **h**) that represents a number.

In the product of a number and a variable, the multiplication sign is usually dropped.

> For example: 3 × T   is written 3T and   5 × z   is written 5z.

----

1. Write a numerical expression for the cost of renting skates for:

   a) 2 hours: __3 × 2__   b) 5 hours: _____   c) 6 hours: _____

   Rent a pair of skates

   $3 for each hour

2. Write an expression for the distance a car would travel at:

   a) Speed: 60 km per hour   b) Speed: 80 km per hour   c) Speed: 70 km per hour
      Time: 2 hours   Time: 3 hours   Time: h hours

      Distance: _____ km   Distance: _____ km   Distance: _____ km

3. Write an algebraic expression for the cost of renting skis for:

   a) h hours: _____ or _____   b) t hours: _____ or _____

   c) x hours: _____ or _____   d) n hours: _____ or _____

   Rent a pair of skis

   $ 5 per hour

4. Write an equation that tells you the relationship between the numbers in column A and column B.

   a)

A	B
1	4
2	5
3	6

   ___A + 3 = B___

   b)

A	B
1	2
2	4
3	6

   ___2 × A = B___

   c)

A	B
1	3
2	4
3	5

   _____

   d)

A	B
1	3
2	6
3	9

   _____

   e)

A	B
1	5
2	10
3	15

   _____

5. Use the variable x to write an expression for the number of apples outside of a box.

   a) There are 10 apples altogether.   b) There are 12 apples altogether.
      4 are outside of a box.   7 are outside of a box.
      How many are in the box?   How many are in the box?

Patterns & Algebra 2

PA5-25: Equations

1. Find the number that makes each equation true (by guessing and checking) and write it in the box.

a) ☐ + 3 = 9

b) ☐ + 2 = 5

c) ☐ + 4 = 10

d) 8 − ☐ = 6

e) 18 − ☐ = 14

f) 10 − ☐ = 7

g) 2 × ☐ = 8

h) 5 × ☐ = 20

i) 3 × ☐ = 12

j) ☐ + 3 = 2

k) ☐ + 5 = 3

l) ☐ + 2 = 5

BONUS

m) 7 + 3 = 6 + ☐

n) 10 − 3 = ☐ + 2

o) ☐ + ☐ + 3 = 7

p) 9 = 1 + 2 + ☐

q) 7 + 8 = ☐ + 2

r) ☐ + 12 = 20 − 7

s) 5 × ☐ = 9 + 11

t) ☐ + 2 = 7 − 4

u) 2 × 3 = ☐ + 5

2. Find a set of numbers that makes each equation true. (Some questions have more than one answer.)
   NOTE: In a given question, congruent shapes represent the **same** number.

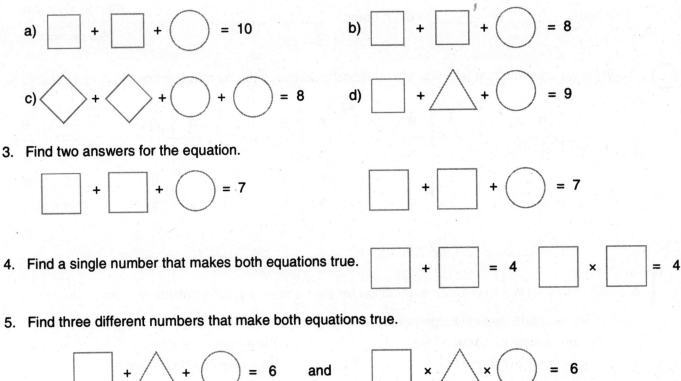

a) ☐ + ☐ + ◯ = 10

b) ☐ + ☐ + ◯ = 8

c) ◇ + ◇ + ◯ + ◯ = 8

d) ☐ + △ + ◯ = 9

3. Find two answers for the equation.

☐ + ☐ + ◯ = 7   ☐ + ☐ + ◯ = 7

4. Find a single number that makes both equations true.   ☐ + ☐ = 4   ☐ × ☐ = 4

5. Find three different numbers that make both equations true.

☐ + △ + ◯ = 6   and   ☐ × △ × ◯ = 6

6. Find a combination of numbers that make the equation true. (You cannot use the number 1.)

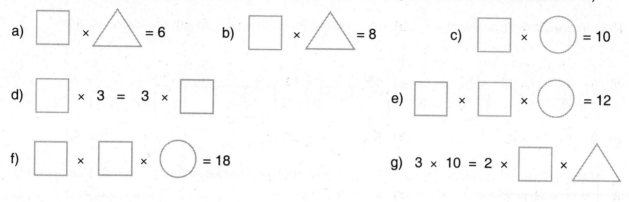

a) ▢ × △ = 6   b) ▢ × △ = 8   c) ▢ × ◯ = 10

d) ▢ × 3 = 3 × ▢   e) ▢ × ▢ × ◯ = 12

f) ▢ × ▢ × ◯ = 18   g) 3 × 10 = 2 × ▢ × △

7. Complete the patterns.

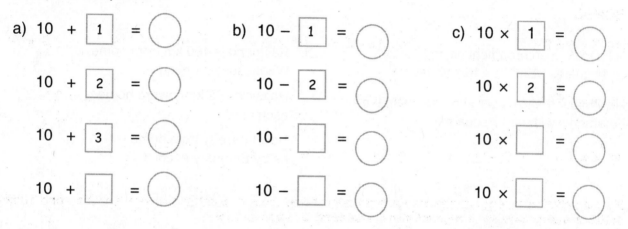

a) 10 + [1] = ◯

    10 + [2] = ◯

    10 + [3] = ◯

    10 + [ ] = ◯

b) 10 − [1] = ◯

    10 − [2] = ◯

    10 − [ ] = ◯

    10 − [ ] = ◯

c) 10 × [1] = ◯

    10 × [2] = ◯

    10 × [ ] = ◯

    10 × [ ] = ◯

8. For each pattern in Question 7, say how the number in the circle changes as the number in the box increases by one.

9. When the number in each box below doubles, what happens to the product? (Use the pattern to fill in the numbers in the last question.)

5 × [ ] = 10   5 × [ ] = 20   5 × [ ] = 40   5 × [ ] = _____

10. Knowing that 6 is double 3, and that $7 × 3 = 21$, how can you find $7 × 6 = 42$ without multiplying $7 × 6$?

11.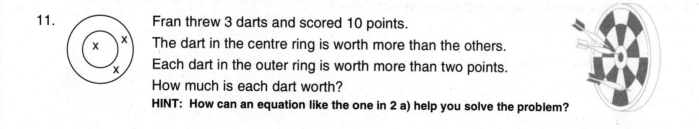

Fran threw 3 darts and scored 10 points.

The dart in the centre ring is worth more than the others.

Each dart in the outer ring is worth more than two points.

How much is each dart worth?

HINT: How can an equation like the one in 2 a) help you solve the problem?

Patterns & Algebra 2

PA5-26: Problems and Puzzles

1. The picture shows how many chairs can be placed at each arrangement of tables.

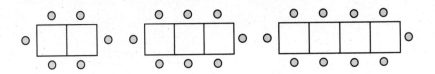

   a) Make a T-table and state a rule that tells the relationship between the number of tables and the number of chairs.

   b) How many chairs can be placed at 15 tables?

---

2. Julia makes an ornament using triangles and squares. She has 16 squares.

   How many triangles will she need to make ornaments with all 16 squares?

3. Raymond is 400 km from home Wednesday morning.

   He cycles 65 km toward home each day.

   How far away from home is he by Saturday evening?

---

4. Explain why the underlined term is or is not the next step in the pattern.

   a) 127, 124, 121, <u>118</u>
   b) 27, 31, 35, <u>40</u>
   c) 7, 5, 8, 6, <u>9</u>

5. A recipe calls for 3 cups of flour for every 4 cups of water.

   How many cups of water will be needed for 18 cups of flour?

---

6. Find the mystery numbers.

   a) I am a 2 digit number. I am a multiple of 4 and 6. My tens digit is 2.

   b) I am between 20 and 40. I am a multiple of 3. My ones digit is 6.

7. Every 6th person who arrives at a book sale receives a free calendar.
   Every 8th person receives a free book.

   Which of the first 50 people receive a book and a calendar?

     Patterns & Algebra 2

8. Describe how each picture was made from the one before.

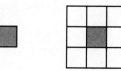

9. What strategy would you use to find the 63rd shape in the pattern below?

What is the shape?

10. Paul shovelled 26 sidewalks in 4 days.

Each day, he shovelled 3 more sidewalks than the day before.

How many sidewalks did he shovel each day?
Guess and check!

11. A camp offers 2 ways to rent a sailboat.

You can pay $8.50 for the first hour and $4.50 for every hour after that.

Or, you can pay $6.00 for every hour.

If you wanted to rent the canoe for 5 hours, which way would you choose to pay?

12. The picture shows how the temperature inside a cloud changes at different heights.

a) Does the temperature increase or decrease at greater heights?

b) What distance does the arrow represent in real life?

c) Measure the length of the arrow.

d) What is the scale of the picture?

_____ cm = _____ m

13. Marlene says she will need 27 blocks to make Figure 7.

Is she right? Explain.

Figure 1   **Figure 2**   **Figure 3**

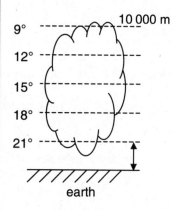

earth

e) Do temperatures change by the same amount each time?

f) If the pattern continued, what would the temperature be at:

i) 12 000 m?

ii) 14 000 m?

NS5-52: Equal Parts and Models of Fractions

Fractions name equal parts of a whole.

The pie is cut into 4 equal parts.

3 parts out of 4 are shaded.

$\frac{3}{4}$ of a pie is shaded.

The **numerator** (3) tells you how many parts are counted.

$\frac{3}{4}$

The **denominator** (4) tells you how many parts are in a whole.

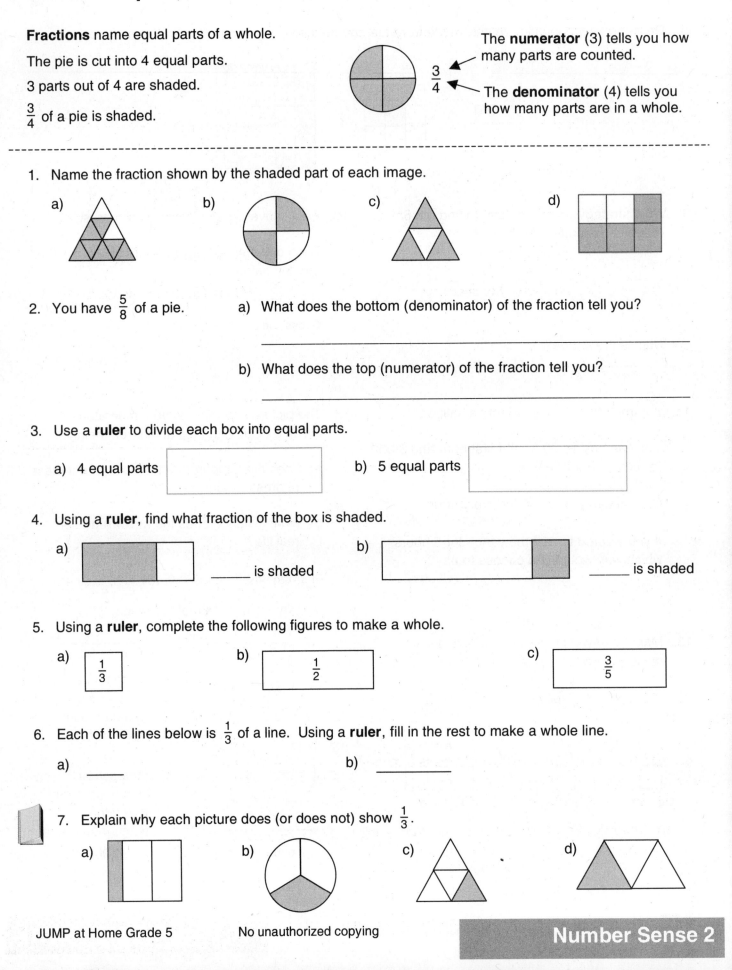

1. Name the fraction shown by the shaded part of each image.

   a)   b)   c)   d)

2. You have $\frac{5}{8}$ of a pie.   a) What does the bottom (denominator) of the fraction tell you?

   _____

   b) What does the top (numerator) of the fraction tell you?

   _____

3. Use a **ruler** to divide each box into equal parts.

   a) 4 equal parts   b) 5 equal parts

4. Using a **ruler**, find what fraction of the box is shaded.

   a)   _____ is shaded   b)   _____ is shaded

5. Using a **ruler**, complete the following figures to make a whole.

   a) $\frac{1}{3}$ b) $\frac{1}{2}$ c) $\frac{3}{5}$

6. Each of the lines below is $\frac{1}{3}$ of a line. Using a **ruler**, fill in the rest to make a whole line.

   a) ____   b) _____

7. Explain why each picture does (or does not) show $\frac{1}{3}$.

   a)   b)   c)   d)

No unauthorized copying   **Number Sense 2**

NS5-53: Equal Parts of a Set

Fractions can name parts of a set: $\frac{3}{5}$ of the figures are triangles, $\frac{1}{5}$ are squares and $\frac{1}{5}$ are circles.

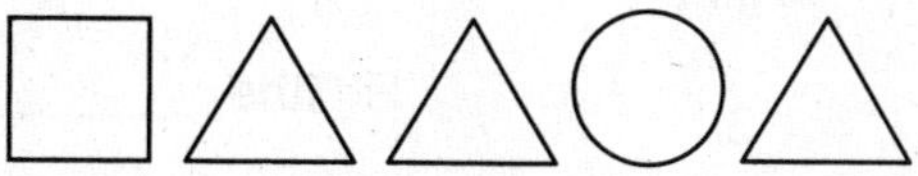

1. Fill in the blanks.

a)

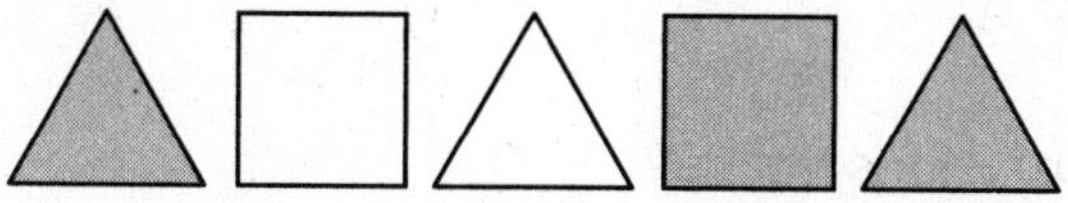

_______ of the figures are triangles.

_______ of the figures are shaded.

b)

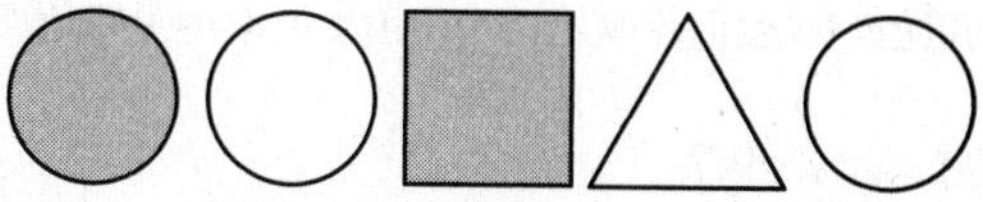

_______ of the figures are squares.

_______ of the figures are shaded.

2. Fill in the blanks.

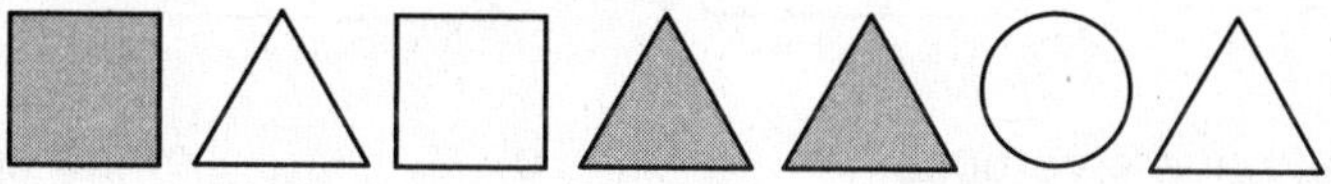

a) $\frac{4}{7}$ of the figures are ____________________

b) $\frac{2}{7}$ of the figures are ____________________

c) $\frac{1}{7}$ of the figures are ____________________

d) $\frac{3}{7}$ of the figures are ____________________

3. Describe this picture in two different ways using the fraction $\frac{3}{5}$.

4. A football team wins 7 games and loses 5 games.

a) How many games did the team play? ______________

b) What <u>fraction</u> of the games did the team win? ______________

c) Did the team win more than half its games? ______________

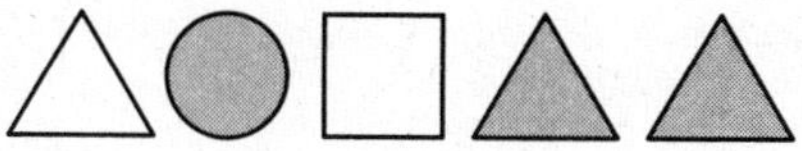

5.

	Number of boys	Number of girls
The Smith Family	2	3
The Sinha Family	1	2

a) What fraction of the children in each family are boys?

Smiths _____ Sinhas _____

b) What fraction of all the children are boys? _____

6. What fraction of the letters in the word "Canada" are:

   a) vowels? _____

   b) consonants? _____

7. Express 7 months as a fraction of one year: _____

8. Write a fraction for each statement.

   a) ☐ of the figures have 4 vertices

   b) ☐ of the figures have more than 4 sides

   c) ☐ of the figures have exactly one right angle

   d) ☐ of the figures have exactly 2 pairs of parallel sides

9. Write two fraction statements for the figures in Question 8 above.

10. Draw a picture to solve the puzzle.

   a) There are 7 circles and squares.

      $\frac{2}{7}$ of the figures are squares.

      $\frac{5}{7}$ of the figures are shaded.

      Three circles are shaded.

   b) There are 8 triangles and squares.

      $\frac{6}{8}$ of the figures are shaded.

      $\frac{2}{8}$ of the figures are triangles.

      One triangle is shaded.

NS5-54: Parts and Wholes

1. 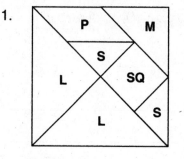 In a tangram:

    ○ 2 small triangles (**S**) cover a medium triangle (**M**)

    ○ 2 small triangles (**S**) cover a square (**SQ**)

    ○ 2 small triangles (**S**) cover a parallelogram (**P**)

    ○ 4 small triangles (**S**) cover a large triangle (**L**)

   What fraction of each shape is covered by a <u>single</u> small triangle?

   a)   b)   c)

   d)   e)   f)

2. What fraction of each shape is shaded? Explain how you know.

   a)   b)   c)   d)

3. What fraction of the trapezoid is covered by a <u>single</u> small triangle?

   Show your work.

4. If ▨ = red and ⬚ = blue, approximately what fraction of each flag is shaded red? Explain.

   a)   b)   c)   d)

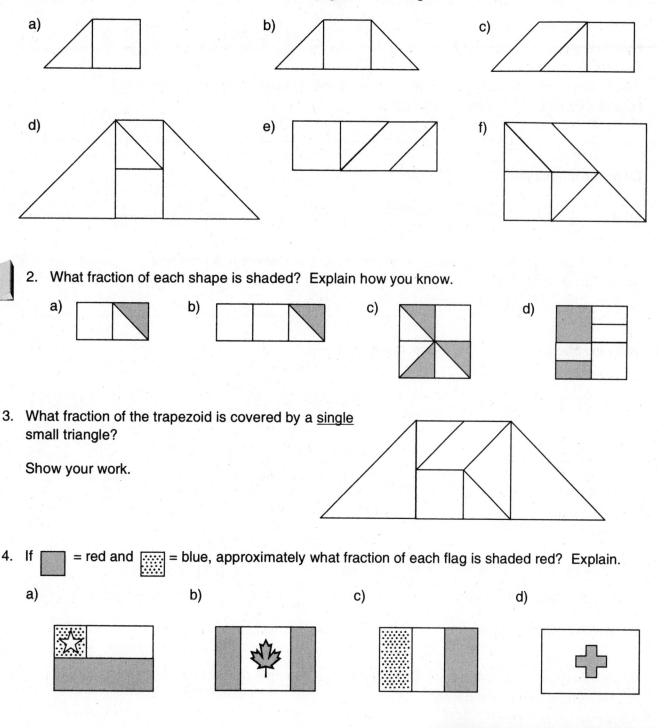

NS5-55: Ordering and Comparing Fractions

1. What fraction has a greater numerator, $\frac{2}{6}$ or $\frac{5}{6}$? _____

   Which fraction is greater? _____

   Explain your thinking. _____

   _____

2. Circle the greater fraction in each pair.

   a) $\frac{6}{16}$ or $\frac{9}{16}$
   b) $\frac{5}{8}$ or $\frac{3}{8}$
   c) $\frac{24}{25}$ or $\frac{22}{25}$
   d) $\frac{37}{53}$ or $\frac{27}{53}$

3. Two fractions have the same <u>denominators</u> (bottoms) but different <u>numerators</u> (tops). How can you tell which fraction is greater?

   _____

4. Circle the greater fraction in each pair.

   a) $\frac{1}{8}$ or $\frac{1}{9}$
   b) $\frac{12}{12}$ or $\frac{12}{13}$
   c) $\frac{5}{225}$ or $\frac{5}{125}$

5. Fraction A and Fraction B have the same <u>numerators</u> but different <u>denominators</u>. How can you tell which fraction is greater?

   _____

6. Write the fractions in order from least to greatest.

   a) $\frac{2}{3}$, $\frac{1}{3}$, $\frac{3}{3}$

   b) $\frac{9}{10}$, $\frac{2}{10}$, $\frac{1}{10}$, $\frac{5}{10}$

   c) $\frac{1}{7}$, $\frac{1}{3}$, $\frac{1}{13}$

   d) $\frac{2}{11}$, $\frac{2}{5}$, $\frac{2}{7}$, $\frac{2}{16}$

7. Circle the greater fraction in each pair.

   a) $\frac{2}{3}$ or $\frac{2}{9}$
   b) $\frac{7}{17}$ or $\frac{11}{17}$
   c) $\frac{6}{288}$ or $\frac{6}{18}$

8. Which fraction is greater, $\frac{1}{2}$ or $\frac{45}{100}$? Explain your thinking.

9. Is it possible for $\frac{2}{3}$ of a pie to be bigger than $\frac{3}{4}$ of another pie? Show your thinking with a picture.

NS5-56: Mixed Fractions

Mattias and his friends ate the amount of pie shown.

They ate three and three quarter pies altogether (or $3\frac{3}{4}$ pies).

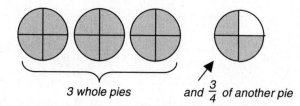

3 whole pies   and $\frac{3}{4}$ of another pie

NOTE: $3\frac{3}{4}$ is called a <u>mixed fraction</u> because it is a mixture of a whole number and a fraction.

----

1. Write how many <u>whole</u> pies are shaded.

   a)

   ___2___ whole pies

   b)

   _____ whole pies

   c)

   _____ whole pie

2. Write the fractions as <u>mixed fractions</u>.

   a)   ____

   b)   ____

   c)   ____

   d)   ____

   e)   ____

   f)   ____

   g)   ____

3. Shade the amount of pie given in bold.
   NOTE: There may be more pies than you need.

   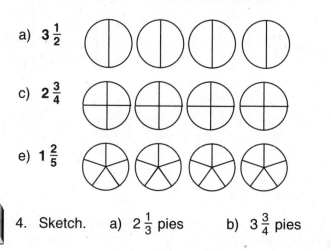

   a) $3\frac{1}{2}$ b) $1\frac{1}{4}$

   c) $2\frac{3}{4}$ d) $3\frac{2}{3}$

   e) $1\frac{2}{5}$

   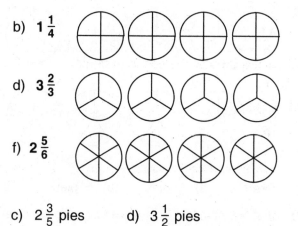

   f) $2\frac{5}{6}$

4. Sketch.   a) $2\frac{1}{3}$ pies   b) $3\frac{3}{4}$ pies   c) $2\frac{3}{5}$ pies   d) $3\frac{1}{2}$ pies

NS5-57: Improper Fractions

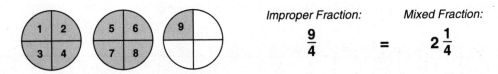

Improper Fraction: $\frac{9}{4}$ **Mixed Fraction:** $2\frac{1}{4}$

Huan-Yue and her friends ate **9** quarter-sized pieces of pizza. Altogether they ate $\frac{9}{4}$ pizzas.

NOTE: When the numerator of a fraction is larger than the denominator, the fraction represents *more than* a whole. Such fractions are called <u>improper fractions</u>.

----

1. Write these fractions as <u>improper</u> fractions.

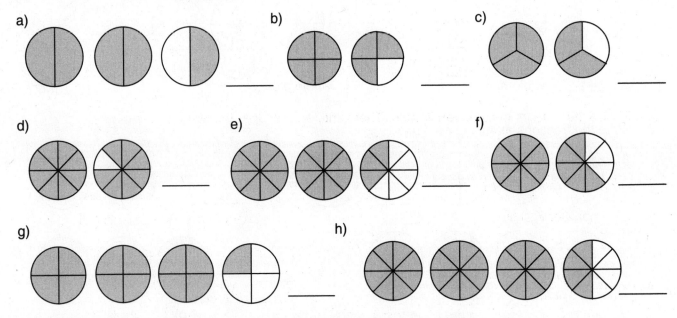

2. Shade one piece at a time until you have shaded the amount of pie given.

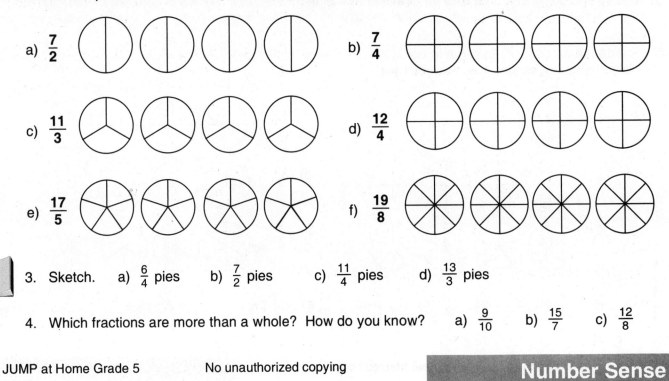

a) $\frac{7}{2}$ b) $\frac{7}{4}$ c) $\frac{11}{3}$ d) $\frac{12}{4}$ e) $\frac{17}{5}$ f) $\frac{19}{8}$

3. Sketch.   a) $\frac{6}{4}$ pies   b) $\frac{7}{2}$ pies   c) $\frac{11}{4}$ pies   d) $\frac{13}{3}$ pies

4. Which fractions are more than a whole? How do you know?   a) $\frac{9}{10}$ b) $\frac{15}{7}$ c) $\frac{12}{8}$

Number Sense 2

NS5-58: Mixed and Improper Fractions

1. Write these fractions as <u>mixed</u> fractions and as <u>improper</u> fractions.

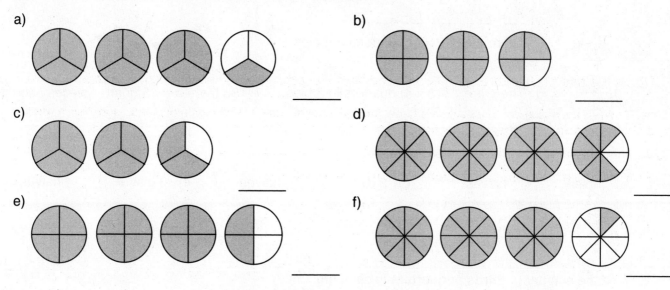

a)

b) _____

c) _____

d) _____

e) _____

f) _____

2. Shade the amount of pie given in bold. Then write an <u>improper</u> fraction for the amount of pie.

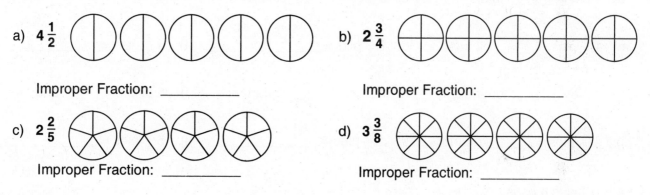

a) $4\frac{1}{2}$

Improper Fraction: _____

b) $2\frac{3}{4}$

Improper Fraction: _____

c) $2\frac{2}{5}$

Improper Fraction: _____

d) $3\frac{3}{8}$

Improper Fraction: _____

3. Shade one piece at a time until you have shaded the amount of pie given in bold. Then write a <u>mixed</u> fraction for the amount of pie.

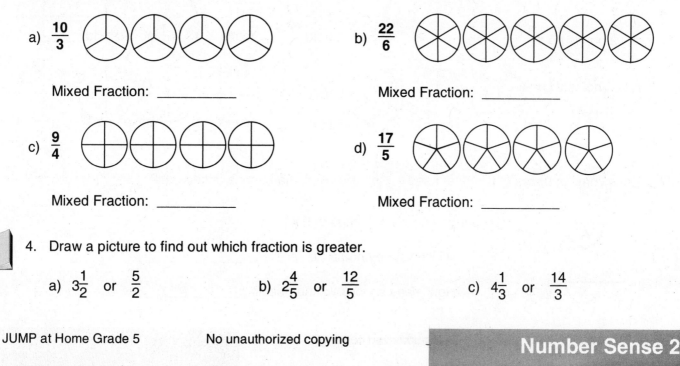

a) $\frac{10}{3}$

Mixed Fraction: _____

b) $\frac{22}{6}$

Mixed Fraction: _____

c) $\frac{9}{4}$

Mixed Fraction: _____

d) $\frac{17}{5}$

Mixed Fraction: _____

4. Draw a picture to find out which fraction is greater.

a) $3\frac{1}{2}$ or $\frac{5}{2}$

b) $2\frac{4}{5}$ or $\frac{12}{5}$

c) $4\frac{1}{3}$ or $\frac{14}{3}$

No unauthorized copying **Number Sense 2**

NS5-59: Mixed Fractions (Advanced)

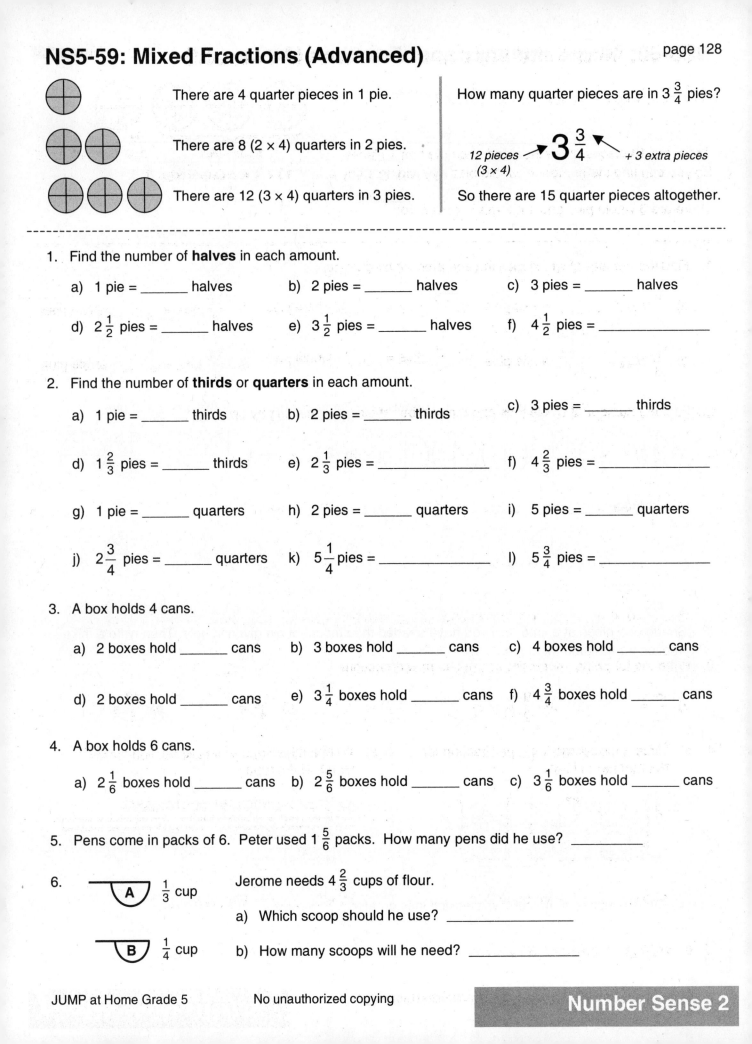

There are 4 quarter pieces in 1 pie.

There are 8 (2 × 4) quarters in 2 pies.

There are 12 (3 × 4) quarters in 3 pies.

How many quarter pieces are in $3\frac{3}{4}$ pies?

12 pieces $\rightarrow 3\frac{3}{4} \leftarrow$ + 3 extra pieces
(3 × 4)

So there are 15 quarter pieces altogether.

---

1. Find the number of **halves** in each amount.

   a) 1 pie = _____ halves

   b) 2 pies = _____ halves

   c) 3 pies = _____ halves

   d) $2\frac{1}{2}$ pies = _____ halves

   e) $3\frac{1}{2}$ pies = _____ halves

   f) $4\frac{1}{2}$ pies = _____

2. Find the number of **thirds** or **quarters** in each amount.

   a) 1 pie = _____ thirds

   b) 2 pies = _____ thirds

   c) 3 pies = _____ thirds

   d) $1\frac{2}{3}$ pies = _____ thirds

   e) $2\frac{1}{3}$ pies = _____

   f) $4\frac{2}{3}$ pies = _____

   g) 1 pie = _____ quarters

   h) 2 pies = _____ quarters

   i) 5 pies = _____ quarters

   j) $2\frac{3}{4}$ pies = _____ quarters

   k) $5\frac{1}{4}$ pies = _____

   l) $5\frac{3}{4}$ pies = _____

3. A box holds 4 cans.

   a) 2 boxes hold _____ cans

   b) 3 boxes hold _____ cans

   c) 4 boxes hold _____ cans

   d) 2 boxes hold _____ cans

   e) $3\frac{1}{4}$ boxes hold _____ cans

   f) $4\frac{3}{4}$ boxes hold _____ cans

4. A box holds 6 cans.

   a) $2\frac{1}{6}$ boxes hold _____ cans

   b) $2\frac{5}{6}$ boxes hold _____ cans

   c) $3\frac{1}{6}$ boxes hold _____ cans

5. Pens come in packs of 6. Peter used $1\frac{5}{6}$ packs. How many pens did he use? _____

6.
   Ⓐ $\frac{1}{3}$ cup

   Ⓑ $\frac{1}{4}$ cup

   Jerome needs $4\frac{2}{3}$ cups of flour.

   a) Which scoop should he use? _____

   b) How many scoops will he need? _____

No unauthorized copying

Number Sense 2

NS5-60: Mixed and Improper Fractions (Advanced)

How many whole pies are there in $\frac{13}{4}$ pies?

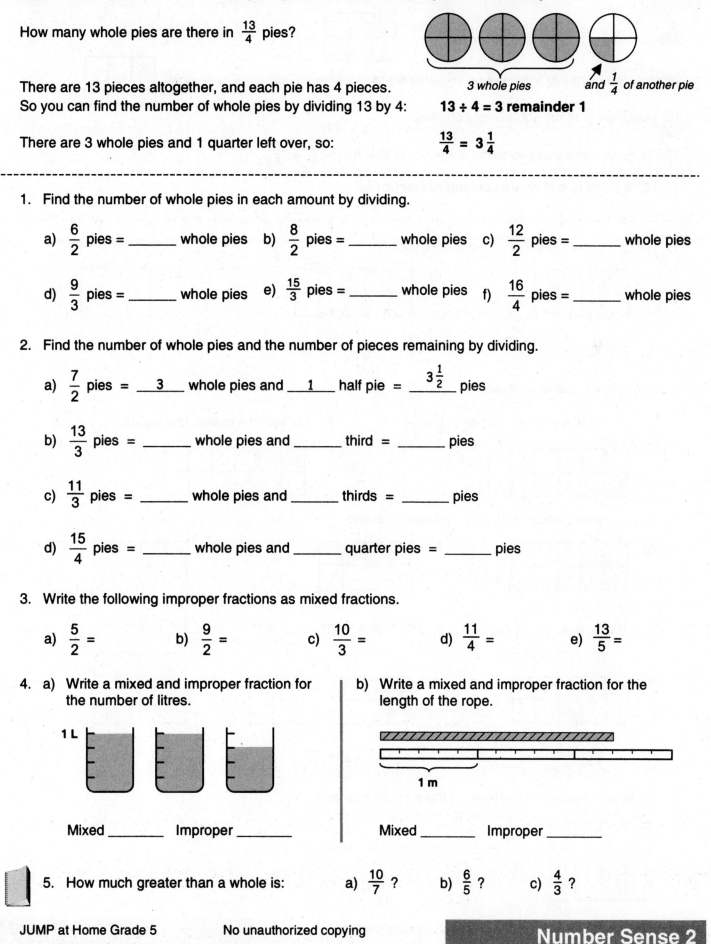

3 whole pies   and $\frac{1}{4}$ of another pie

There are 13 pieces altogether, and each pie has 4 pieces.
So you can find the number of whole pies by dividing 13 by 4:   **13 ÷ 4 = 3 remainder 1**

There are 3 whole pies and 1 quarter left over, so: $\frac{13}{4} = 3\frac{1}{4}$

---

1. Find the number of whole pies in each amount by dividing.

   a) $\frac{6}{2}$ pies = _____ whole pies   b) $\frac{8}{2}$ pies = _____ whole pies   c) $\frac{12}{2}$ pies = _____ whole pies

   d) $\frac{9}{3}$ pies = _____ whole pies   e) $\frac{15}{3}$ pies = _____ whole pies   f) $\frac{16}{4}$ pies = _____ whole pies

2. Find the number of whole pies and the number of pieces remaining by dividing.

   a) $\frac{7}{2}$ pies = ___3___ whole pies and ___1___ half pie = ___$3\frac{1}{2}$___ pies

   b) $\frac{13}{3}$ pies = _____ whole pies and _____ third = _____ pies

   c) $\frac{11}{3}$ pies = _____ whole pies and _____ thirds = _____ pies

   d) $\frac{15}{4}$ pies = _____ whole pies and _____ quarter pies = _____ pies

3. Write the following improper fractions as mixed fractions.

   a) $\frac{5}{2}$ =   b) $\frac{9}{2}$ =   c) $\frac{10}{3}$ =   d) $\frac{11}{4}$ =   e) $\frac{13}{5}$ =

4. a) Write a mixed and improper fraction for the number of litres.

   b) Write a mixed and improper fraction for the length of the rope.

   Mixed _____   Improper _____

   Mixed _____   Improper _____

5. How much greater than a whole is: a) $\frac{10}{7}$?   b) $\frac{6}{5}$?   c) $\frac{4}{3}$?

NS5-61: Equivalent Fractions

Aidan shades $\frac{2}{6}$ of the squares in an array:

He then draws heavy lines around the squares to group them into 3 equal groups:

He sees that $\frac{1}{3}$ of the squares are shaded.

The pictures show that two sixths are equal to one third: $\frac{2}{6} = \frac{1}{3}$

Two sixths and one third are **equivalent fractions**.

---

1. Group squares to show an equivalent fraction.

   a)

   $\frac{2}{8} = \frac{}{4}$

   b)

   $\frac{6}{10} = \frac{}{5}$

   c)

   $\frac{3}{9} = \frac{}{3}$

2. Group the squares to show:

   a) Six twelfths equals one half ($\frac{6}{12} = \frac{1}{2}$)

   b) Six twelfths equals three sixths ($\frac{6}{12} = \frac{3}{6}$)

3. Group the squares to make an equivalent fraction.

   a)

   $\frac{8}{10} = \frac{}{5}$

   b)

   $\frac{4}{8} = \frac{}{2}$

   c)

   $\frac{4}{12} = \frac{}{3}$

   d)

   $\frac{9}{15} = \frac{}{}$

   e)

   $\frac{6}{14} = \frac{}{}$

   f)

   $\frac{8}{12} = \frac{}{}$

4. Write four equivalent fractions for the amount shaded here.

   _____ _____ _____ _____

Candice has a set of grey and white buttons.
Four of the six buttons are grey.

Candice groups buttons to show
that two thirds of the buttons are grey:

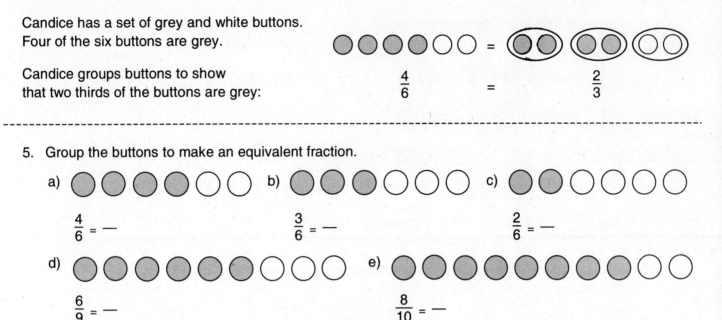

$$\frac{4}{6} = \frac{2}{3}$$

---

5. Group the buttons to make an equivalent fraction.

a) 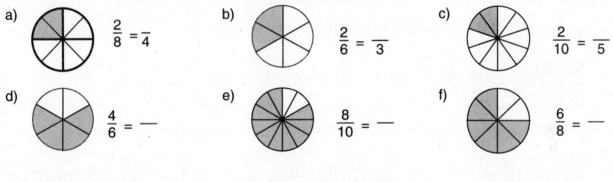 $\frac{4}{6} = \frac{}{}$

b) $\frac{3}{6} = \frac{}{}$

c) $\frac{2}{6} = \frac{}{}$

d) $\frac{6}{9} = \frac{}{}$

e) $\frac{8}{10} = \frac{}{}$

6. Group the pie pieces to make an equivalent fraction.
   The grouping in the first question has already been done for you.

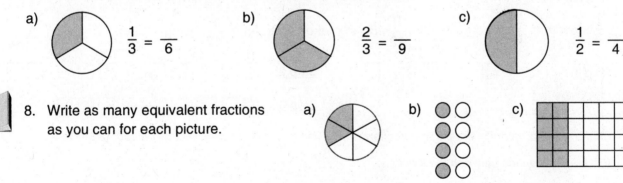

a) $\frac{2}{8} = \frac{}{4}$

b) $\frac{2}{6} = \frac{}{3}$

c) $\frac{2}{10} = \frac{}{5}$

d) $\frac{4}{6} = \frac{}{}$

e) $\frac{8}{10} = \frac{}{}$

f) $\frac{6}{8} = \frac{}{}$

7. Cut each pie into smaller pieces to make an equivalent fraction.

a) $\frac{1}{3} = \frac{}{6}$

b) $\frac{2}{3} = \frac{}{9}$

c) $\frac{1}{2} = \frac{}{4}$

8. Write as many equivalent fractions as you can for each picture.

a)   b)   c)

9. A pizza is cut into 8 pieces. Each piece is covered with olives, mushrooms or both.

$\frac{1}{4}$ of the pizza is covered in olives.

$\frac{7}{8}$ of the pizza is covered in mushrooms.

Draw a picture to show how many pieces have both olives and mushrooms on them.

1. Draw lines to cut the pies into more pieces.

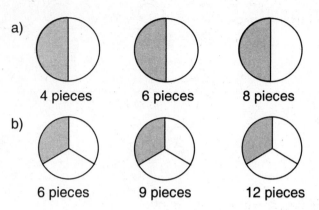

a)

4 pieces   6 pieces   8 pieces

b)

6 pieces   9 pieces   12 pieces

Then fill in the numerators of the equivalent fractions:

$$\frac{1}{2} = \frac{}{4} = \frac{}{6} = \frac{}{8}$$

$$\frac{1}{3} = \frac{}{6} = \frac{}{9} = \frac{}{12}$$

2. Cut each pie into more pieces. Then fill in the missing numbers.

a)

$$\frac{2}{3} \overset{\times 2}{\underset{\times 2}{=}} \frac{}{6}$$

b)

$$\frac{3}{4} \overset{\times 2}{\underset{\times 2}{=}} \frac{}{8}$$

c)

$$\frac{2}{3} \overset{\times}{\underset{\times}{=}} \frac{}{9}$$

This number tells you how many pieces to cut the pie into.

3. Use multiplication to find the equivalent fractions below.

a) $\frac{1}{3} \overset{\times 2}{\underset{\times 2}{=}} \frac{}{6}$ b) $\frac{1}{2} = \frac{}{10}$ c) $\frac{2}{5} = \frac{}{10}$ d) $\frac{3}{4} = \frac{}{8}$ e) $\frac{1}{4} = \frac{}{12}$

4. Use the patterns in the numerators and denominators to find 6 equivalent fractions.

a) $\frac{1}{2} = \frac{2}{4} = \frac{3}{} = \frac{}{8} = \frac{}{10} = \frac{}{}$ b) $\frac{3}{5} = \frac{6}{} = \frac{9}{15} = \frac{12}{20} = \frac{}{} = \frac{}{}$

5. To show that $\frac{3}{4}$ is equivalent to $\frac{9}{12}$, Brian makes a model of $\frac{9}{12}$ using blocks.

Step 1: 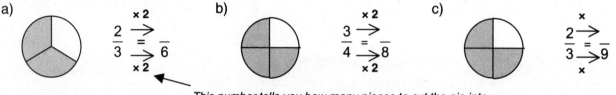

Step 2:

Step 3:

Brian makes a model of the original fraction $\frac{3}{4}$.

(He leaves a space between the blocks.)

He adds blocks until he has placed 12 blocks.

From Step 3, Brian can see $\frac{3}{4}$ is equivalent to $\frac{9}{12}$:

Use Brian's method to show that the fractions are equivalent.

a) $\frac{3}{5}$ and $\frac{9}{15}$ b) $\frac{2}{3}$ and $\frac{8}{12}$ c) $\frac{3}{4}$ and $\frac{12}{16}$

NS5-63: Fractions of Whole Numbers

Dan has 6 cookies. He wants to give $\frac{2}{3}$ of his cookies to his friends. To do so, he shares the cookies equally onto 3 plates:

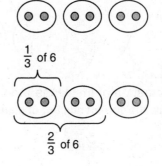

There are 3 equal groups, so each group is $\frac{1}{3}$ of 6.

$\frac{1}{3}$ of 6

There are 2 cookies in each group, so $\frac{1}{3}$ of 6 is 2.

There are 4 cookies in two groups, so $\frac{2}{3}$ of 6 is 4.

$\frac{2}{3}$ of 6

----

1. Write a fraction for the amount of dots shown. The first one has been done for you.

a) $\boxed{\dfrac{3}{4}}$ of 8

b) $\boxed{}$ of 15

2. Fill in the missing numbers.

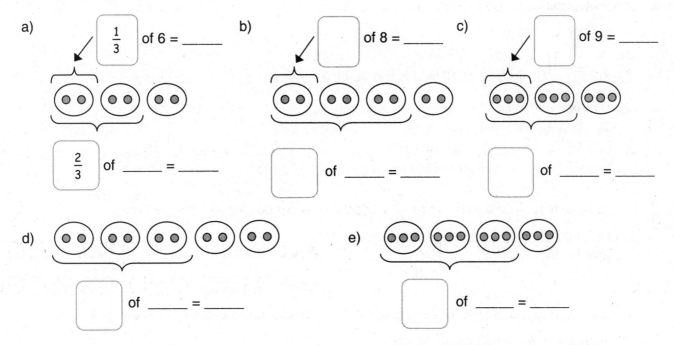

a) $\boxed{\dfrac{1}{3}}$ of 6 = _____

$\boxed{\dfrac{2}{3}}$ of _____ = _____

b) $\boxed{}$ of 8 = _____

$\boxed{}$ of _____ = _____

c) $\boxed{}$ of 9 = _____

$\boxed{}$ of _____ = _____

d) $\boxed{}$ of _____ = _____

e) $\boxed{}$ of _____ = _____

3. Draw a circle to show the given amount. The first one has been done for you.

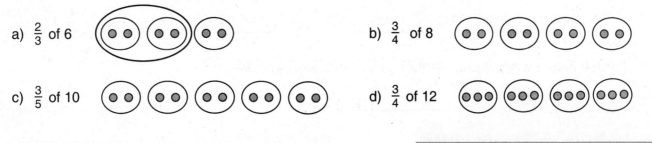

a) $\frac{2}{3}$ of 6

b) $\frac{3}{4}$ of 8

c) $\frac{3}{5}$ of 10

d) $\frac{3}{4}$ of 12

Number Sense 2

4. Fill in the correct number of dots in each circle, then draw a larger circle to show the given amount.

   a) $\frac{2}{3}$ of 12 ◯ ◯ ◯   b) $\frac{2}{3}$ of 9 ◯ ◯ ◯

5. Find the fraction of the whole amount by sharing the cookies equally.
   HINT: Draw the correct number of plates, then place the cookies one at a time. Then circle the correct amount.

   a) Find $\frac{1}{4}$ of 8 cookies.

   b) Find $\frac{1}{2}$ of 10 cookies.

   $\frac{1}{4}$ of 8 is _____

   $\frac{1}{2}$ of 10 is _____

   c) Find $\frac{2}{3}$ of 6 cookies.

   d) Find $\frac{3}{4}$ of 12 cookies.

   $\frac{2}{3}$ of 6 is _____

   $\frac{3}{4}$ of 12 is _____

6. Andy finds $\frac{2}{3}$ of 12 as follows:

   Step 1: *He finds $\frac{1}{3}$ of 12 by dividing 12 by 3.* (●●●●) (●●●●) (●●●●)

   12 ÷ 3 = 4 (4 is $\frac{1}{3}$ of 12)

   Step 2: *Then he multiplies the result by 2.* (●●●●) (●●●●) (●●●●)

   4 × 2 = 8 (8 is $\frac{2}{3}$ of 12)

   Find the following amounts using Andy's method.

   a) $\frac{2}{3}$ of 9   b) $\frac{3}{4}$ of 8   c) $\frac{2}{3}$ of 15   d) $\frac{2}{5}$ of 10

   _____   _____   _____   _____

   e) $\frac{3}{5}$ of 25   f) $\frac{2}{7}$ of 14   g) $\frac{1}{6}$ of 18   h) $\frac{1}{2}$ of 12

   _____   _____   _____   _____

   i) $\frac{3}{4}$ of 12   j) $\frac{2}{3}$ of 21   k) $\frac{3}{8}$ of 16   l) $\frac{3}{7}$ of 21

   _____   _____   _____   _____

NS5-63: Fractions of Whole Numbers (continued)

7. a) Shade $\frac{2}{5}$ of the boxes.

    b) Shade $\frac{2}{3}$ of the boxes.

    c) Shade $\frac{3}{4}$ of the boxes.

    d) Shade $\frac{5}{6}$ of the boxes.

    e) Shade $\frac{2}{7}$ of the boxes.

8. a) Shade $\frac{1}{4}$ of the boxes.

        Draw stripes in $\frac{1}{6}$ of the boxes.

    b) Shade $\frac{1}{3}$ of the boxes.

        Draw stripes in $\frac{1}{6}$ of the boxes.

        Put dots in $\frac{1}{8}$ of the boxes.

9. In the problems below, each circle represents a child. Solve the problem by writing **J** for "juice" and **W** for "water" on the correct number of circles. The first one is done for you.

    a) 8 children had drinks at lunch.
        $\frac{1}{2}$ drank juice and $\frac{1}{4}$ drank water.

        (J)(J)(W)( )
        (J)(J)(W)( )

        How many didn't drink juice or water? __2 didn't drink juice or water__

    b) 6 children had drinks at lunch.
        $\frac{1}{2}$ drank juice and $\frac{1}{3}$ drank water.

        ( )( )( )
        ( )( )( )

        How many didn't drink juice or water? _____

10. 12 children had drinks.
    $\frac{1}{4}$ drank juice and $\frac{2}{3}$ drank water.

    How many didn't drink juice or water?

11. Carol has a collection of 12 shells. $\frac{1}{3}$ of the shells are scallop shells.

    $\frac{1}{4}$ of the shells are conch shells. The rest of the shells are cone shells.

    How many of Carol's shells are cone shells?

conch

1. A kilogram of nuts costs $8.

    How much would $\frac{3}{4}$ of a kilogram cost? _____

2. Gerald has 10 oranges.
    He gives away $\frac{3}{5}$ of the oranges.

    a) How many oranges did he give away? _____   b) How many did he keep? _____

3. Shade $\frac{1}{3}$ of the squares.

    Draw stripes in $\frac{1}{6}$ of the squares.

    How many squares are blank? _____

4. Sapin has 20 marbles.
    $\frac{2}{5}$ are blue. $\frac{1}{4}$ are yellow.
    The rest are green.
    How many are green?

5. Which is longer:
    17 months or $1\frac{3}{4}$ years?

6. How many months are in $\frac{3}{4}$ of a year?

7. How many minutes are in $\frac{2}{3}$ of an hour?

8. Fong had 28 stickers.
    She kept $\frac{1}{7}$ herself and divided the rest evenly among 6 friends.
    How many stickers did each friend get?

9. Nancy put 4 of her 10 shells on a shelf.
    Explain how you know she put $\frac{2}{5}$ of her shells on the shelf.

10. Karl started studying at 7:15.
    He studied for $\frac{3}{5}$ of an hour.
    At what time did he stop studying?

11. Linda had 12 apples.
    She gave $\frac{1}{4}$ to Nandita and she gave 2 to Amy.
    She says that she has half left.
    Is she correct?

CHALLENGING:

12. Draw a picture or make a model to solve this problem.

    ♣ $\frac{2}{5}$ of Kim's marbles are yellow   ♣ $\frac{3}{5}$ are blue   ♣ 8 are yellow

    How many of Kim's marbles are blue?

NS5-65: Comparing and Ordering Fractions

Use the fraction strips below to answer Questions 1 to 3.

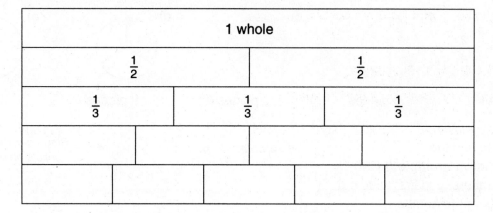

1. Fill in the missing numbers on the fraction strips above. Then write > (greater than) or < (less than) between each pair of numbers below.

   a) $\frac{1}{2}$ ☐ $\frac{2}{3}$ b) $\frac{3}{4}$ ☐ $\frac{2}{3}$ c) $\frac{2}{5}$ ☐ $\frac{3}{4}$ d) $\frac{4}{5}$ ☐ $\frac{3}{4}$

2. Circle the fractions that are greater than $\frac{1}{3}$.

   $\frac{1}{5}$ $\frac{2}{5}$ $\frac{1}{2}$

3. Circle the fractions that are greater than $\frac{1}{2}$.

   $\frac{3}{5}$ $\frac{2}{5}$ $\frac{3}{4}$

4. Draw lines to cut the left-hand pie into the same number of pieces as the right-hand pie. Then circle the greater fraction.

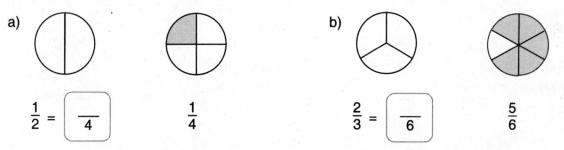

   a) $\frac{1}{2}$ = ☐$\frac{}{4}$ $\frac{1}{4}$

   b) $\frac{2}{3}$ = ☐$\frac{}{6}$ $\frac{5}{6}$

5. Turn each fraction on the left into an equivalent fraction with the same denominator as the fraction on the right. Then write > or < to show which fraction is greater.

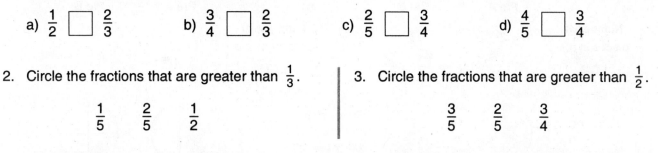

   a) $\frac{1 \times 3}{2 \times 3} = \frac{3}{6}$ ☒< $\frac{4}{6}$ b) $\frac{1 \times}{2 \times} = \frac{}{8}$ ☐ $\frac{5}{8}$ c) $\frac{1}{2} = \frac{}{}$ ☐ $\frac{3}{4}$

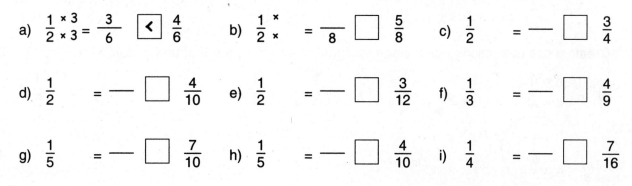

   d) $\frac{1}{2} = \frac{}{}$ ☐ $\frac{4}{10}$ e) $\frac{1}{2} = \frac{}{}$ ☐ $\frac{3}{12}$ f) $\frac{1}{3} = \frac{}{}$ ☐ $\frac{4}{9}$

   g) $\frac{1}{5} = \frac{}{}$ ☐ $\frac{7}{10}$ h) $\frac{1}{5} = \frac{}{}$ ☐ $\frac{4}{10}$ i) $\frac{1}{4} = \frac{}{}$ ☐ $\frac{7}{16}$

Number Sense 2

1. Cut each pie evenly into the given number of pieces. Then write a fraction for the result.

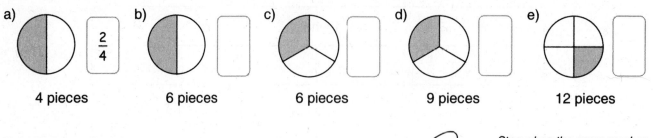

| a) | b) | c) | d) | e) |
| 4 pieces | 6 pieces | 6 pieces | 9 pieces | 12 pieces |

2. Recall that to find the **lowest common multiple** (LCM) of a pair of numbers, you first write out the multiples of the number.

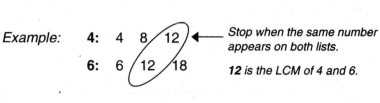

Example: 4: 4 8 12 ← Stop when the same number appears on both lists.

6: 6 12 18

12 is the LCM of 4 and 6.

Follow the steps in chart a) below to cut each pair of pies into the same number of pieces.

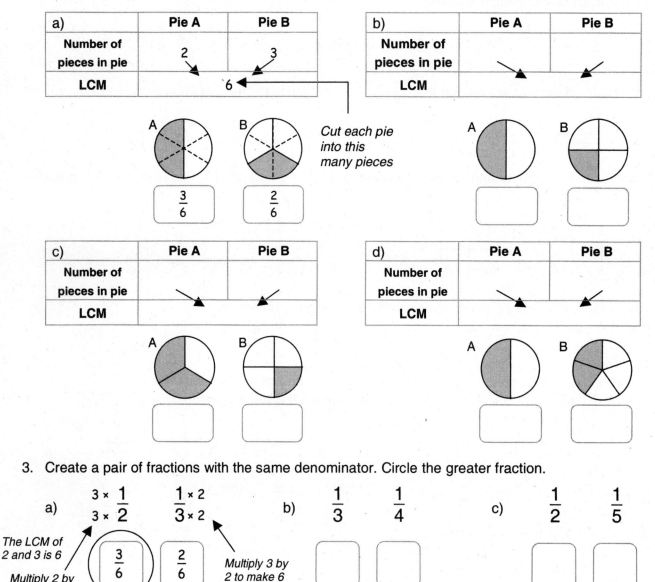

3. Create a pair of fractions with the same denominator. Circle the greater fraction.

a) $\frac{3 \times 1}{3 \times 2}$ $\frac{1 \times 2}{3 \times 2}$

The LCM of 2 and 3 is 6

Multiply 2 by 3 to make 6

$\frac{3}{6}$ $\frac{2}{6}$

Multiply 3 by 2 to make 6

b) $\frac{1}{3}$ $\frac{1}{4}$

c) $\frac{1}{2}$ $\frac{1}{5}$

NS5-67: Adding and Subtracting Fractions

1. Imagine moving the shaded pieces from pies A and B onto pie plate C. Show how much of pie C would be filled and then write a fraction for pie C.

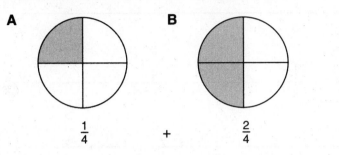

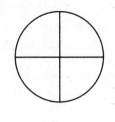

$$\frac{1}{4} \qquad + \qquad \frac{2}{4} \qquad = \qquad \underline{\quad}$$

2. Imagine pouring the liquid from cups A and B into cup C.
   Shade the amount of liquid that would be in C.
   Then complete the addition statements.

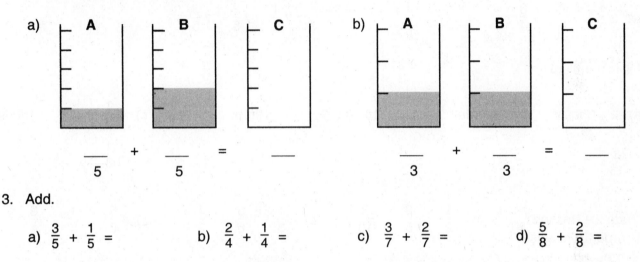

a) $\underline{\quad} + \underline{\quad} = \underline{\quad}$
      5   5

b) $\underline{\quad} + \underline{\quad} = \underline{\quad}$
      3   3

3. Add.

a) $\frac{3}{5} + \frac{1}{5} =$

b) $\frac{2}{4} + \frac{1}{4} =$

c) $\frac{3}{7} + \frac{2}{7} =$

d) $\frac{5}{8} + \frac{2}{8} =$

e) $\frac{3}{11} + \frac{7}{11} =$

f) $\frac{5}{17} + \frac{9}{17} =$

g) $\frac{11}{24} + \frac{10}{24} =$

h) $\frac{18}{57} + \frac{13}{57} =$

4. Show how much pie would be left if you took away the amount shown.
   Then complete the fraction statement.

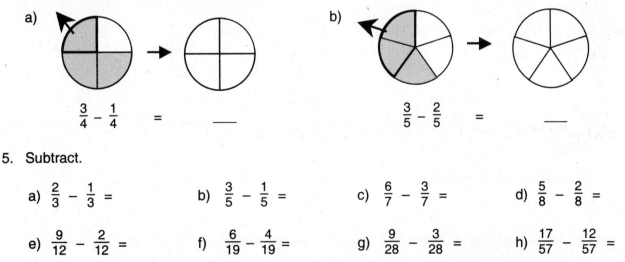

a) $\frac{3}{4} - \frac{1}{4} \qquad = \qquad \underline{\quad}$

b) $\frac{3}{5} - \frac{2}{5} \qquad = \qquad \underline{\quad}$

5. Subtract.

a) $\frac{2}{3} - \frac{1}{3} =$

b) $\frac{3}{5} - \frac{1}{5} =$

c) $\frac{6}{7} - \frac{3}{7} =$

d) $\frac{5}{8} - \frac{2}{8} =$

e) $\frac{9}{12} - \frac{2}{12} =$

f) $\frac{6}{19} - \frac{4}{19} =$

g) $\frac{9}{28} - \frac{3}{28} =$

h) $\frac{17}{57} - \frac{12}{57} =$

1. Fill in the missing mixed fractions on the number line.

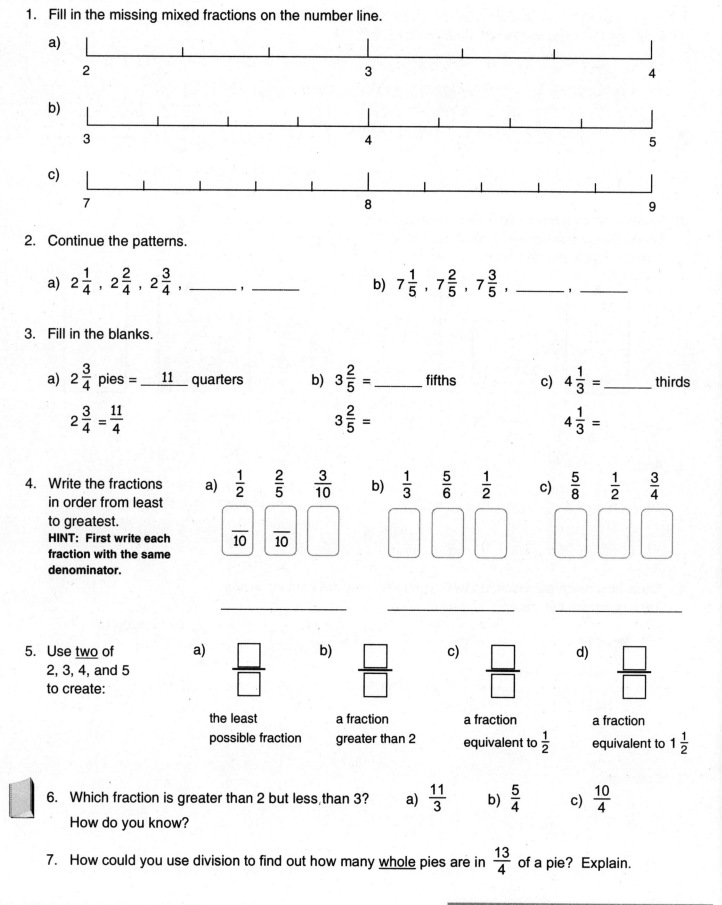

a)

```
2          3          4
```

b)

```
3          4          5
```

c)

```
7          8          9
```

2. Continue the patterns.

a) $2\frac{1}{4}$, $2\frac{2}{4}$, $2\frac{3}{4}$, _____ , _____

b) $7\frac{1}{5}$, $7\frac{2}{5}$, $7\frac{3}{5}$, _____ , _____

3. Fill in the blanks.

a) $2\frac{3}{4}$ pies = ___11___ quarters

$2\frac{3}{4} = \frac{11}{4}$

b) $3\frac{2}{5}$ = _____ fifths

$3\frac{2}{5}$ =

c) $4\frac{1}{3}$ = _____ thirds

$4\frac{1}{3}$ =

4. Write the fractions in order from least to greatest.

HINT: First write each fraction with the same denominator.

a) $\frac{1}{2}$ $\frac{2}{5}$ $\frac{3}{10}$

$\overline{10}$ $\overline{10}$ ☐

_____

b) $\frac{1}{3}$ $\frac{5}{6}$ $\frac{1}{2}$

☐   ☐   ☐

_____

c) $\frac{5}{8}$ $\frac{1}{2}$ $\frac{3}{4}$

☐   ☐   ☐

_____

5. Use two of 2, 3, 4, and 5 to create:

a) ☐/☐

the least possible fraction

b) ☐/☐

a fraction greater than 2

c) ☐/☐

a fraction equivalent to $\frac{1}{2}$

d) ☐/☐

a fraction equivalent to $1\frac{1}{2}$

6. Which fraction is greater than 2 but less than 3?   a) $\frac{11}{3}$ b) $\frac{5}{4}$ c) $\frac{10}{4}$

How do you know?

7. How could you use division to find out how many whole pies are in $\frac{13}{4}$ of a pie? Explain.

NS5-69: Place Value: Decimals

Fractions with denominators that are multiples of ten (tenths, hundredths) commonly appear in units of measurement.

- A millimetre is a tenth of a centimetre (10 mm = 1 cm)
- A centimetre is a tenth of a decimetre (10 cm = 1 dm)
- A decimeter is a tenth of a metre (10 dm = 1 m)
- A centimetre is a hundredth of a metre (100 cm = 1 m)

REMEMBER:

3. 7 5

ones | tenths | hundredths

Decimals are short forms for fractions. The chart shows the value of the decimal digits.

1. Write the place value of the underlined digit.

a) 3.72 hundredths b) 3.21 c) 7.52

d) 5.29 e) 9.98 f) 1.05

g) 0.32 h) 5.55 i) 6.42

2. Give the place value of the number 6 in each of the numbers below.

a) 3.65 b) 2.36 c) 0.63

d) 9.06 e) 0.06 f) 3.61

g) 1.60 h) 6.48 i) 7.26

3. Write the following numbers into the place value chart.

	Ones	Tenths	Hundredths
a) 5.03	5	0	3
b) 9.47			
c) 0.36			
d) 2.30			
e) 0.05			

NS5-70: Decimal Hundredths

1. Count the number of shaded squares. Write a fraction for the shaded part of the hundreds square. Then write the fraction as a decimal.

    HINT: Count by 10s for each column or row that is shaded.

    a)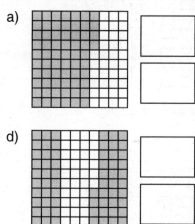

    b)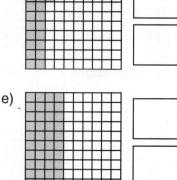

    c)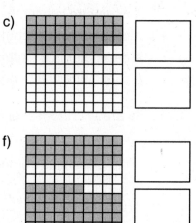

    d)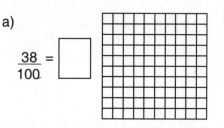

    e)

    f)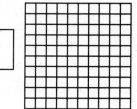

2. Convert the fraction to a decimal. Then shade.

    a) $\frac{38}{100}$ = ☐

    b) $\frac{45}{100}$ = ☐

    c) $\frac{5}{100}$ = ☐

3. The picture shows a floor plan of a museum. Write a fraction and a decimal for each shaded part.

    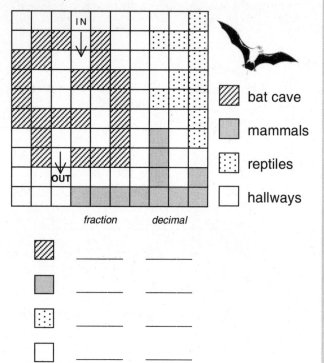

    ▨ bat cave

    ▣ mammals

    ⬚ reptiles

    ☐ hallways

    fraction   decimal

    ▨ ____ ____

    ▣ ____ ____

    ⬚ ____ ____

    ☐ ____ ____

4. Make your own floor plan for a museum. Write a fraction and a decimal for each shaded part.

    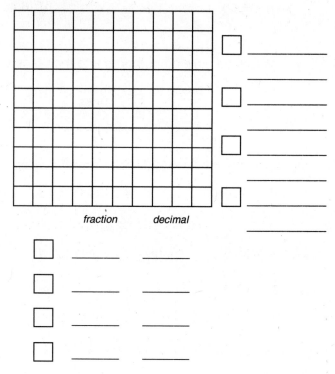

    fraction   decimal

    ☐ ____ ____

    ☐ ____ ____

    ☐ ____ ____

    ☐ ____ ____

NS5-71: Tenths and Hundredths

1. Draw lines around the columns to show tenths, as shown in a). Then write a fraction and a decimal to represent the number of shaded squares.

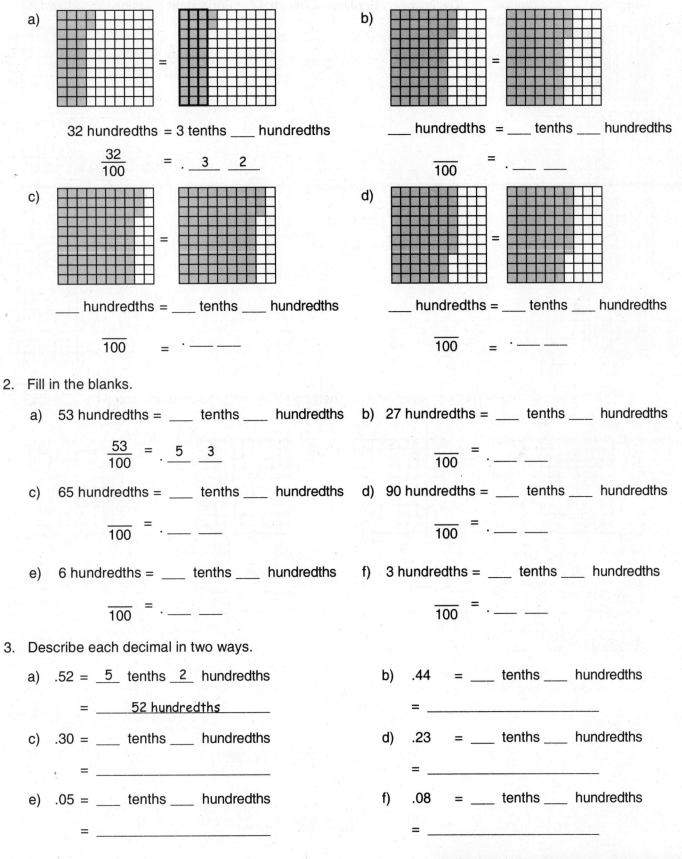

a)

32 hundredths = 3 tenths ___ hundredths

$\frac{32}{100}$ = . _3_ _2_

b)

___ hundredths = ___ tenths ___ hundredths

$\frac{}{100}$ = . ___ ___

c)

___ hundredths = ___ tenths ___ hundredths

$\frac{}{100}$ = . ___ ___

d)

___ hundredths = ___ tenths ___ hundredths

$\frac{}{100}$ = . ___ ___

2. Fill in the blanks.

a) 53 hundredths = ___ tenths ___ hundredths

$\frac{53}{100}$ = . _5_ _3_

b) 27 hundredths = ___ tenths ___ hundredths

$\frac{}{100}$ = . ___ ___

c) 65 hundredths = ___ tenths ___ hundredths

$\frac{}{100}$ = . ___ ___

d) 90 hundredths = ___ tenths ___ hundredths

$\frac{}{100}$ = . ___ ___

e) 6 hundredths = ___ tenths ___ hundredths

$\frac{}{100}$ = . ___ ___

f) 3 hundredths = ___ tenths ___ hundredths

$\frac{}{100}$ = . ___ ___

3. Describe each decimal in two ways.

a) .52 = _5_ tenths _2_ hundredths

= ___52 hundredths___

b) .44 = ___ tenths ___ hundredths

= _____

c) .30 = ___ tenths ___ hundredths

= _____

d) .23 = ___ tenths ___ hundredths

= _____

e) .05 = ___ tenths ___ hundredths

= _____

f) .08 = ___ tenths ___ hundredths

= _____

NS5-72: Changing Tenths to Hundredths

1. Fill in the chart below. The first one has been done for you.

Drawing	Fraction	Decimal	Equivalent Decimal	Equivalent Fraction	Drawing
	$\frac{4}{10}$	0.4	0.40	$\frac{40}{100}$	

2. Write a fraction for the number of <u>hundredths</u>. Then count the shaded columns and write a fraction for the number of <u>tenths</u>.

a) $\overline{100} = \overline{10}$ b) $\overline{100} = \overline{10}$ c) $\overline{100} = \overline{10}$ d) $\overline{100} = \overline{10}$

3. Fill in the missing numbers.

REMEMBER: $\frac{10}{100} = \frac{1}{10}$

a) $.8 = \frac{8}{10} = \overline{100} = .\underline{\ }\,\underline{\ }$

b) $.\underline{\ } = \frac{2}{10} = \overline{100} = .20$

c) $.\underline{\ } = \frac{6}{10} = \overline{100} = .60$

d) $.\underline{\ } = \frac{7}{10} = \overline{100} = .\underline{\ }\,\underline{\ }$

e) $.\underline{\ } = \overline{10} = \frac{40}{100} = .\underline{\ }\,\underline{\ }$

f) $.\underline{\ } = \overline{10} = \frac{30}{100} = .\underline{\ }\,\underline{\ }$

g) $.\underline{\ } = \frac{4}{10} = \overline{100} = .\underline{\ }\,\underline{\ }$

h) $.\underline{\ } = \frac{9}{10} = \overline{100} = .\underline{\ }\,\underline{\ }$

i) $.3 = \overline{10} = \overline{100} = .\underline{\ }\,\underline{\ }$

Number Sense 2

A **dime** is **one tenth** of a dollar. A **penny** is **one hundredth** of a dollar.

1. Express the value of each decimal in four different ways.

    a) .64

        6 dimes 4 pennies

        6 tenths 4 hundredths

        64 pennies

        64 hundredths

    b) .62

        _____

        _____

        _____

        _____

    c) .57

        _____

        _____

        _____

        _____

    d) .05

        _____

        _____

        _____

        _____

    e) .08

        _____

        _____

        _____

        _____

    f) .13

        _____

        _____

        _____

        _____

2. Express the value of each decimal in 4 different ways.
    HINT: First add a zero in the hundredths place.

    a) .4 ____ dimes ____ pennies

        ____ tenths ____ hundredths

        ____ pennies

        ____ hundredths

    b) .9 ____ dimes ____ pennies

        ____ tenths ____ hundredths

        ____ pennies

        ____ hundredths

3. Express the value of each decimal in four different ways. Then circle the greater number.

    .17 ____ dimes ____ pennies

    ____ tenths ____ hundredths

    ____ pennies

    ____ hundredths

    .2 ____ dimes ____ pennies

    ____ tenths ____ hundredths

    ____ pennies

    ____ hundredths

4. Tanya says **.53** is greater than **.7** because 53 is greater than 7. Can you explain her mistake?

1. Fill in the missing numbers.

a)

tenths	hundredths

b)

tenths	hundredths

c)

tenths	hundredths

d)

tenths	hundredths

$\overline{}$/100 = . ____ ____
        tenths hundredths

$\overline{}$/100 = . ____ ____

$\overline{}$/100 = . ____ ____

$\overline{}$/100 = . ____ ____

2. Write the following decimals as fractions.

a) $.5 = \overline{10}$　　b) $.3 = \overline{10}$　　c) $.6 = \overline{10}$　　d) $.2 = \overline{10}$　　e) $.1 = \overline{10}$

f) $.34 = \overline{100}$　　g) $.59 = \overline{100}$　　h) $.77 = \overline{100}$　　i) $.84 = \overline{100}$　　j) $.31 = \overline{100}$

k) $.08 = \overline{100}$　　l) $.03 = \overline{100}$　　m) $.09 = \overline{100}$　　n) $.05 = \overline{100}$　　o) $.01 = \overline{100}$

p) $.7 =$　　q) $.3 =$　　r) $.06 =$　　s) $.8 =$　　t) $.08 =$

u) $.6 =$　　v) $.46 =$　　w) $.05 =$　　x) $.9 =$　　y) $.6 =$

3. Change the following fractions to decimals.

a) $\frac{5}{10} = .$ ____　　b) $\frac{4}{10} = .$ ____　　c) $\frac{6}{10} = .$ ____　　d) $\frac{9}{10} = .$ ____

e) $\frac{93}{100} = .$ __ __　　f) $\frac{8}{100} = .$ __ __　　g) $\frac{88}{100} = .$ __ __　　h) $\frac{4}{100} = .$ __ __

4. Circle the equalities that are incorrect.

a) $.63 = \frac{63}{100}$　　b) $.9 = \frac{9}{10}$　　c) $.6 = \frac{6}{100}$　　d) $\frac{27}{100} = .27$　　e) $\frac{4}{100} = .04$

f) $.7 = \frac{7}{100}$　　g) $.64 = \frac{64}{10}$　　h) $.75 = \frac{75}{100}$　　i) $.06 = \frac{6}{100}$　　j) $.03 = \frac{3}{10}$

5. Explain how you know .7 is equal to .70.

A hundreds block may be used to represent a whole. 10 is a tenth of 100, so a tens block represents a tenth of the whole. 1 is a hundredth of 100, so a ones block represents a hundredth of the whole.

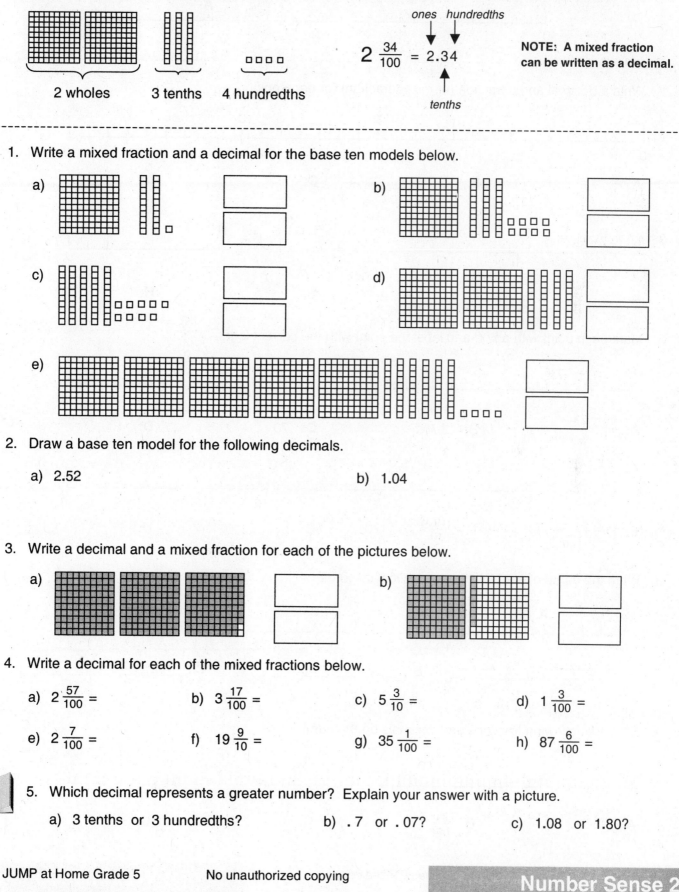

2 wholes   3 tenths   4 hundredths

ones   hundredths

$2 \frac{34}{100} = 2.34$

tenths

NOTE: A mixed fraction can be written as a decimal.

1. Write a mixed fraction and a decimal for the base ten models below.

a)

b)

c)

d)

e)

2. Draw a base ten model for the following decimals.

a) 2.52

b) 1.04

3. Write a decimal and a mixed fraction for each of the pictures below.

a)

b)

4. Write a decimal for each of the mixed fractions below.

a) $2\frac{57}{100} =$

b) $3\frac{17}{100} =$

c) $5\frac{3}{10} =$

d) $1\frac{3}{100} =$

e) $2\frac{7}{100} =$

f) $19\frac{9}{10} =$

g) $35\frac{1}{100} =$

h) $87\frac{6}{100} =$

5. Which decimal represents a greater number? Explain your answer with a picture.

a) 3 tenths or 3 hundredths?

b) .7 or .07?

c) 1.08 or 1.80?

NS5-76: Decimals and Fractions on Number Lines

This number line is divided into tenths. The number represented by Point A is $2\frac{3}{10}$ or 2.3:

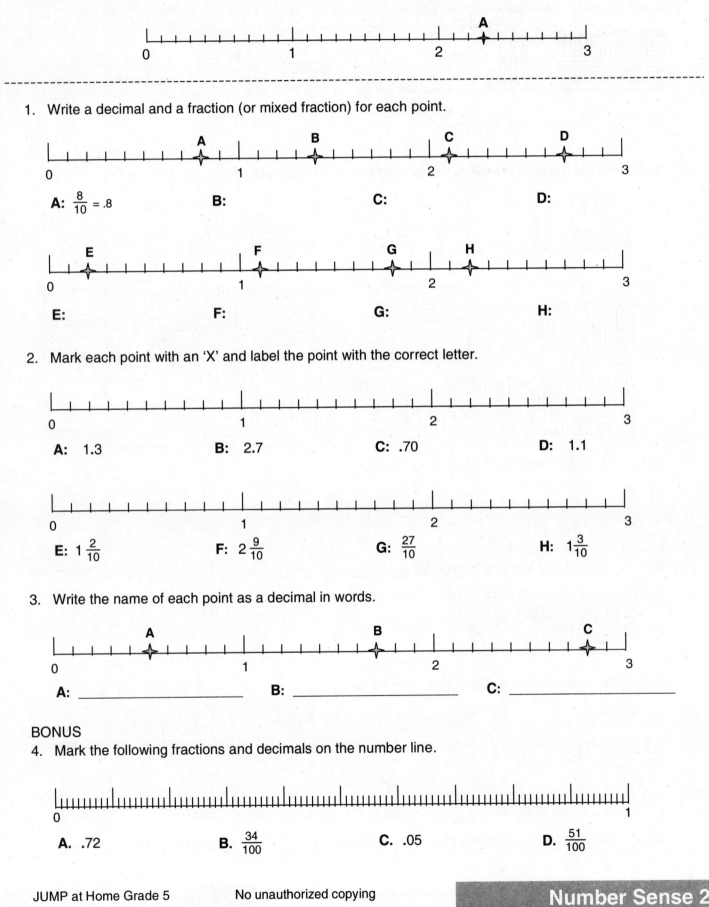

1. Write a decimal and a fraction (or mixed fraction) for each point.

A: $\frac{8}{10}$ = .8   B: C: D:

E: F: G: H:

2. Mark each point with an 'X' and label the point with the correct letter.

A: 1.3   B: 2.7   C: .70   D: 1.1

E: $1\frac{2}{10}$ F: $2\frac{9}{10}$ G: $\frac{27}{10}$ H: $1\frac{3}{10}$

3. Write the name of each point as a decimal in words.

A: _____   B: _____   C: _____

BONUS
4. Mark the following fractions and decimals on the number line.

A. .72   B. $\frac{34}{100}$ C. .05   D. $\frac{51}{100}$

1.

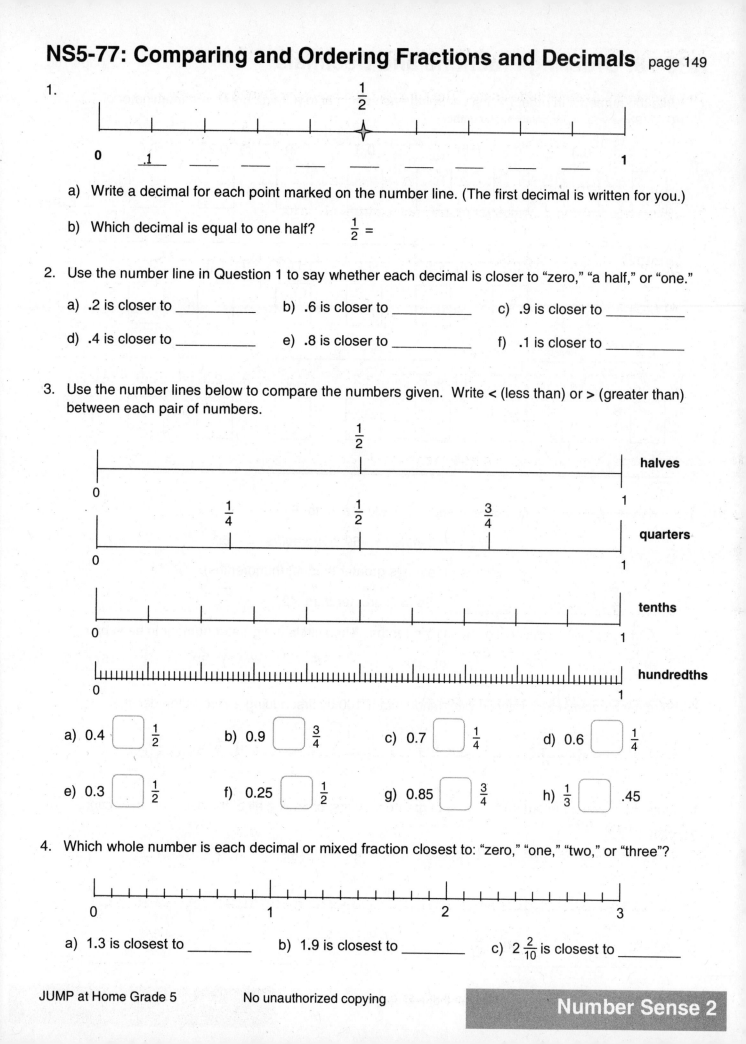

a) Write a decimal for each point marked on the number line. (The first decimal is written for you.)

b) Which decimal is equal to one half? $\frac{1}{2}$ =

2. Use the number line in Question 1 to say whether each decimal is closer to "zero," "a half," or "one."

a) .2 is closer to _____   b) .6 is closer to _____   c) .9 is closer to _____

d) .4 is closer to _____   e) .8 is closer to _____   f) .1 is closer to _____

3. Use the number lines below to compare the numbers given. Write < (less than) or > (greater than) between each pair of numbers.

a) 0.4 ☐ $\frac{1}{2}$ b) 0.9 ☐ $\frac{3}{4}$ c) 0.7 ☐ $\frac{1}{4}$ d) 0.6 ☐ $\frac{1}{4}$

e) 0.3 ☐ $\frac{1}{2}$ f) 0.25 ☐ $\frac{1}{2}$ g) 0.85 ☐ $\frac{3}{4}$ h) $\frac{1}{3}$ ☐ .45

4. Which whole number is each decimal or mixed fraction closest to: "zero," "one," "two," or "three"?

a) 1.3 is closest to _____   b) 1.9 is closest to _____   c) $2\frac{2}{10}$ is closest to _____

NS5-78: Ordering Fractions and Decimals

1. Write the numbers in order by first changing each decimal to a fraction with a denominator of 10.
   NOTE: Show your work below each number.

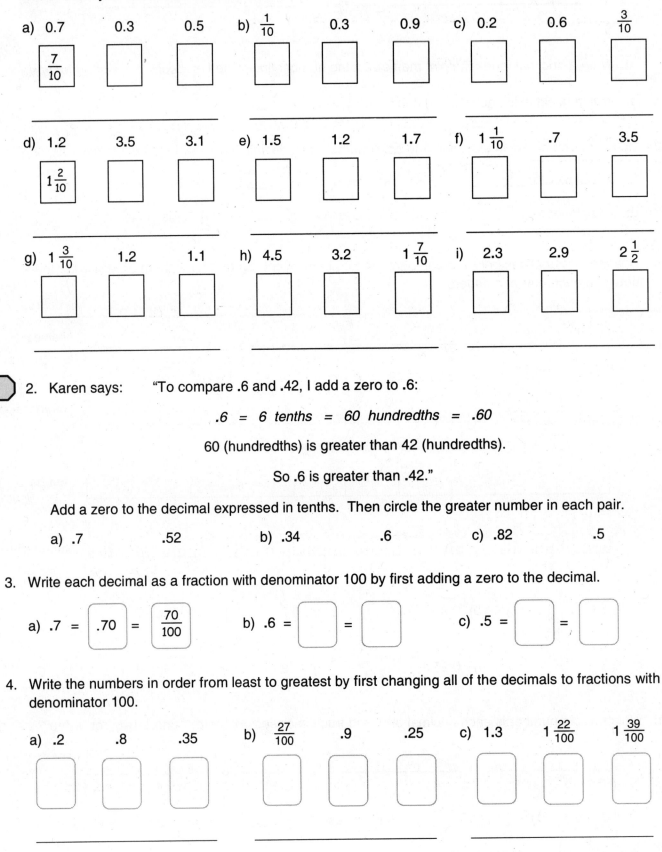

   a) 0.7   0.3   0.5   b) $\frac{1}{10}$ 0.3   0.9   c) 0.2   0.6 $\frac{3}{10}$

   $\frac{7}{10}$

   d) 1.2   3.5   3.1   e) 1.5   1.2   1.7   f) $1\frac{1}{10}$ .7   3.5

   $1\frac{2}{10}$

   g) $1\frac{3}{10}$ 1.2   1.1   h) 4.5   3.2 $1\frac{7}{10}$ i) 2.3   2.9 $2\frac{1}{2}$

2. Karen says: "To compare .6 and .42, I add a zero to .6:

   .6 = 6 tenths = 60 hundredths = .60

   60 (hundredths) is greater than 42 (hundredths).

   So .6 is greater than .42."

   Add a zero to the decimal expressed in tenths. Then circle the greater number in each pair.

   a) .7   .52   b) .34   .6   c) .82   .5

3. Write each decimal as a fraction with denominator 100 by first adding a zero to the decimal.

   a) .7 = .70 = $\frac{70}{100}$ b) .6 = ☐ = ☐   c) .5 = ☐ = ☐

4. Write the numbers in order from least to greatest by first changing all of the decimals to fractions with denominator 100.

   a) .2   .8   .35   b) $\frac{27}{100}$ .9   .25   c) 1.3 $1\frac{22}{100}$ $1\frac{39}{100}$

5. Shade $\frac{1}{2}$ of the squares. Write 2 fractions and 2 decimals for $\frac{1}{2}$.

Fractions: $\frac{1}{2}$ = $\frac{}{10}$ = $\frac{}{100}$

Decimals: $\frac{1}{2}$ = .____ = .____

6. Shade $\frac{1}{5}$ of the boxes. Write 2 fractions and 2 decimals for $\frac{1}{5}$.

Fractions: $\frac{1}{5}$ = $\frac{}{10}$ = $\frac{}{100}$

Decimals: $\frac{1}{5}$ = .____ = .____

7. Write equivalent fractions.

a) $\frac{2}{5}$ = $\frac{}{10}$ = $\frac{}{100}$ b) $\frac{3}{5}$ = $\frac{}{10}$ = $\frac{}{100}$ c) $\frac{4}{5}$ = $\frac{}{10}$ = $\frac{}{100}$

8. Shade $\frac{1}{4}$ of the squares. Write a fraction and a decimal for $\frac{1}{4}$.

Fraction: $\frac{1}{4}$ = $\frac{}{100}$ Decimal: $\frac{1}{4}$ = .____

Fraction: $\frac{3}{4}$ = $\frac{}{100}$ Decimal: $\frac{3}{4}$ = .____

9. Circle the greater number.
   HINT: First change all fractions and decimals to fractions with denominator 100.

a) $\frac{1}{2}$ .37   b) $\frac{1}{4}$ .52   c) $\frac{2}{5}$ .42

$\frac{50}{100}$ ☐   ☐   ☐   ☐   ☐   ☐

d) .7 $\frac{3}{5}$ e) .23 $\frac{1}{5}$ f) .52 $\frac{1}{2}$

☐   ☐   ☐   ☐   ☐   ☐

10. Write the numbers in order from least to greatest. Explain how you found your answers.

a) .7   .32 $\frac{1}{2}$ b) $\frac{1}{4}$ $\frac{3}{5}$ .63   c) $\frac{2}{5}$ .35 $\frac{1}{2}$

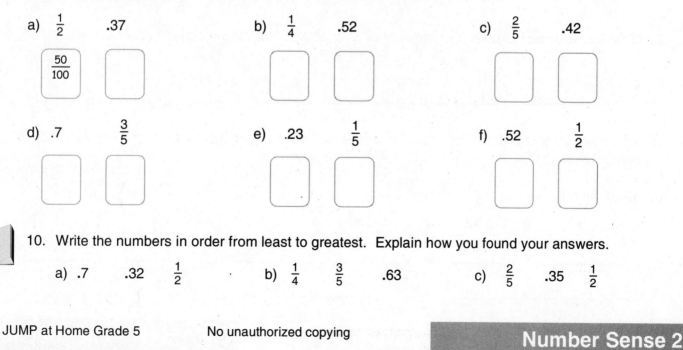

NS5-79: Adding and Subtracting Tenths

1. 1.3 is one whole and 3 tenths. How many tenths is that altogether? _____

2. a) 4.7 = _____ tenths   b) 7. 1 = _____ tenths   c) 3. 0 = _____ tenths

   d) _____ = 38 tenths   e) _____ = 42 tenths   f) _____ = 7 tenths

3. Add or subtract the decimals by first writing them as whole numbers of tenths.

   a)   2.1   _21_ tenths   b)   1.3   ____ tenths   c)   1.4   ____ tenths
        + 1.0   _10_ tenths   + 1.1   ____ tenths   + 7.3   ____ tenths
        [3.1] ← _31_ tenths   [   ] ← ____ tenths   [   ] ← ____ tenths

   d)   2.5   ____ tenths   e)   7.6   ____ tenths   f)   8.9   ____ tenths
        − 1.0   ____ tenths   − 4.2   ____ tenths   − 1.4   ____ tenths
        [   ] ← ____ tenths   [   ] ← ____ tenths   [   ] ← ____ tenths

4. Find the sum or difference.

   a)   0.7   1.0   b)   1.8   ← 0.6
      |0_____1_____2| |0_____1_____2|

      .7 + 1.0 = _____   1.8 − .6 = _____

   Now draw your own arrows.

   c) |0_____1_____2_____3_____4|

                    2.5 + 1.2 = _____

   d) |0_____1_____2_____3_____4|

                    2.7 − 1.9 = _____

5. Add or subtract.

   a)   3.5   b)   4.6   c)   5.4   d)   9.2   e)   3.7   f)   2.8
        − 1.2   + 3.2   + 1.7   − 4.9   + 4.9   − 1.9
        [   ]   [   ]   [   ]   [   ]   [   ]   [   ]

NS5-80: Adding Hundredths

1. Write a fraction for each shaded part. Then add the fractions, and shade your answer. The first one has been done for you.

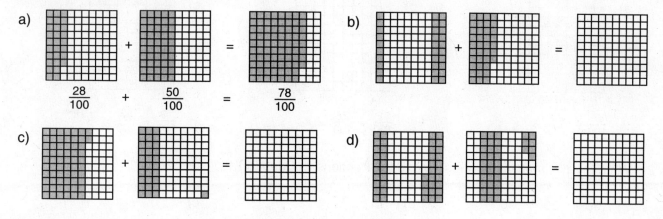

a) $\dfrac{28}{100}$ + $\dfrac{50}{100}$ = $\dfrac{78}{100}$

b)

c)

d)

2. Write the decimals that correspond to the fractions in Question 1.

a) .28 + .50 = .78	b)
c)	d)

3. Add the decimals by lining up the digits. Be sure that your final answer is expressed as a decimal.

a) 0.42 + 0.36   b) 0.91 + 0.04   c) 0.42 + 0.72   d) 0.22 + 0.57

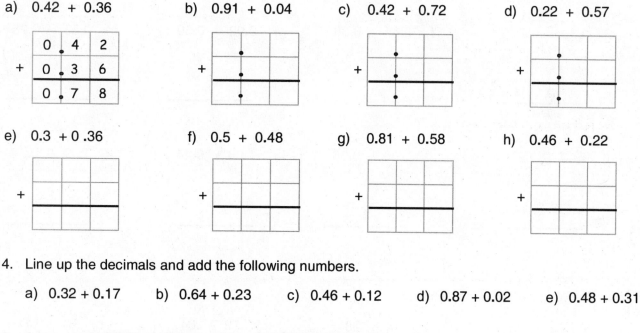

	0	4	2
+	0	3	6
	0	7	8

e) 0.3 + 0.36   f) 0.5 + 0.48   g) 0.81 + 0.58   h) 0.46 + 0.22

4. Line up the decimals and add the following numbers.

a) 0.32 + 0.17   b) 0.64 + 0.23   c) 0.46 + 0.12   d) 0.87 + 0.02   e) 0.48 + 0.31

5. Anne mixed .63 litres of juice with .36 litres of ginger ale.
   How many litres of punch did she make?

6. A snake is .56 metres long.

   What fraction of a metre is this?
   If two snakes of the same length lay end to end, would they be more or less than a metre long?

Number Sense 2

NS5-81: Subtracting Hundredths

1. Subtract by crossing out the correct number of boxes.

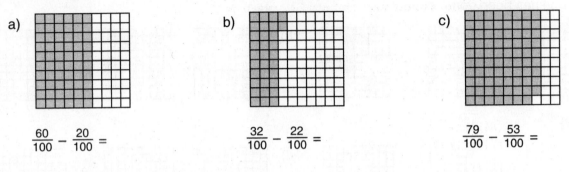

a) $\frac{60}{100} - \frac{20}{100} =$

b) $\frac{32}{100} - \frac{22}{100} =$

c) $\frac{79}{100} - \frac{53}{100} =$

2. Write the decimals that correspond to the fractions in Question 1.

a) .60 - .20 = .40

b)

c)

3. Subtract the decimals by lining up the digits.

a) 0.74 − 0.31

	0 . 7	4
−	0 . 3	1
	0 . 4	3

b) 0.88 − 0.34

c) 0.46 − 0.23

d) 0.75 − 0.21

e) 0.33 − .17

f) 0.64 − 0.38

g) 0.92 − 0.59

h) 0.53 − 0.26

i) 1.00 − .82

j) 1.00 − 0.36

k) 1.00 − 0.44

l) 1.00 − 0.29

4. Subtract the following decimals.

a) .82 − .45

b) .97 − .38

c) .72 − .64

d) .31 − .17

e) .58 − .3

f) .62 − .6

g) .98 − .03

h) .53 − .09

5. Find the missing decimal in each of the following.

a) 1 = .35 +

b) 1 = .72 +

c) 1 = .41 +

Number Sense 2

1. Add by drawing a base ten model. Then, using the chart provided, line up the decimal points and add.
    NOTE: Use a hundreds block for a whole and a tens block for one tenth.

    a) 1.32 + 1.15   b) 1.46 + 1.33

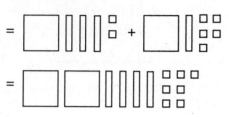

+	ones		tenths	hundredths
+		.		
		.		
		.		

+	ones		tenths	hundredths
+		.		
		.		
		.		

2. Subtract by drawing a base ten model of the greater number and then crossing out as many
    ones, tenths and hundredths as are in the lesser number, as shown in part a).

    a) 2.15 – 1.13   b) 2.33 – 1.12

 = 1.02

3. Add or subtract.

    a) ⎡ 3 . 1 2 ⎤   b) ⎡ 5 . 8 9 ⎤   c) ⎡ 3 . 8 6 ⎤   d) ⎡ 4 . 2 3 ⎤   e) ⎡ 1 8 . 0 5 ⎤
      + ⎣ 4 . 5 7 ⎦   + ⎣ 1 . 3 4 ⎦   – ⎣ 2 . 1 5 ⎦   – ⎣ 2 . 1 9 ⎦   – ⎣ 1 2 . 7 3 ⎦

    f) ⎡ 7 . 8 7 ⎤   g) ⎡ 9 . 7 4 ⎤   h) ⎡ 2 . 7 5 ⎤   i) ⎡ 8 . 7 1 ⎤   j) ⎡ 1 7 . 9   ⎤
      + ⎣ 4 . 0 3 ⎦   + ⎣ 6 . 3 5 ⎦   – ⎣   . 2 8 ⎦   – ⎣   . 1 4 ⎦   – ⎣   4 . 2 9 ⎦

4. Bamboo can grow up to 0.3 m in a single day in ideal conditions.
    How high could it grow in 3 days?

5. The largest axe in the world is 18.28 m long.
    If a regular axe is 1.5 metres long, how much longer is the world's largest axe?

6. Continue the patterns.   a) .2 , .4 , .6 , _____ , _____ , _____   b) .3 , .6 , .9 , _____ , _____ , _____

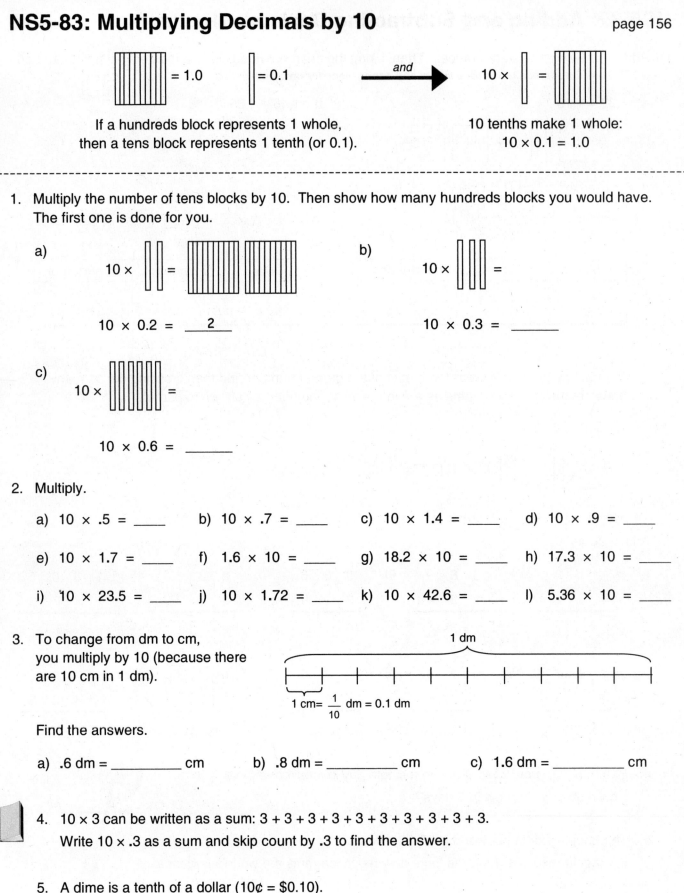

If a hundreds block represents 1 whole,
then a tens block represents 1 tenth (or 0.1).

10 tenths make 1 whole:
10 × 0.1 = 1.0

----

1. Multiply the number of tens blocks by 10. Then show how many hundreds blocks you would have. The first one is done for you.

a)

10 × 0.2 = ___2___

b)

10 × 0.3 = _____

c)

10 × 0.6 = _____

2. Multiply.

a) 10 × .5 = ____   b) 10 × .7 = ____   c) 10 × 1.4 = ____   d) 10 × .9 = ____

e) 10 × 1.7 = ____   f) 1.6 × 10 = ____   g) 18.2 × 10 = ____   h) 17.3 × 10 = ____

i) 10 × 23.5 = ____   j) 10 × 1.72 = ____   k) 10 × 42.6 = ____   l) 5.36 × 10 = ____

3. To change from dm to cm, you multiply by 10 (because there are 10 cm in 1 dm).

1 dm

$1 \text{ cm} = \frac{1}{10} \text{ dm} = 0.1 \text{ dm}$

Find the answers.

a) .6 dm = _____ cm   b) .8 dm = _____ cm   c) 1.6 dm = _____ cm

4. 10 × 3 can be written as a sum: 3 + 3 + 3 + 3 + 3 + 3 + 3 + 3 + 3 + 3.
   Write 10 × .3 as a sum and skip count by .3 to find the answer.

5. A dime is a tenth of a dollar (10¢ = $0.10).
   Draw a picture or use play money to show that 10 × $0.20 = $2.00.

NS5-84: Multiplying Decimals by 100

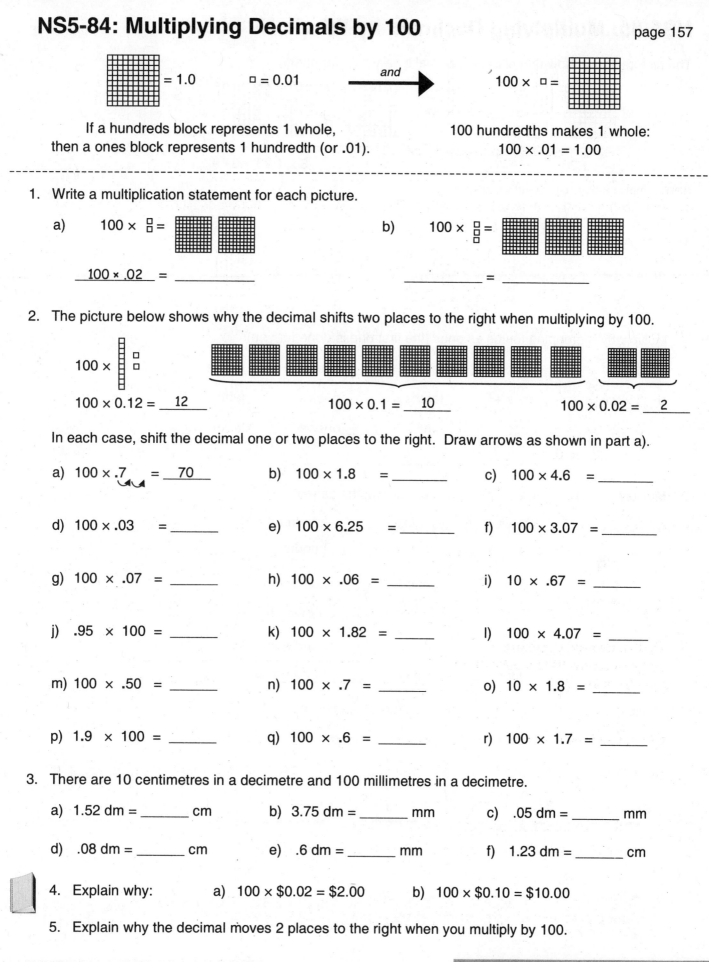

If a hundreds block represents 1 whole,
then a ones block represents 1 hundredth (or .01).

100 hundredths makes 1 whole:
100 × .01 = 1.00

----

1. Write a multiplication statement for each picture.

a) 100 × ⊟ =

100 × .02 = _____

b) 100 × ⊟ =

_____ = _____

2. The picture below shows why the decimal shifts two places to the right when multiplying by 100.

100 × ⊟

100 × 0.12 = __12__   100 × 0.1 = __10__   100 × 0.02 = __2__

In each case, shift the decimal one or two places to the right. Draw arrows as shown in part a).

a) 100 × .7 = __70__

b) 100 × 1.8 = _____

c) 100 × 4.6 = _____

d) 100 × .03 = _____

e) 100 × 6.25 = _____

f) 100 × 3.07 = _____

g) 100 × .07 = _____

h) 100 × .06 = _____

i) 10 × .67 = _____

j) .95 × 100 = _____

k) 100 × 1.82 = _____

l) 100 × 4.07 = _____

m) 100 × .50 = _____

n) 100 × .7 = _____

o) 10 × 1.8 = _____

p) 1.9 × 100 = _____

q) 100 × .6 = _____

r) 100 × 1.7 = _____

3. There are 10 centimetres in a decimetre and 100 millimetres in a decimetre.

a) 1.52 dm = _____ cm

b) 3.75 dm = _____ mm

c) .05 dm = _____ mm

d) .08 dm = _____ cm

e) .6 dm = _____ mm

f) 1.23 dm = _____ cm

4. Explain why: a) 100 × $0.02 = $2.00   b) 100 × $0.10 = $10.00

5. Explain why the decimal moves 2 places to the right when you multiply by 100.

No unauthorized copying   **Number Sense 2**

The picture shows how to multiply a decimal by a whole number.

1.23   ×3   3 × 1.23 = 3.69

HINT: Simply multiply each digit separately.

1. Multiply mentally.

   a) 2 × 1.43 = _____   b) 3 × 1.2 = _____   c) 5 × 1.01 = _____   d) 4 × 2.1 = _____

   e) 2 × 5.34 = _____   f) 4 × 2.1 = _____   g) 3 × 3.12 = _____   h) 3 × 4.32 = _____

2. Multiply by regrouping tenths as ones (the first one is done for you).

   a) 6 × 1.4 = __6__ ones + __24__ tenths = __8__ ones + __4__ tenths = __8.4__

   b) 3 × 2.5 = _____ ones + _____ tenths = _____ ones + _____ tenths = _____

   c) 3 × 2.7 = _____ ones + _____ tenths = _____ ones + _____ tenths = _____

   d) 4 × 2.6 = _____

3. Multiply by regrouping tenths as ones or hundredths as tenths.

   a) 3 × 2.51 = _____ ones + _____ tenths + _____ hundredths

        = _____ ones + _____ tenths + _____ hundredths = _____

   b) 4 × 2.14 = _____ ones + _____ tenths + _____ hundredths

        = _____ ones + _____ tenths + _____ hundredths = _____

   c) 5 × 1.41 = _____ ones + _____ tenths + _____ hundredths

        = _____ ones + _____ tenths + _____ hundredths = _____

4. Multiply. In some questions you will have to regroup twice.

   a)   b)   c)   d)

   | 3 | 4 | 5 | | 7 | 6 | 2 | | 4 | 3 | 1 | | 3 | 2 | 5 |
   × | | 3 | × | | 4 | × | | 6 | × | | 3 |

5. Find the products.

   a) 5 × 2.1   b) 3 × 8.3   c) 5 × 7.5   d) 9 × 2.81   e) 7 × 3.6   f) 6 × 3.4

   g) 4 × 3.2   h) 5 × 6.35   i) 6 × 3.95   j) 8 × 2.63   k) 3 × 31.21   l) 4 × 12.32

NS5-86: Dividing Decimals by 10

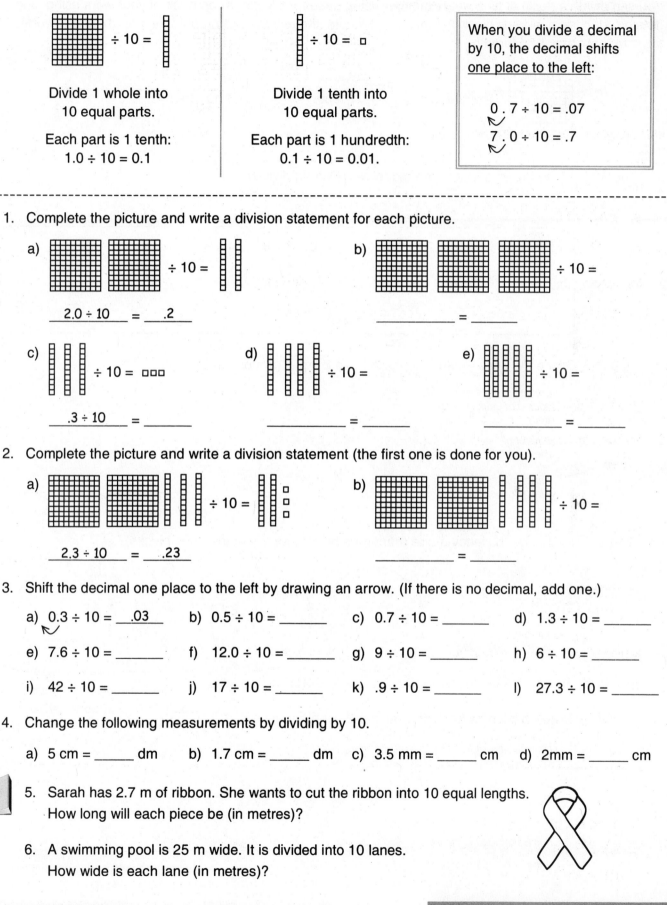

1. Complete the picture and write a division statement for each picture.

    a) ÷ 10 =

    2.0 ÷ 10 = .2

    b) ÷ 10 =

    _____ = _____

    c) ÷ 10 = □□□

    .3 ÷ 10 = _____

    d) ÷ 10 =

    _____ = _____

    e) ÷ 10 =

    _____ = _____

2. Complete the picture and write a division statement (the first one is done for you).

    a) ÷ 10 =

    2.3 ÷ 10 = .23

    b) ÷ 10 =

    _____ = _____

3. Shift the decimal one place to the left by drawing an arrow. (If there is no decimal, add one.)

    a) 0.3 ÷ 10 = .03   b) 0.5 ÷ 10 = _____   c) 0.7 ÷ 10 = _____   d) 1.3 ÷ 10 = _____

    e) 7.6 ÷ 10 = _____   f) 12.0 ÷ 10 = _____   g) 9 ÷ 10 = _____   h) 6 ÷ 10 = _____

    i) 42 ÷ 10 = _____   j) 17 ÷ 10 = _____   k) .9 ÷ 10 = _____   l) 27.3 ÷ 10 = _____

4. Change the following measurements by dividing by 10.

    a) 5 cm = _____ dm   b) 1.7 cm = _____ dm   c) 3.5 mm = _____ cm   d) 2mm = _____ cm

5. Sarah has 2.7 m of ribbon. She wants to cut the ribbon into 10 equal lengths. How long will each piece be (in metres)?

6. A swimming pool is 25 m wide. It is divided into 10 lanes. How wide is each lane (in metres)?

JUMP at Home Grade 5   No unauthorized copying

Number Sense 2

NS5-87: Dividing Decimals by Whole Numbers

You can divide a decimal by a whole number using base ten blocks. Keep track of your work using long division. Use the hundreds block to represent 1 whole, the tens block to represent 1 tenth, and the ones block to represent 1 hundredth.

1 whole   1 tenth   □ 1 hundredth

---

1. Find **5.12 ÷ 2** by drawing a base ten model and by long division.

Step 1:   Draw a base ten model of 5.12.

Draw your model here.

Step 2:   Divide the ones (hundreds blocks) into 2 equal groups.

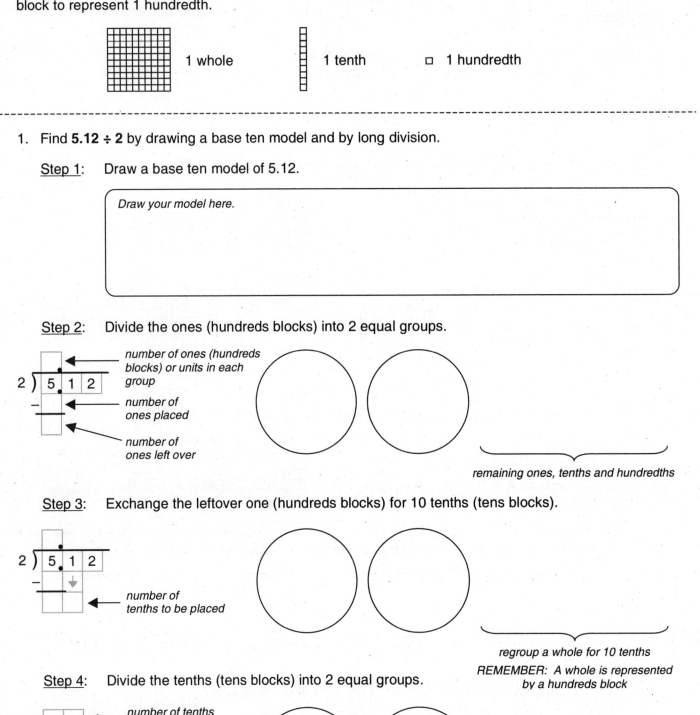

number of ones (hundreds blocks) or units in each group

number of ones placed

number of ones left over

remaining ones, tenths and hundredths

Step 3:   Exchange the leftover one (hundreds blocks) for 10 tenths (tens blocks).

number of tenths to be placed

regroup a whole for 10 tenths
REMEMBER: A whole is represented by a hundreds block

Step 4:   Divide the tenths (tens blocks) into 2 equal groups.

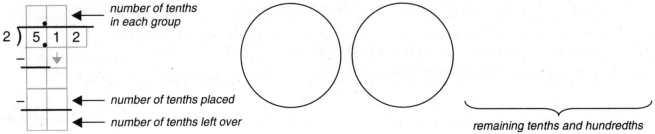

number of tenths in each group

number of tenths placed

number of tenths left over

remaining tenths and hundredths

Number Sense 2

Step 5:   Regroup the leftover tenths (tens blocks) as 10 hundredths (ones blocks).

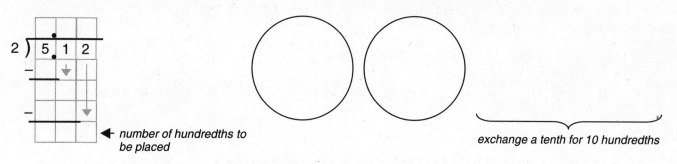

← number of hundredths to be placed

exchange a tenth for 10 hundredths

Steps 6 and 7:   Divide the hundredths (ones blocks) into 2 equal groups.

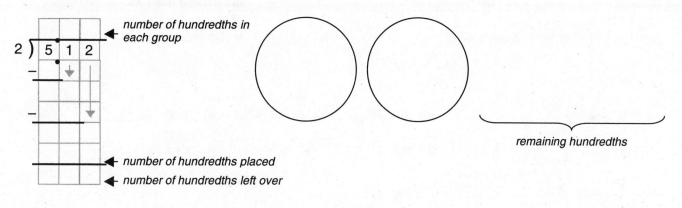

← number of hundredths in each group

remaining hundredths

← number of hundredths placed

← number of hundredths left over

2.   Divide.

a)   3) 4 . 3 2

b)   4) 6 . 2 5

c)   5) 6 . 2 3

d)   2) 3 . 3 2

3.   Divide.   a) 8) 1.44   b) 7) 9.4   c) 8) 2.72   d) 9) 6.13   e) 5) 20.5

4.   Five apples cost $2.75. How much does each apple cost?

5.   Karen cycled 62.4 km in 4 hours. How many kilometres did she cycle in an hour?

6.   Four friends earn a total of $29.16 shovelling snow. How much does each friend earn?

7.   Which is a better deal: 6 pens for $4.98 or 8 pens for $6.96?

NS5-88: Differences of 0.1 and 0.01

1. Fill in the blanks.

   a) .64 + .1 = _____   b) .35 + .1 = _____   c) .06 + .1 = _____

   d) .89 + .1 = _____   e) .73 + .01 = _____   f) .40 + .01 = _____

   g) 4.23 + .01 = _____   h) 2.87 + .1 = _____   i) 11.95 + .01 = _____

2. Fill in the blanks.

   a) _____ is .1 more than .7   b) _____ is .1 more than 2.6

   c) _____ is .1 more than 1.32   d) _____ is .1 more than .63

   e) _____ is .01 more than .35   f) _____ is .01 more than .2

3. Fill in the blanks.

   a) 1.35 + _____ = 1.36   b) 2.3 + _____ = 2.4   c) 3.06 − _____ = 3.05

   d) 4.95 − _____ = 4.94   e) 3.7 + _____ = 4.7   f) 7.85 + _____ = 7.95

4. Fill in the missing numbers on the number lines.

   a)
   5.0   6.0

   b)
   3.8   4.8

   c)
   4.14   4.24

5. Continue the patterns.

   a) .2, .3, .4, _____, _____, _____   b) 6.6, 6.7, 6.8, _____, _____, _____

   c) 3.5, 3.6, 3.7, _____, _____, _____   d) 9.6, 9.7, 9.8, _____, _____, _____

   e) 4.71, 4.72, 4.73, _____, _____, _____   f) 5.96, 5.97, 5.98, _____, _____, _____

6. Fill in the blanks.

   a) 3.9 + .1 = _____   b) 4.9 + .1 = _____   c) 8.93 + .1 = _____

   d) 3.79 + .01 = _____   e) 6.09 + .01 = _____   f) 7.99 + .01 = _____

NS5-89: Decimals (Review)

The size of a unit of measurement depends on which unit has been selected as the **whole**.

A millimetre is a **tenth** of a centimetre, but it is only a **hundredth** of a decimetre.

1 cm   1 mm

1 dm

---

1. Draw a picture in the space provided to show 1 tenth of each whole.

   a)

   1 whole   1 tenth

   b)

   1 whole   1 tenth

   c)

   1 whole   1 tenth

2. Write each measurement as a fraction then as a decimal.

   a) 1 cm = $\frac{1}{10}$ dm = ___.1___ dm

   b) 100 cm = ☐ dm = _____ dm

   c) 1 mm = ☐ cm = _____ cm

   d) 16 mm = ☐ cm = _____ cm

   e) 77 mm = ☐ dm = _____ dm

   f) 83 cm = ☐ m = _____ m

3. Add by first changing the <u>smaller unit</u> into a decimal in the <u>larger unit</u>.

   a) 4 cm + 9.2 dm = ___0.4 dm + 9.2 dm = 9.6 dm___

   b) 6 cm + 2.9 dm = _____

   c) 9 mm + 8.4 cm = _____

   d) 33 cm + 1.64 m = _____

4. What amount is represented by the tenths digits?

   a) 7.52 m _____5 dm_____

   b) $6.29 _____

   c) 2.32 m _____

   d) 3.7 million _____

   e) 2.8 thousand _____

   f) 5.35 dm _____

5. Round each decimal to the nearest tenth.
   HINT: Underline the hundredths digit first. It will tell you whether you round up or down.

   a) .2<u>5</u> _____

   b) .32 _____

   c) .68 _____

   d) 1.35 _____

6. Round each decimal to the nearest whole number. **HINT: Underline the tenths digit first.**

   a) 3.<u>2</u>5 _____

   b) 4.13 _____

   c) 2.95 _____

   d) 8.3 _____

Number Sense 2

7. The diagram shows a section of measuring tape.

    Round each measurement to the nearest tenth of a metre.
    Write your answer in words.

A: _____Five and two tenths_____   B: _____

C: _____   D: _____

8. Write a decimal for each description.

    a) Between 3.52 and 3.57:   ___ . ___ ___   b) Between 1.70 and 1.80: ___ . ___ ___

    c) Between 12.65 and 12.7: ___ ___ . ___ ___   d) Between 2.6 and 2.7:   ___ . ___ ___

9. Add.

    a) $3\,000 + 200 + 7 + 0.02 =$ _____   b) $10\,000 + 500 + 20 + 0.1 + 0.05 =$ _____

    c) $6\,000 + 300 + 8 + 0.1 \ =$ _____   d) $400 + 7 + .02 =$ _____

10. Write < or > to show which decimal is greater.

    a) 3.7 ☐ 3.5   b) 2.32 ☐ 2.37   c) 1.7 ☐ 1.69   d) 0.5 ☐ 0.55

11. If you divide a number by 10, the result is 12.9.
     What was the original number? Explain.

12. The Olympic gold medal throw for the shot put in 2004 was 21.16 m.
     The bronze throw was 21.07 m.

    a) Was the difference in the throws more or less than 0.1 m?

    b) Round both throws to the nearest tenth.
        What is the difference in the rounded amounts?

    c) Make up two throws which would round to the same number (when rounded to the tenths).

    d) Why are Olympic shot put throws measured so precisely?

Answer the following questions in your notebook.

1. Giant Kelp is the fastest growing ocean plant.
   It can grow 0.67 m in a day.
   How much could it grow in a week?

2. Lichen grows slowly at a rate of 3.4 mm a year.
   Could it grow 1 cm in 3 years?

3. How much do 7 books
   cost at $8.99 per book?

4. Under which deal do you pay less for 1 pen:
   4 pens for $2.96 or 6 pens for $4.99?

5. On a map, 1 cm represents 15 km.

   Two towns are 2.3 cm apart on the map.

   How far apart are the towns?

6.
$$\begin{array}{r} 6\ .\ 4\ 2 \\ +\ 7\ .\ 1\ 9 \\ \hline 7\ 8\ .\ 3\ 2 \end{array}$$

   Tim added the numbers on his calculator.

   What mistake do you think Tim made pressing the buttons on the calculator?

7. $0.45 means 4 dimes and 5 pennies.
   Why do we use decimal notation for money?
   What is a dime a tenth of?
   What is a penny a hundredth of?

8. Here are the greatest lengths of some sea creatures.

   a) How much longer than the great white shark is the blue whale?

   b) About how many times longer than the turtle is the great white shark?

   c) About how long would 3 ocean sunfish be if they swam in a row?

Animal	Length (m)
Blue Whale	34
Great White Shark	7.9
Pacific Leather Back Turtle	2.1
Ocean Sunfish	2.9

NS5-91: Unit Rates

A **rate** is a comparison of two quantities in different units.

In a **unit rate**, one of the quantities is equal to one.
For instance, "1 apple costs 30¢" is a unit rate.

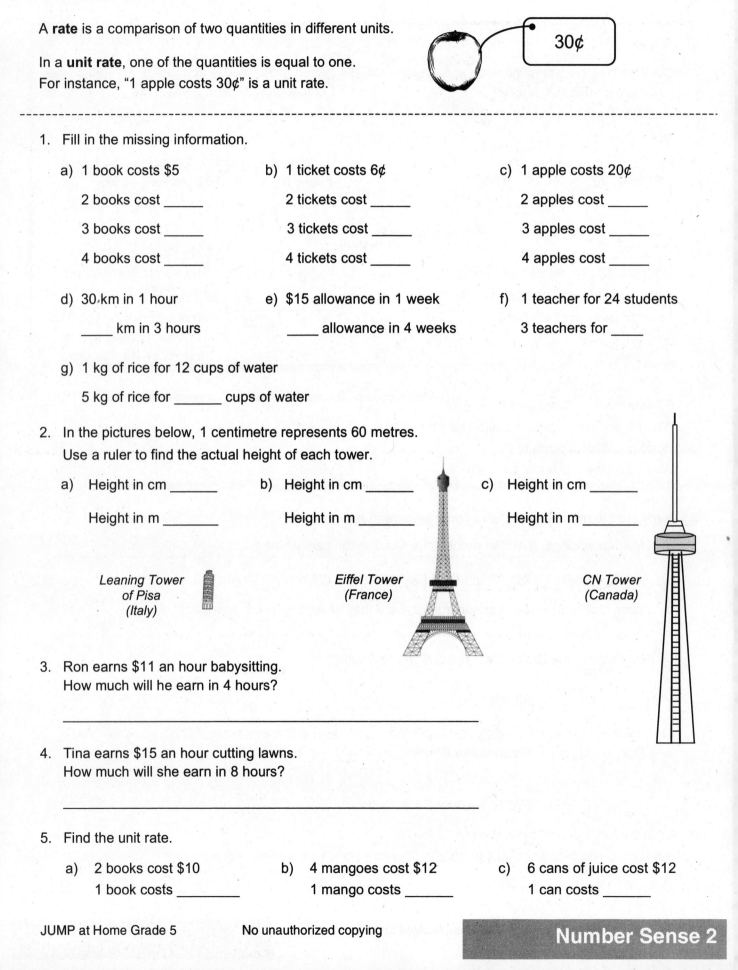

---

1. Fill in the missing information.

   a) 1 book costs $5

      2 books cost _____

      3 books cost _____

      4 books cost _____

   b) 1 ticket costs 6¢

      2 tickets cost _____

      3 tickets cost _____

      4 tickets cost _____

   c) 1 apple costs 20¢

      2 apples cost _____

      3 apples cost _____

      4 apples cost _____

   d) 30 km in 1 hour

      _____ km in 3 hours

   e) $15 allowance in 1 week

      _____ allowance in 4 weeks

   f) 1 teacher for 24 students

      3 teachers for _____

   g) 1 kg of rice for 12 cups of water

      5 kg of rice for _____ cups of water

2. In the pictures below, 1 centimetre represents 60 metres.
   Use a ruler to find the actual height of each tower.

   a) Height in cm _____

      Height in m _____

   b) Height in cm _____

      Height in m _____

   c) Height in cm _____

      Height in m _____

   *Leaning Tower
   of Pisa
   (Italy)*

   *Eiffel Tower
   (France)*

   *CN Tower
   (Canada)*

3. Ron earns $11 an hour babysitting.
   How much will he earn in 4 hours?

   _____

4. Tina earns $15 an hour cutting lawns.
   How much will she earn in 8 hours?

   _____

5. Find the unit rate.

   a) 2 books cost $10
       1 book costs _____

   b) 4 mangoes cost $12
       1 mango costs _____

   c) 6 cans of juice cost $12
       1 can costs _____

Number Sense 2

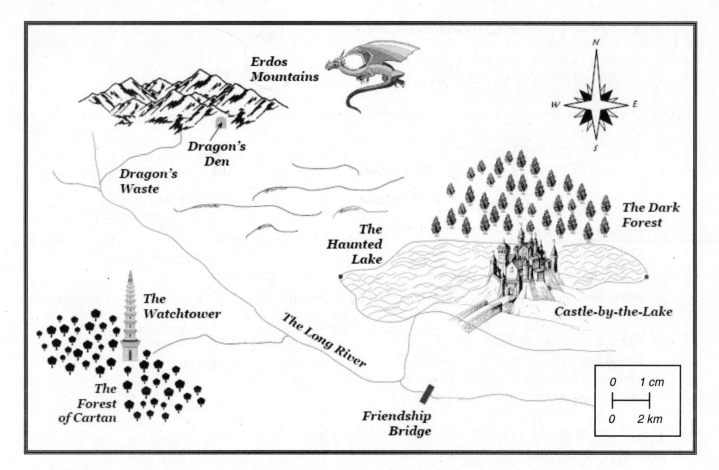

1. Sharon has drawn a map of a fantasy world. Use the scale to answer the questions below.

   a) How many kilometres must the dragon fly from its den to reach Castle-by-the-Lake's entrance?

   _____

   b) How long is the Haunted Lake (from East to West)?

   _____

   c) How wide is the Dark Forest (from North to South)?

   _____

   d) How far must a knight ride to get from the Watchtower to the entrance of Castle-by-the-Lake?
      (Assume the only way across the river is by Friendship Bridge.)

   _____

2. On a map that Jacob drew, 2 cm = 50 km.
   How many kilometres would each of the following distances on the map represent?

   a) 8 cm: _____   b) 10 cm: _____   c) 1 cm: _____   d) 5 cm: _____   e) 9 cm: _____

Answer the following questions in your notebook.

1. On a 3-day canoe trip, Pamela canoed 25.5 km on the first day, 32.6 km on the second, and 17.25 km on the third.

   a) How far did she canoe in total?

   b) What was the average distance she paddled each day?

   c) If she canoes for 6 hours each day, about how many kilometres does she travel each hour?

   d) Pamela's canoe can hold 100 kg. Pamela weighs 45 kg, her tent weighs 10 kg and her supplies weigh 15 kg. How much more weight can the canoe carry?

2. Jessica has 78 beads.

   She gave her 3 friends 23 beads each.

   How many did she have left over?

3. James bought a slice of pizza for $3.21, a video game for $15.87, a bottle of pop for $1.56, and a bag of chips for $1.37.

   How much change did he get from $25.00?

4. Six classes went skating.

   There are 24 students in each class.

   Each bus holds 30 students.

   The teachers ordered 4 buses.

   Will there be enough room?

   Explain.

5. Janice earned $28.35 on Monday. On Thursday, she spent $17.52 for a shirt.

   She now has $32.23.

   How much money did she have before she started work Monday?

   HINT: Work backwards. How much money did she have before she bought the shirt?

6. Sue spent half of her money on a book. Then she spent $1.25 on a pen. She has $3.20 left.

   How much did she start with?

7. Anne travelled 12.5 m in 10 steps.

   How many metres was each step?

8. Gravity on Jupiter is 2.3 times as strong as gravity on Earth.

   How much more would a 7 kg dog weigh on Jupiter than on Earth?

9. Ruby lives 2.4 km from the park. She walks to the park and back each day.

   How many kilometres does she walk to and from the park in a week?

10. Encke's Comet appears in our sky every 3.3 years. It was first seen in 1786.

    When was the last time the comet was seen in the 1700s (i.e. before 1800)?

    Show your work.

Glossary

add to find the total when combining two or more numbers together

area the amount of space occupied by the face or surface of an object

array an arrangement of things (for example, objects, symbols, or numbers) in rows and columns

base-10 materials materials used to represent ones (ones squares or cubes), tens (tens strips or rods), hundreds (hundreds squares or flats), and thousands (thousands cubes)

centimetre (cm) a unit of measurement used to describe length, height, or thickness

cent notation a way to express an amount of money (for example, 40¢)

column things (for example, objects, symbols, numbers) that run up and down

consecutive numbers numbers that occur one after the other on a number line

coordinate system a grid with labelled rows and columns, used to describe the location of a dot or object, for example the dot is at (A,3)

core the part of a pattern that repeats

decimal a short form for tenths (for example, 0.2) or hundredths (for example, 0.02), and so on

decimetre (dm) a unit of measurement used to describe length, height, or thickness; equal to 10 cm

decreasing sequence a sequence where each number is less than the one before it

denominator the number on the bottom portion of a fraction; tells you how many parts are in a whole

diagonal things (for example, objects, symbols, or numbers) that are in a line from one corner to another corner

difference the "gap" between two numbers; the remainder left after subtraction

divide to find how many times one number contains another number

dividend in a division problem, the number that is being divided or shared

divisible by containing a number a specific number of times without having a remainder (for example, 15 is divisible by 5 and 3)

divisor in a division problem, the number that is divided into another number

dollar notation a way to express an amount of money (for example, $4.50)

equivalent fractions fractions that represent the same amount, but have different denominators (for example, $\frac{2}{3} = \frac{4}{6}$)

estimate a guess or calculation of an approximate number

expanded form a way to write a number that shows the place value of each digit (for example, 27 in expanded form can be written as 2 tens + 7 ones, or 20 + 7)

factors whole numbers that are multiplied to give a number

fraction a number used to name a part of a set or a region

greater than a term used to describe a number that is higher in value than another number

growing pattern a pattern in which each term is greater than the previous term

improper fraction a fraction that has a numerator that is larger than the denominator; this represents more than a whole

Glossary

increasing sequence a sequence where each number is greater than the one before it

kilometre (km) a unit of measurement for length; equal to 1000 cm

less than a term used to describe a number that is lower in value than another number

litre (L) a unit of measurement used to describe capacity; equal to 1000 mL

lowest common multiple (LCM) the least nonzero number that two numbers can divide into evenly (for example, 6 is the LCM of 2 and 3)

metre (m) a unit of measurement used to describe length, height, or thickness; equal to 100 cm

millilitre (mL) a unit of measurement used to describe capacity

millimetre (mm) a unit of measurement used to describe length, height, or thickness; equal to 0.1 cm

mixed fraction a mixture of a whole number and a fraction

model a physical representation (for example, using base-10 materials to represent a number)

multiple of a number that is the result of multiplying one number by another specific number (for example, the multiples of 5 are 0, 5, 10, 15, and so on)

multiply to find the total of a number times another number

number line a line with numbers marked at intervals, used to help with skip counting

numerator the number on the top portion of a fraction; tells you how many parts are counted

pattern (repeating pattern) the same repeating group of objects, numbers, or attributes

perimeter the distance around the outside of a shape

period the part of a pattern that repeats; the core of the pattern

product the result from multiplying two or more numbers together

quotient the result from dividing one number by another number

regroup to exchange one place value for another place value (for example, 10 ones squares for 1 tens strip)

remainder the number left over after dividing or subtracting (for example, $10 \div 3 = 3$ R1)

row things (for example, objects, symbols, or numbers) that run left to right

set a group of like objects

skip counting counting by a number (for example, 2s, 3s, 4s) by "skipping" over the numbers in between

square centimetre (cm2) a unit of measurement used to describe area

subtract to take away one or more numbers from another number

sum the result from adding two or more numbers together

T-table a chart used to compare two sequences of numbers

About the Authors

JOHN MIGHTON is a mathematician, author, and playwright. He completed a Ph.D. in mathematics at the University of Toronto and is currently a fellow of the Fields Institute for Mathematical Research. The founder of JUMP Math (www.jumpmath.org), Mighton also gives lectures to student teachers at York University and the Ontario Institute for Studies in Education, and invited talks and training sessions for parents and educators. He is the author of the *JUMP at Home* workbooks and the national bestsellers *The Myth of Ability* and *The End of Ignorance*. He has won the Governor General's Literary Award and the Siminovitch Prize for his plays.

DR. ANNA KLEBANOV received her B.Sc., M.Sc., Ph.D., and teaching certificate from the Technion – Israel Institute of Technology. She is the recipient of three teaching awards for excellence. She began her career at JUMP Math as a curriculum writer in 2007, working with Dr. John Mighton and Dr. Sindi Sabourin on JUMP Math's broad range of publications.

DR. SINDI SABOURIN received her Ph.D. in mathematics from Queen's University, specializing in commutative algebra. She is the recipient of the Governor General's Gold Medal Award from Queen's University and a National Sciences and Research Council Postdoctoral Fellowship. Her career with JUMP Math began in 2003 as a volunteer doing in-class tutoring, one-on-one tutoring, as well as working on answer keys. In 2006, she became a curriculum writer working on JUMP Math's broad range of publications.